ASP 3

fast&easy™
web development

Send Us Your Comments

To comment on this book or any other PRIMA TECH title, visit our reader response page on the Web at www.prima-tech.com/comments.

How to Order

For information on quantity discounts, contact the publisher: Prima Publishing, P.O. Box 1260BK, Rocklin, CA 95677-1260; (916) 787-7000. On your letterhead, include information concerning the intended use of the books and the number of books you want to purchase.

ASP 3

fast&easy™
web development

Michael D. Thomasson

A DIVISION OF PRIMA PUBLISHING

A Division of Prima Publishing

Prima Publishing and colophon are registered trademarks of Prima Communications, Inc. PRIMA TECH and fast & easy are trademarks of Prima Communications, Inc., Roseville, California 95661.

Publisher: Stacy L. Hiquet

Marketing Manager: Judi Taylor

Associate Marketing Manager: Heather Buzzingham

Managing Editor: Sandy Doell

Acquisitions Editor: Kim Spilker

Project Editor: Brian Thomasson

Technical Editor: Ian Feaveryear

Copy Editor: Tom Dinse

Interior Layout: Shawn Morningstar

Cover Design: Barbara Kordesh

Indexer: Joy Dean Lee

Microsoft, Windows, Windows 2000, Internet Explorer, VBScript, ActiveX, Visual Interdev, Internet Information Server, and Visual Studio are trademarks or registered trademarks of Microsoft Corporation.

Important: Prima Publishing cannot provide software support. Please contact the appropriate software manufacturer's technical support line or Web site for assistance.

Prima Publishing and the author have attempted throughout this book to distinguish proprietary trademarks from descriptive terms by following the capitalization style used by the manufacturer.

Information contained in this book has been obtained by Prima Publishing from sources believed to be reliable. However, because of the possibility of human or mechanical error by our sources, Prima Publishing, or others, the Publisher does not guarantee the accuracy, adequacy, or completeness of any information and is not responsible for any errors or omissions or the results obtained from the use of such information. Readers should be particularly aware of the fact that the Internet is an ever-changing entity. Some facts may have changed since this book went to press.

ISBN: 0-7615-2854-7

Library of Congress Catalog Card Number: 00-104860

Printed in the United States of America

00 01 02 03 04 DD 10 9 8 7 6 5 4 3 2 1

To my beloved wife Evelyn, whose smile seldom wanes and whose love ever waxes.

Acknowledgments

My wife Evelyn and children Sophia and Nathanael have been a great encouragement to me as I've brought this book to life. They've rejoiced with me as each chapter made its way out of the outline and onto to the Zip disk. Evelyn, thanks for "living" this book with me. I'd also like to thank my Project Editor, Brian Thomasson who also happens to be my younger brother. Bri, you're a great boss, but don't let it go to your head! Thank you Mom and Dad (Jim and Melody Thomasson) for periodically allowing me to escape to the solitude of your family room and for allowing me to cool my brain in your pool. You guys are a blessing! Bri, Jon and Dad…I couldn't have done it without those walks along the canal! Thanks to all the techies at PCOE. Thank you Kim Spilker for giving me this opportunity. And to my Technical Editor and fellow ASP programmer Ian Feaveryear…live by THE CODE!

About the Author

Michael Thomasson lives in the foothills of the Sierra Nevadas of Northern California along with his lovely wife Evelyn, daughter Sophia and son Nathanael. Michael designs web-enabled database applications for the Placer County Office of Education. He started programming with BASIC in junior high and still considers objects, stored procedures, classes, functions, variables, and the like, toys to be played with. When not at work, Mike can often be found swinging with his wife and kids at the park, hiking with his brothers and father in the woods or catching early morning coffee at Starbucks with some friends from church.

Contents at a Glance

Contents

Introduction

ASP (*Active Server Pages*) is one of the hottest web technologies around. You don't have to browse too many web pages before you realize that a good number of them end with the .asp extension. That's because ASP is not that difficult to learn and provides outstanding performance, scalability and flexibility. ASP is no longer just a "Microsoft thing" either, companies like Chili!Soft have successfully ported ASP to several non-Microsoft platforms. Now's the time to join the ASP revolution if you haven't already! This book will teach you everything you need to know to become proficient at ASP!

ASP is not a standalone technology. ASP is a server-side scripting platform. It is the glue that holds together web applications that contain HTML, VBScript, SQL, ADO and COM/COM+ components. *ASP 3 fast & easy web development* will not only teach you how to program in ASP, but how to effectively use and incorporate the other technologies that are necessary to produce powerful web applications.

Who Should Read This Book

This book is geared toward the reader who has some experience with HTML. Perhaps you're someone who has designed several websites and would like to learn how to take your sites beyond the constraints of static HTML into the realm of the Web application. This is the book for you! If you already know something about Visual Basic, SQL or even ASP then this book will show you how to pull it all together to create customized web sites that will not only present information to the user but interact with the user! This book lays out the essentials of ASP, VBScript, SQL, ADO and COM so that someone who's not familiar with these technologies will be able to get started. However, this book won't bore the person that's already used these technologies either, since it delves into some fairly advanced topics and presents several useful "tricks of the trade."

Additional Features

This book not only ships with a CD-ROM containing all of the code used in the book, but it also contains a full-featured 90 day trial version of Microsoft's Visual InterDev 6.0 which is the industry standard ASP development platform! Additionally, the CD-ROM has Microsoft's Web Application Stress Tool (WAS) that enables you to test how your web application will perform while being hit by hundreds or even thousands of concurrent users. The last few chapters of this book will show you how to use the WAS tool as well as give you several tips on how to maximize the performance and scalability of your ASP web applications. The book also has three useful appendices. One shows step-by-step how to implement SSL encryption on your website. The other appendix lists and explains several useful ASP and web development resources on the web.

Software Requirements

One of the goals of this book is to show you how to develop cutting edge, industrial-strength ASP 3 web applications. ASP 3 requires Windows 2000 (Professional or Server) running Internet Information Server (IIS) 5.0 or higher. However, many of the examples will run on Windows NT 4 or Windows 98 using IIS 4.0 or Personal Web Server (PWS). I point out which code features are new to ASP 3 and VB Script 5 as programming concepts are introduced. Several of the chapters toward the end of the book make use of Visual Basic 6, Access 2000 and SQL Server 7. I included the code for the examples that use these products on the CD-ROM as well. There is a Readme file on the CD-ROM. You must follow the instructions in the Readme file to get the sample scripts to work properly.

1

Getting Started with Visual InterDev

All you really need to create active server pages is a text editor like Notepad. That being said however, there are many reasons why you might want to go with an active server page development tool like Microsoft's Visual InterDev. Just the keyword coloration and auto complete features of Visual InterDev alone make the development of active server pages significantly easier. In this chapter, you'll learn how to:

- Install Visual InterDev
- Create a project
- Use key features of Visual InterDev

Installation

The CD-ROM that came with this book includes a 90-day trial version of Microsoft's Visual InterDev 6.0. Follow these instructions to install Visual InterDev and Microsoft's Internet Information Server (IIS) or Personal Web Server (PWS).

NOTE

Even if you decide not to use Visual InterDev you will still need to have Microsoft's Personal Web Server or Internet Information Server running on your machine in order to view the active server page examples.

Software Requirements

Visual InterDev provides different levels of functionality, depending on the platform it's on. Visual InterDev will run on Windows 95, 98, NT or 2000. However, after running it on each of these platforms, I've found that it works significantly better and has more features when it's run on Windows NT or 2000 machines.

In addition to the operating system, Web server software is required on the development machine if you want to run and debug your active server pages with Visual InterDev.

If you're running Windows 95 or 98, you can run Microsoft's PWS (*Personal Web Server*). To install PWS on Windows 95, you must download it from the Microsoft Web site. To add it to your installation of Windows 98:

1. Open Control Panel and click on Add/Remove Programs.

2. Click on the Windows Setup tab.

3. Click on Internet Tools in the List box, then click on the Details button.

4. Check the Personal Web Server check box if it isn't already, then click on OK.

5. If you're asked to put in your Windows 98 installation disks, do so and follow the instructions from there.

You can use Microsoft Internet Information Server with Windows NT or 2000. Windows NT 4 supports up to IIS 4.0; Windows 2000 supports up to IIS 5.0. To install IIS on Windows 2000:

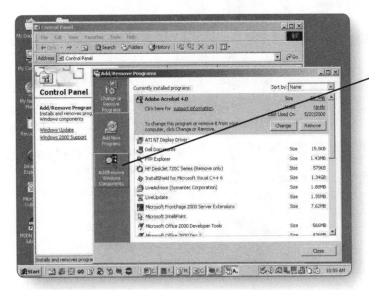

1. Open Control Panel and click on Add/Remove Programs.

2. Click on Add/Remove Windows Components.

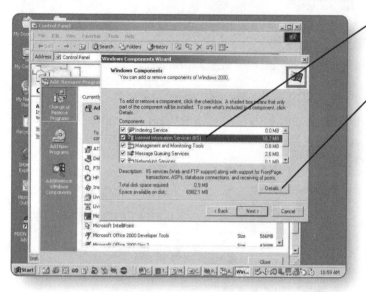

3. Check the Internet Information Services check box if it isn't already.

4. Highlight Internet Information Services by clicking on it. Then click on the Details button.

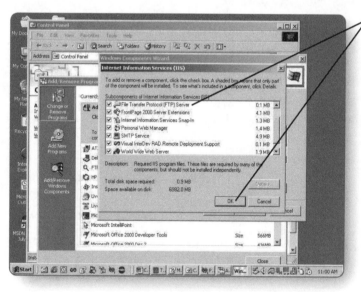

5. Click on all the check boxes. You must have the Front Page Server Extensions to publish your projects. Click on OK.

6. Click on Next to begin the installation.

7. If you're prompted to put in the Windows 2000 Installation disk, do so and follow the directions from there.

NOTE

IIS 5.0 has the ASP 3.0 interpreter. All of the examples in this book were created on Windows 2000 running IIS 5.0. If you are using another configuration, some of the pages will not work.

Installing Visual InterDev

You need to install both the client and the server components of Visual InterDev to use all its features. The following steps take you through the installation process on Windows 2000 and Windows NT. (Look at the Readme file on the Visual InterDev installation disk for information on installing it on Windows 95 or 98.)

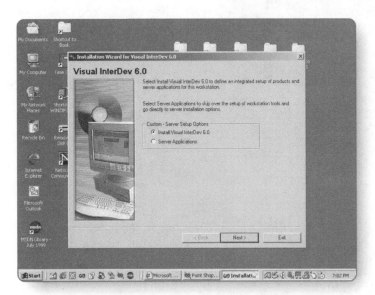

1. Put in the CD-ROM that came with this book. Open the contents of your CD-ROM in Windows Explorer and double-click on Start-Here.html to start the Prima Tech CD-ROM interface. After agreeing to the license, click on Programs from the left column of the interface. Click on Visual InterDev. Click on the Click Here to Install! link on the Visual InterDev page.

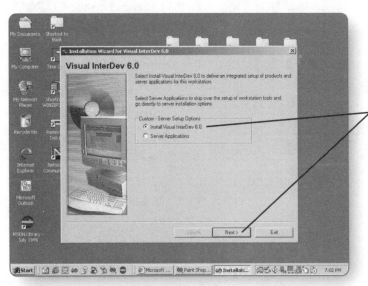

2. Go through the wizard until you get to a screen that allows you to select Custom Server Setup Options.

3. Click on Install Visual InterDev 6.0, then click on Next to begin the client installation.

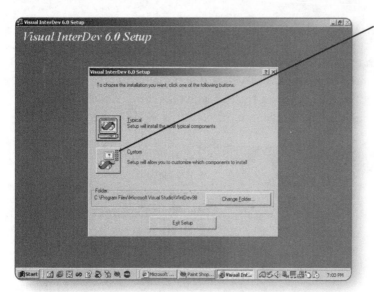

4. Choose Custom and click on Next to select the default install directory on the screen that appears.

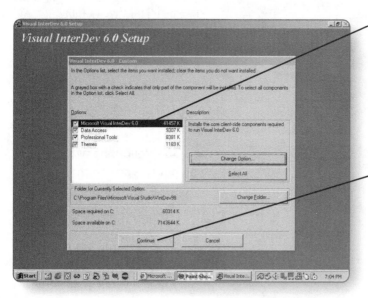

5. Choose the components you want to install. Themes are not required. You should periodically get the latest Microsoft Data Access Components (MDAC) from the Microsoft site. For now, install just those on the CD-ROM.

6. Click on Continue and follow the instructions to complete the installation process.

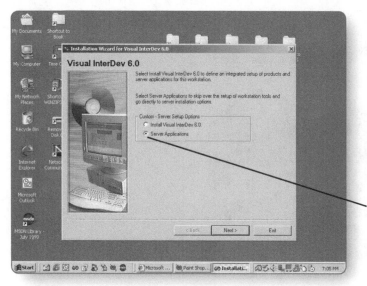

7. After you're done installing the client components, you need to install the server components. If setup does not resume automatically, insert the Prima Tech CD-ROM return to the screen that allows you to select Custom Server Setup Options.

8. This time, click on Server Applications, then click on Next.

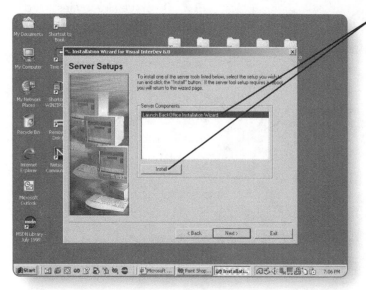

9. Click on Launch Back Office Installation Wizard, then click on Install.

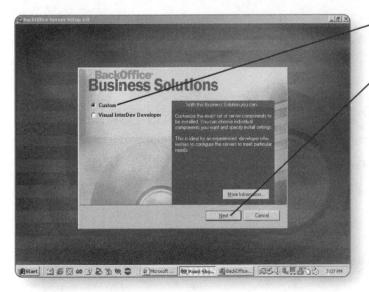

10. Click on Custom, then click on Next.

11. Click on Next again.

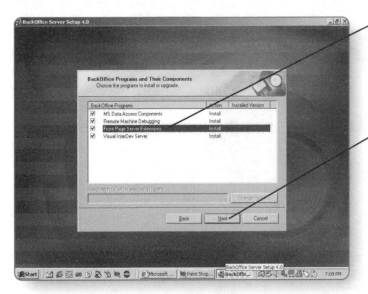

12. If you've already installed IIS 5.0 and Front Page 2000 server extensions, you can uncheck the Front Page Server Extensions checkbox.

13. Click on Next and follow the instructions to finish the installation wizard.

Creating a Project

The main reason to create a project is to deploy your files to the Web server. If you are going to copy and paste or ftp your .asp pages to the Web server manually, you don't need to create a project. If you are using InterDev on a platform that doesn't support creating projects, you can save a collection of files as a *solution*. Now that you have installed Visual InterDev, launch the program from the Start menu. Here are the steps you need to take to create a project:

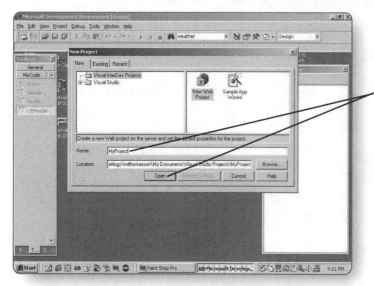

1. Click on File, New Project. The New Project dialog box will appear.

2. Type a name for your project and browse for a location to create the project files. Then click on the Open button.

NOTE

If this is the first time you have launched Visual InterDev, the New Project dialog box will automatically appear.

3. Type the name of the Web server on which you want to create the Web project. I typically create the project on the same computer on which Visual InterDev is running, and manually copy the active server pages to a production Web server after I've tested it. If you create the project locally, you can type **localhost** (or the computer name) in the text box.

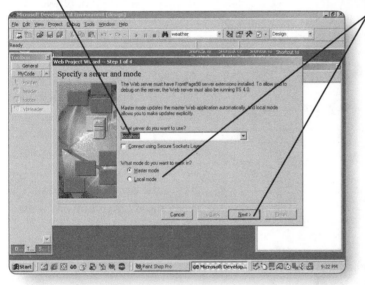

4. Below the server text box are two radio buttons having to do with the *mode* that you want to work in. If you choose Local mode, you have to explicitly synchronize the active server pages you create with the pages on the Web server. If you choose Master mode, any changes you make while developing your .asp pages are automatically updated on the Web server. Master mode is the default, and usually that's what I go with. Click on Next when you've made a decision.

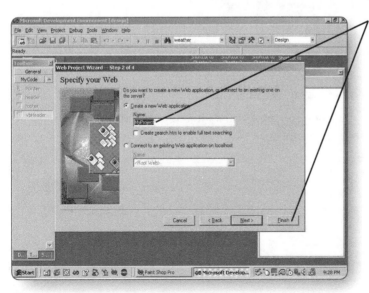

5. On the wizard's next screen you can type the name of your Web application or you can connect to an existing application on the server. The name you choose becomes the name of the virtual directory created on the Web server for your Web application. At this point you can click on Finish and create the project.

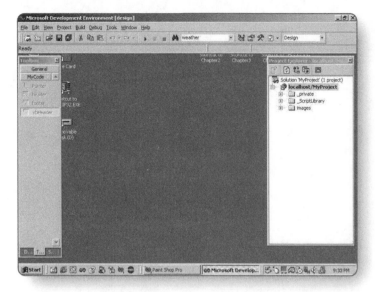

6. After you click on finish, the computer begins cranking away, creating the project files. When it's done, your new project looks like this.

Two copies of every file are created when you make a project. One copy is stored in the location you specified when you created your project. The files are in a folder with the same name as your project.

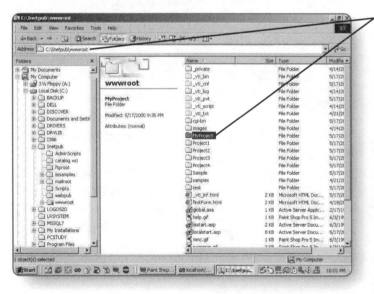

The other copy of the files are in a folder in the Inetpub directory of the Web server on which you created your project. This folder also has the same name as the project.

NOTE

If your configuration doesn't support project creation, you need to copy and paste your active server pages into the Inetpub directory manually. The ASP interpreter automatically processes active server pages in this directory. You can put your active server pages in another directory if you create a Virtual Directory in IIS that points to the directory with the .asp pages.

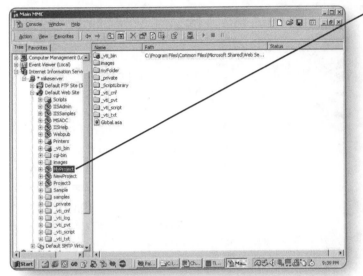

In IIS, a Virtual Directory is also created under the Default Web Site. The virtual directory has the name you entered in the Web Application text box of the Web Project Wizard. Thus the root directory for your web application will be http://<Name of your web server>/<name of web application>.

Adding Files to Your Project

After you've created a new project, you're ready to add folders and files. The project already has an images folder in which you can put your images.

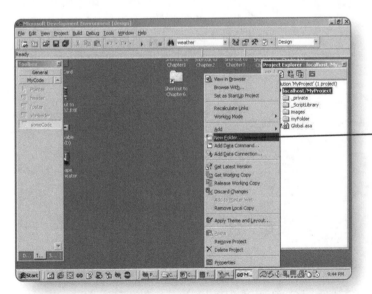

1. To add a folder to your project, right-click on the name of the project in the Project Explorer on the right side of the screen and click on New Folder. Type a name for the folder in the dialog box, and click on OK.

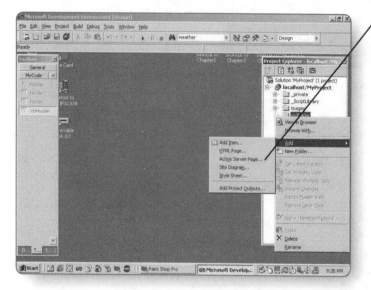

2. To add an active server page to a folder, right-click on the folder and hold the mouse pointer over Add. Another menu will appear that will show the kinds of files that can be added to the folder. The Add Item option is for adding any kind of file (for example .gif or .jpg). Click on Active Server Page.

NOTE

To add an active server page to the root folder right click on the name of the project and hold the mouse pointer over Add. Click on Active Server Page.

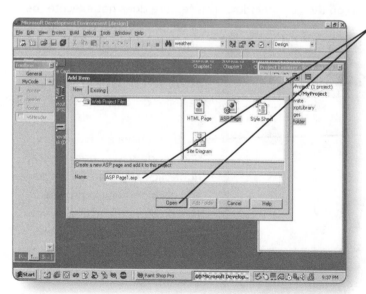

3. In the dialog box that opens you can type the name of an active server page to create or click on the Existing tab to browse for an already existing active server page. Click on Open when you're done.

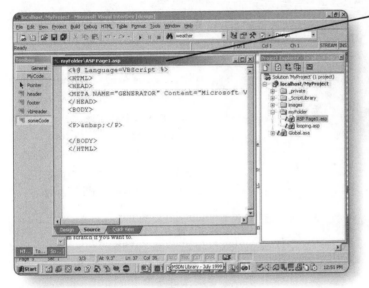

By default, Visual InterDev will insert some "starter" code. You can delete this and start from scratch if you want to. You are now ready to start creating your ASP application.

Previewing Your Pages

After you've created an active server page, you'll want to see if it works. Visual InterDev provides ways to do that. First, you can look at the HTML for the page by clicking on the Design tab on the code window. This feature does not execute the page, however, and is more useful for looking at plain HTML pages. If you want to view the active server page in action, here are the steps to take.

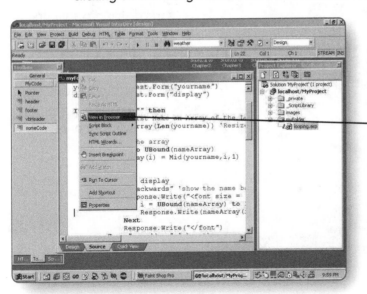

1. If you have an active server page code page open, you can right-click anywhere in the page and click on View in Browser. This displays the active server page in the default browser you've identified.

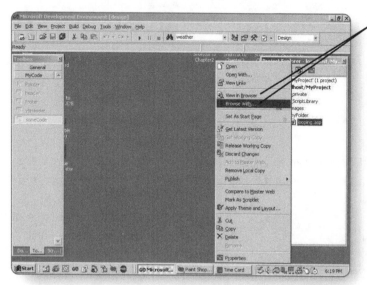

2. Alternatively, you can right-click on the name of the active server page in the Project Explorer. Notice that you can choose View in Browser or Browse With. Select Browse With.

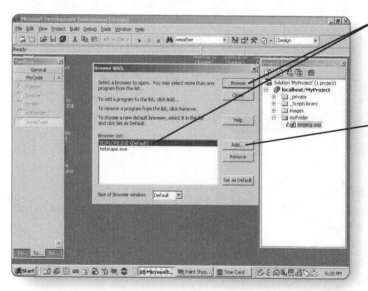

3. Click on the browser in the list and click on Browse.

NOTE

To add browsers to the list, you first must have the browser installed on your computer. Next, click on the Add button and find the browser's executable. After you've done that, you can view your active server pages in the new browser as well. This feature makes it easy to create and test cross-browser Web applications.

Useful Features in Visual InterDev

Visual InterDev is full of features. I am only going to go over those which are most essential to understand.

Options

By clicking on Tools, Options, you can select various settings that affect the way Visual InterDev looks and operates. Here are a few of the options that I usually change:

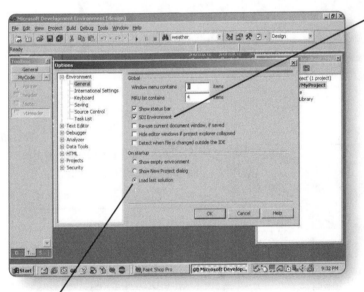

1. Under the General section of the Environment options, click on the SDI environment check box. This changes the look of the development environment. In the SDI(*Single Document*) environment, the windows on the screen *float*, and you can size the code window however you want. The default setting is the MDI (*Multiple Document*) environment. Try both settings to see which you prefer.

2. In the General section under On Startup, check the box that says Load last solution. This option specifies that Visual InterDev should open the last project you were working on when it starts.

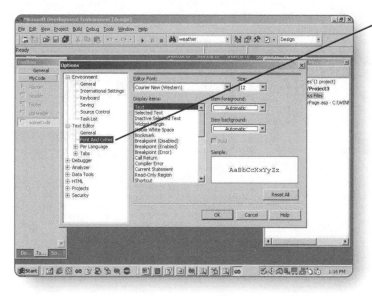

3. If you expand the Text Editor section and click on Font and Colors. You can specify the fonts you want to use when working in the code window. You might want to bump the font up to 11 or 12 points to make it easier to read your code.

Toolbox

One nice feature of Visual InterDev is the Toolbox. The Toolbox is a place to store code snippets. The first time you create a project using Visual InterDev, there are several tabs created in the Toolbox. Each tab contains several code snippets of a certain type (for example, HTML form elements). I usually delete all these tabs and create my own code snippets as I work. Here are the steps for creating tabs and adding and using code snippets in the Toolbox.

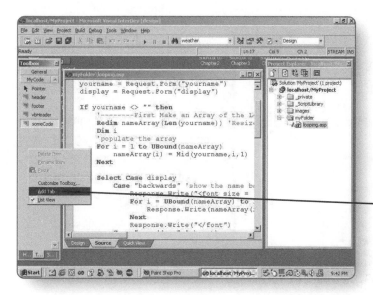

1. Right-click in the Toolbox and click on Add Tab.

2. Type a name for the tab. You might want to have several tabs. For example, an ADO tab to hold ActiveX Data Object code, an HTML tab to hold HTML code, and so on. Alternatively, you can create one tab, like I have, and call it something like "My Code."

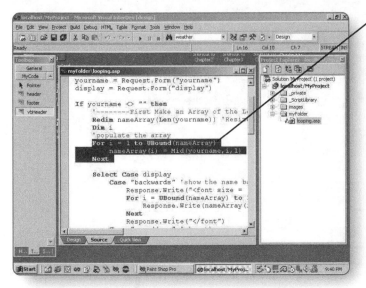

3. To add a code snippet to your Toolbox tab, simply click and drag to highlight the code you want to copy. Then click on the highlighted region and drag the code to the Toolbox. When you release the mouse button the code will be called "HTML Fragment."

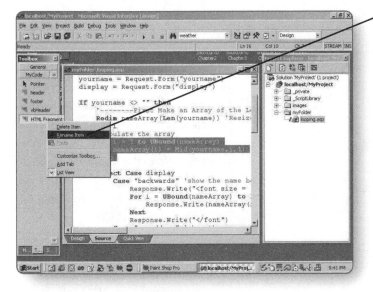

4. Right-click on the new HTML Fragment and click on Rename Item. Name the code something descriptive.

5. To use a code fragment, simply click on the fragment and drag it onto the code page. Let go of the mouse button where you want to place the code.

Style Sheets

Cascading Style Sheets (CSS) are part of the HTML 4.0 specification. They provide a way to apply consistent formatting to your Web pages. Most newer browsers (versions 4.0 or higher of Netscape or IE) support CSS. Visual InterDev has a CSS designer that makes very good cross-browser style sheets. Here's how to make one.

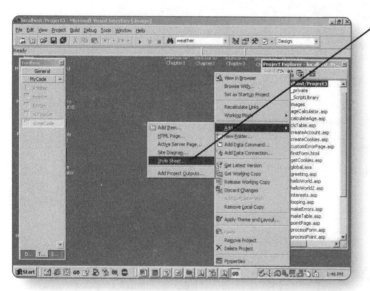

1. Right-click on the folder where you want to put the style sheet and move the mouse pointer over Add. Click on Style Sheet. I usually put my style sheets in the root directory of my application. To do that, right-click on the name of your project in the Project Explorer.

2. You will be prompted to type a name for the style sheet or to select an existing one. Type a name and click on Open.

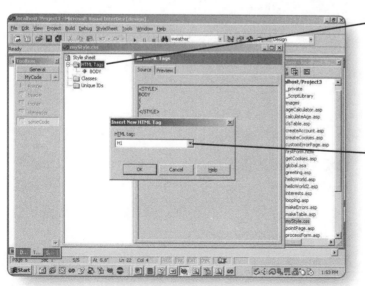

3. On the left hand side you'll notice three folders (HTML Tags, Classes, and Unique ID's). If you right-click on one of the folders, you can add an HTML Tag, Class, or Unique ID respectively.

4. To add "style" to an HTML tag, right-click on the HTML Tag folder and click on Insert HTML Tag. Then select the HTML tag from the drop down list box.

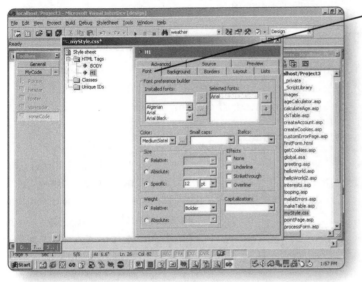

5. Under the Font tab you can specify the attributes this element should have. When this style sheet is applied to a Web page, all the tags specified by it are displayed according to its specifications.

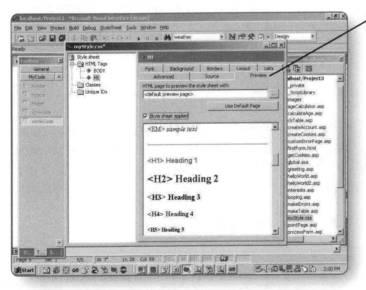

6. To preview your style sheet, click on the Preview tab. You can specify a page to preview with or you can use the default preview page.

7. If you click on the Source tab, you can see the actual HTML code that was produced for your style sheet.

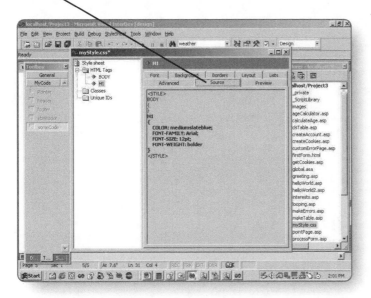

My recommendation is that you keep your style sheets simple. The more "Advanced" features you use, the more browser specific your style sheets become. Be sure to test your style sheets in all the browsers that you are targeting. When you're done with your style sheet, close the window. You are prompted to save the changes to the sheet.

Code Coloration

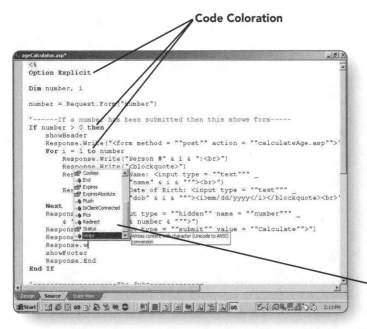

Auto Complete

Auto Complete and Code Coloration

Two other features that make Visual InterDev a great active server page development tool are Auto Complete (Intellisense) and Code Coloration. These features make active server pages easier to write and easier to read.

2

Requesting Information from a Client Using the Request Object

Perhaps the most significant difference between a standard HTML page and a server-side scripting page is the degree of interaction that can occur between the client and the server. In a static HTML page, the conversation is essentially one-sided. The Web's potential uses are greatly increased by the capability to receive information back from the client. This functionality allows ASP to turn regular Web pages into Web applications such as online ordering systems, shopping carts, search screens, customized news pages and the like. Instruction for accomplishing the basic tasks of sending and receiving information to and from the client serves as this chapter's launching point into Active Server Page Web application development. In this chapter, you'll learn how to:

- Use the ASP Request Object to gather information from HTML forms
- Use the ASP Request Object to gather query string information
- Use the ASP Request Object to gather information from other sources

Would you like to select news headlines better suited to the interests of individual users? Do you need your customer's credit card number to fulfill an order? Or do you just want to know who's out there looking at your page? The good news is that with ASP you can do all this and more without too much effort. The ASP Request object provides numerous ways to request information from a client. Information can be gathered from forms that an online user fills out, from pictures or hyperlinks they click on, from information in the HTTP headers, from cookies stored on their computer, or from a client certificate installed on their machine. Knowing when and where to use a particular method of requesting information is something of an art. Learning how to use the particular methods of gathering information, however, is not difficult at all.

There are five collections (categories of information) associated with the Request object. They are the Form, Query String, Cookies, Server Variables, and Client Certificate collections. The following syntax is used to request a particular value from one of these collections:

```
Request[.Collection]("Name of Item in Collection")
```

For example, to request the value of a form element named "customerName", the following syntax is used :

```
Request.Form("customerName")
```

We'll examine each of these collections in more detail in the following sections.

Requesting Information from Forms

Perhaps the most typical place to request information from a Web page is from an HTML form. In this section, you'll learn how to use the ASP Request object to retrieve information sent from an HTML form.

HTML Form Basics

Since forms play such an important roll in a Web application, we'll go over the fundamentals of HTML forms. You're probably already familiar with HTML forms. But here's a little refresher just in case you forgot.

Anatomy of a Form

This form contains the elements you'll use most often.

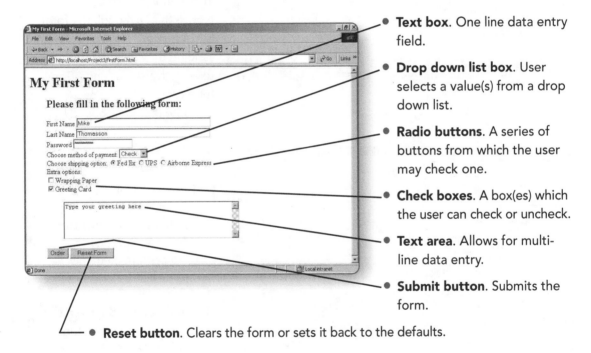

- **Text box**. One line data entry field.

- **Drop down list box**. User selects a value(s) from a drop down list.

- **Radio buttons**. A series of buttons from which the user may check one.

- **Check boxes**. A box(es) which the user can check or uncheck.

- **Text area**. Allows for multi-line data entry.

- **Submit button**. Submits the form.

- **Reset button**. Clears the form or sets it back to the defaults.

```
firstform.html
<HTML>
<HEAD>
<title>My First Form</title>
</HEAD>
<BODY>
<h1>My First Form</h1>
<blockquote>
    <h2>Please fill in the following form:</h2>
    <form method = "post" action = "processForm.asp">
        First Name <input type = "text" size = "50" name = "fname"><br>
        Last Name <input type = "text" size = "50" name = "lname"><br>
        Password <input type = "password" maxlength = "20"
        name = "password"><br>

        Choose method of payment:
        <select name = "payment">
            <option SELECTED>Check
            <option>Charge
        </select><br>

        Choose shipping option:
        <input type = "radio" name = "shipping" CHECKED
        value = "fedex">Fed Ex
        <input type = "radio" name = "shipping" value = "ups">UPS
        <input type = "radio" name = "shipping" value = "air">
        Airborne Express
        <br>

        Extra options:</br>
```
Design   Source   Quick View

The `<form>` tag indicates the beginning of the form. Notice the attributes of the tag. `method` refers to how the information in the form should be sent. This can be `"post"` or `"get"` (see "The Get versus the Post Method" later in this chapter). The `action` attribute refers to where the information should be sent. Notice that, although the form is in a normal HTML page, we are sending the output of the form to an active server page. The form can also have a `name` attribute (it's not required).

```
firstform.html
<HTML>
<HEAD>
<title>My First Form</title>
</HEAD>
<BODY>
<h1>My First Form</h1>
<blockquote>
    <h2>Please fill in the following form:</h2>
    <form method = "post" action = "processForm.asp">
        First Name <input type = "text" size = "50" name = "fname"><br>
        Last Name <input type = "text" size = "50" name = "lname"><br>
        Password <input type = "password" maxlength = "20"
        name = "password"><br>

        Choose method of payment:
        <select name = "payment">
            <option SELECTED>Check
            <option>Charge
        </select><br>

        Choose shipping option:
        <input type = "radio" name = "shipping" CHECKED
        value = "fedex">Fed Ex
        <input type = "radio" name = "shipping" value = "ups">UPS
        <input type = "radio" name = "shipping" value = "air">
        Airborne Express
        <br>

        Extra options:</br>
```
Design   Source   Quick View

NOTE

The `name` attribute becomes important when you're using JavaScript to reference a particular form or form element.

Notice that after the form tag there are several other tags (which I've indented). The `<input>`, `<select>`, and `<textarea>` tags are all referred to as the "elements" of the form.

`<input>` tags are the most common elements of a form. The `type` attribute can be "text", "radio", "checkbox", "password", "file", "hidden", "button", "reset", or "submit". All of the elements in a form should also have a `name` attribute. This attribute allows both client and server-side scripts to reference the form elements.

```
firstForm.html
<HTML>
<HEAD>
<title>My First Form</title>
</HEAD>
<BODY>
<h1>My First Form</h1>
<blockquote>
    <h2>Please fill in the following form:</h2>
    <form method = "post" action = "processForm.asp">
        First Name <input type = "text" size = "50" name = "fname"><br>
        Last Name <input type = "text" size = "50" name = "lname"><br>
        Password <input type = "password" maxlength = "20"
        name = "password"><br>

        Choose method of payment:
        <select name = "payment">
            <option SELECTED>Check
            <option>Charge
        </select><br>

        Choose shipping option:
        <input type = "radio" name = "shipping" CHECKED
        value = "fedex">Fed Ex
        <input type = "radio" name = "shipping" value = "ups">UPS
        <input type = "radio" name = "shipping" value = "air">
        Airborne Express
        <br>

        Extra options:<br>
```

The `<input type = "text" name = "someName">` line creates a text box. This tag can have many attributes. Those most frequently used are size, maxlength, and value. The size is how many characters wide the text box should be. The maxlength refers to how many characters the box will allow the user to input. The value is the default text that shows up in the text box.

```
firstForm.html
<HTML>
<HEAD>
<title>My First Form</title>
</HEAD>
<BODY>
<h1>My First Form</h1>
<blockquote>
    <h2>Please fill in the following form:</h2>
    <form method = "post" action = "processForm.asp">
        First Name <input type = "text" size = "50" name = "fname"><br>
        Last Name <input type = "text" size = "50" name = "lname"><br>
        Password <input type = "password" maxlength = "20"
        name = "password"><br>

        Choose method of payment:
        <select name = "payment">
            <option SELECTED>Check
            <option>Charge
        </select><br>

        Choose shipping option:
        <input type = "radio" name = "shipping" CHECKED
        value = "fedex">Fed Ex
        <input type = "radio" name = "shipping" value = "ups">UPS
        <input type = "radio" name = "shipping" value = "air">
        Airborne Express
        <br>

        Extra options:<br>
```

To hide the text while it is being typed, use type = "password" with the `<input>` tag. The only difference between this and a normal text box is that characters show up as asterisks on the screen so that an onlooker won't be able to see what's being typed.

NOTE

Data entered in a password field is still sent over the wire in plain text. If password privacy is important, then the site should be encrypted using SSL. For more information, see Appendix A, "Setting up SSL Encryption on IIS."

```
firstForm.html
    <HEAD>
    <title>My First Form</title>
    </HEAD>
    <BODY>
    <h1>My First Form</h1>
    <blockquote>
        <h2>Please fill in the following form:</h2>
        <form method = "post" action = "processForm.asp">
            First Name <input type = "text" size = "50" name = "fname"><br>
            Last Name <input type = "text" size = "50" name = "lname"><br>
            Password <input type = "password" maxlength = "20"
            name = "password"><br>

            Choose method of payment:
            <select name = "payment">
                <option SELECTED>Check
                <option>Charge
            </select><br>

            Choose shipping option:
            <input type = "radio" name = "shipping" CHECKED
            value = "fedex">Fed Ex
            <input type = "radio" name = "shipping" value = "ups">UPS
            <input type = "radio" name = "shipping" value = "air">
            Airborne Express
            <br>

            Extra options:<br>
            <input type = "checkbox" name = "paper">Wrapping Paper<br>
```

```
Design   Source   Quick View
```

Another frequently used form element is the <select> tag and its child element, the <option> tag. This tag creates a drop down list box from which users can select an option. The <option> tag can be used with or without a value attribute. If you use the value attribute then the information specified by the value attribute will be sent with the form. If you don't use the value attribute then the text after the <option> tag will be sent. The text after each <option> tag shows up in the list. Notice that a closing </option> tag is not necessary. The multiple keyword with the <select> tag enables users to select multiple members of the drop down list when they hold either the CTRL key or the SHIFT key while selecting (usage: <select multiple>). The size attribute of the <select> tag refers to the number of list items shown in the list box while it is not being clicked. The default value of the size attribute is 1. As for the <option> tag, the keyword selected refers to the list member that should be selected by default. Remember to put a closing </select> tag after the last option.

```
firstForm.html
<HEAD>
<title>My First Form</title>
</HEAD>
<BODY>
<h1>My First Form</h1>
<blockquote>
    <h2>Please fill in the following form:</h2>
    <form method = "post" action = "processForm.asp">
        First Name <input type = "text" size = "50" name = "fname"><br>
        Last Name <input type = "text" size = "50" name = "lname"><br>
        Password <input type = "password" maxlength = "20"
        name = "password"><br>

        Choose method of payment:
        <select name = "payment">
            <option SELECTED>Check
            <option>Charge
        </select><br>

        Choose shipping option:
        <input type = "radio" name = "shipping" CHECKED
        value = "fedex">Fed Ex
        <input type = "radio" name = "shipping" value = "ups">UPS
        <input type = "radio" name = "shipping" value = "air">
        Airborne Express
        <br>

        Extra options:<br>
        <input type = "checkbox" name = "paper">Wrapping Paper<br>
```

```
Design    Source    Quick View
```

Radio buttons are useful when you want to present users with an assortment of options from which only one can be chosen. The radio buttons are created using the <input> tag with the type attribute set to "radio". Radio buttons require both the name and value attributes. Note that the name attribute has to be the same for every member of a set of radio buttons. Use the checked keyword to identify which radio button is checked by default.

```
firstForm.html
        Choose shipping option:
        <input type = "radio" name = "shipping" CHECKED
        value = "fedex">Fed Ex
        <input type = "radio" name = "shipping" value = "ups">UPS
        <input type = "radio" name = "shipping" value = "air">
        Airborne Express
        <br>

        Extra options:<br>
        <input type = "checkbox" name = "paper">Wrapping Paper<br>
        <input type = "checkbox" CHECKED name = "card">Greeting Card<br>
            <blockquote>
                <textarea name = "greeting" rows = "5"
                cols = "50" wrap = "soft">Type your greeting here
                </textarea>
            </blockquote>

        <input type = "submit" value = "Order">
        <input type = "reset" value = "Reset Form"><br>
    </form>
</blockquote>
</BODY>
</HTML>
```

```
Design    Source    Quick View
```

Check boxes are similar to radio buttons, however, they are not bound together. Any check box can be checked or unchecked without affecting the state of other check boxes. There is no value attribute for this element. The checked keyword can be used to make the check box checked by default.

```
firstForm.html

        Choose shipping option:
        <input type = "radio" name = "shipping" CHECKED
        value = "fedex">Fed Ex
        <input type = "radio" name = "shipping" value = "ups">UPS
        <input type = "radio" name = "shipping" value = "air">
        Airborne Express
        <br>

        Extra options:<br>
        <input type = "checkbox" name = "paper">Wrapping Paper<br>
        <input type = "checkbox" CHECKED name = "card">Greeting Card<br>
            <blockquote>
                <textarea name = "greeting" rows = "5"
                cols = "50" wrap = "soft">Type your greeting here
                </textarea>
            </blockquote>

        <input type = "submit" value = "Order">
        <input type = "reset" value = "Reset Form"><br>
    </form>
</blockquote>
</BODY>
</HTML>

Design   Source   Quick View
```

For the wordy among you, there's the <textarea> tag. While text boxes are intended for one-line inputs, text areas can contain multiple lines of text. The rows attribute sets how many characters high the text area should be, and the cols attribute sets how many characters wide the text area should be. Any default text should be placed between the <textarea></textarea> tags.

CAUTION

For the sake of those using Netscape browsers, consider using the following attribute: wrap = "soft", otherwise the text in the text area doesn't wrap.

```
firstForm.html

        Choose shipping option:
        <input type = "radio" name = "shipping" CHECKED
        value = "fedex">Fed Ex
        <input type = "radio" name = "shipping" value = "ups">UPS
        <input type = "radio" name = "shipping" value = "air">
        Airborne Express
        <br>

        Extra options:<br>
        <input type = "checkbox" name = "paper">Wrapping Paper<br>
        <input type = "checkbox" CHECKED name = "card">Greeting Card<br>
            <blockquote>
                <textarea name = "greeting" rows = "5"
                cols = "50" wrap = "soft">Type your greeting here
                </textarea>
            </blockquote>

        <input type = "submit" value = "Order">
        <input type = "reset" value = "Reset Form"><br>
    </form>
</blockquote>
</BODY>
</HTML>

Design   Source   Quick View
```

Finally, the end of the form comes with the Submit and Reset buttons. These are both defined within an <input> tag with the type attribute set to "submit" or "reset" respectively. The value attribute of the buttons determines what text will show up in the button itself. A submit button sends the information in the form to the page specified by the action attribute of the <form> tag. A reset button is not required. When clicked on, it clears the form or sets it back to the defaults.

There are three other elements that are sometimes useful. The "hidden" element, `<input type = "hidden">`, is useful in multi-page forms to pass data from one page to the next. The "button" element, `<input type = "button">`, simply puts on the form a button that looks like a submit or reset button. The JavaScript `onclick` event of the button can be used to build in desired functionality. Finally, the "file" element, `<input type = "file">`, can be used to upload files from the client machine to the server.

The Get Method versus the Post Method

Recall that the `<form>` tag's `method` attribute can have two different values: "get" or "post". The `post` method sends the data in HTTP format to the server. The `get` method, on the other hand, sends the data in a query string attached to the URL. A query string is assortment of characters starting with a "?" that follows the name of the Web page in a URL (for example, `myPage.html?something=yes&else=no`). Consider the following guidelines when you're deciding which method to use:

- Some older browsers limit how long the query string can be. For this reason, you wouldn't want to use the `get` method when the form has a lot of data in it.

- Data sent using the `get` method will show up in plain text as a query string in the address bar of the browser. Hidden fields and password fields will be visible to the user and those who might be looking on.

- If you want to be able to pass data into a form from a hyperlink, use the `get` method because a query string can be put in a hyperlink.

Based on these considerations, plan on using the `post` method by default, and the `get` method when information will be passed into the form from a hyperlink.

Getting Information from a Form

Now that we've reviewed the basic principles of HTML forms, we're ready to get down to what you're really after: how to get that credit card number from the form. This is where the ASP Request object comes in. Referencing the `Request.Form` collection allows you to retrieve data sent from a form using the `post` method.

The simplest way to request information from the Form collection is to refer by name to the individual elements of the form. For example, the value that was entered for the form element named "payment" can be obtained through `Request.Form("payment")`.

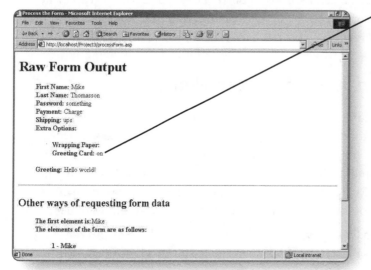

This screen shot of processForm.asp shows the "raw output" of the form in the firstForm.html page. Notice that all of the elements in the form with the exception of the checkbox elements returned the actual text that was entered, checked, or selected. The checkbox elements that were "checked" in the form return a value of "on".

I'll explain the <%= …%> marks more in Chapter 3," Responding from the Server Using the Response Object." For now, just notice that the value of the form element named by the `Request.Form("element")` method is returned as HTML to the client.

```
 processForm.asp                                                    _|B|X|
          <blockquote>
              <b>Wrapping Paper:</b> <%=Request.Form("paper")%><br>
              <b>Greeting Card:</b> <%=Request.Form("card")%><br>
          </blockquote>
          <b>Greeting:</b> <%=Request.Form("greeting")%><br>
      </blockquote>
      <hr>
      <h2>Other ways of requesting form data</h2>
      <blockquote>
          <b>The first element is:</b><%=Request.Form(1)%><br>
          <b>The elements of the form are as follows:</b><br>
              <blockquote>
                  <%
                  theCount = Request.Form.Count
                  For i = 1 to theCount
                      Response.Write("<b>" & i & " - " & Request.Form(i) & "</b>
                  Next
                  %>
              </blockquote>
      </blockquote>
      </body>
      </html>
 Design   Source   Quick View
```

There are some other ways of requesting form data that sometimes come in handy. One method is to refer to each element of the form by a number. Each element of the form is numbered in the order that it appears in the form, starting from 1. Therefore, the value of the first element of a form can be referenced by `Request.Form(1)`.

```
 processForm.asp                                                    _|B|X|
          <blockquote>
              <b>Wrapping Paper:</b> <%=Request.Form("paper")%><br>
              <b>Greeting Card:</b> <%=Request.Form("card")%><br>
          </blockquote>
          <b>Greeting:</b> <%=Request.Form("greeting")%><br>
      </blockquote>
      <hr>
      <h2>Other ways of requesting form data</h2>
      <blockquote>
          <b>The first element is:</b><%=Request.Form(1)%><br>
          <b>The elements of the form are as follows:</b><br>
              <blockquote>
                  <%
                  theCount = Request.Form.Count
                  For i = 1 to theCount
                      Response.Write("<b>" & i & " - " & Request.Form(i) & "</b>
                  Next
                  %>
              </blockquote>
      </blockquote>
      </body>
      </html>
 Design   Source   Quick View
```

Sometimes it's useful to loop through all elements in a form and take action according to the value of each element. One way to create such a loop is to find the total number of elements returned by the form and loop until the final element is reached. You can get the count of all elements sent by a form using `Request.Form.Count`. Next, simply loop through the elements from 1 to `Request.Form.Count`. Don't worry about the `For...Next` loop and `Response.Write` stuff for now; I'll discuss these in detail in later chapters. The purpose of this example is to show that `Request.Form.Count` can be a useful tool to get information out of a form.

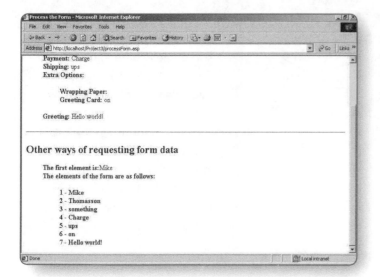

Now you see the first element of the form using `Request.Form(1)` followed by the output of the `For...Next` loop.

Requesting Information from Point and Click Pages

Although online forms are great for gathering data entry type information from a user, it's often useful to gather information through the hyperlinks that a user clicks. Suppose, for example, you have an online magazine. While you could create a separate HTML page for every article in your magazine, it would be much easier to create one active server page as a template for displaying all the articles. The magazine's home page could have hyperlinks with the titles of this month's articles. When a user clicks on a title, the name of the article could be sent to the active server page that displays the articles. That particular article could then be pulled out of a database and displayed in the page. Another common scenario is an online marketplace in which a user clicks on the picture of the product they want to purchase. When the user clicks on the picture, the product's ID might be sent to an order page where the appropriate ordering information could be gathered. These "point and click" options can be implemented in ASP through the `Request.QueryString` collection.

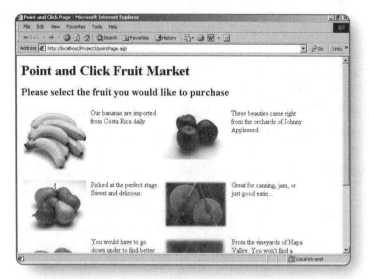

Welcome to my online fruit stand! Yes, you can buy anything on the Web! In this simple example, an online customer clicks on the produce he/she wants to purchase. The selection is then sent to another page where the ordering process can begin.

Notice that every picture on the page is a hyperlink pointing to the active server page, processPoint.asp. Each hyperlink has a query string appended to it that indicates the kind of fruit the customer wants to purchase and what color the fruit is. Let's consider each part of the query string.

First, every query string starts with the "?" character, which immediately follows the name of the Web page the hyperlink points to. After that is the name of the first element in the query string (in this case, "fruit"). Following an "=" is the value of the element (grapes, apples, and so on). Each additional element in the query string is preceded by an "&" character. This query string has only two elements (fruit and color), so it needs only one "&" to separate them.

> ### NOTE
>
> Although I've hard coded the values of these query strings, the values usually come from a database, cookie, server variable, session variable, or the like. We'll see plenty of examples later in the book. This example introduces you to the concept of creating a query string.

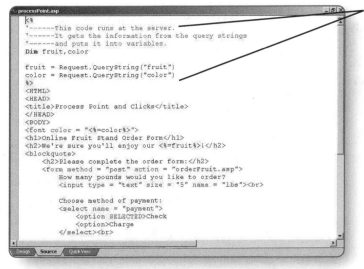

Now you need to see how to retrieve the information from the query string in the processPoint.asp page. First, notice that the top of the page has some non-HTML looking information between <% and %>. That information is server-side script. Information within the bracket/ percent block is processed on the server. Microsoft IIS is set up to process server-side script as VBScript by default (I'll talk more about VBScript in Chapter 4, "VBScript Basics").

> ### NOTE
>
> You can explicitly specify that a page use VBScript by putting the following line at the top of the page `<%@LANGUAGE=VBScript%>`. Such a statement is known as an "@directive." It tells the ASP interpreter how a page should be processed. There are five @directives in ASP. We'll be looking at the `@ENABLESESSIONSTATE` directive in Chapter 7 and the `@TRANSACTION` directive in Chapter 11.

```
processPoint.asp
<%
'------This code runs at the server.
'------It gets the information from the query strings
'------and puts it into variables.
Dim fruit,color

fruit = Request.QueryString("fruit")
color = Request.QueryString("color")
%>
<HTML>
<HEAD>
<title>Process Point and Clicks</title>
</HEAD>
<BODY>
<font color = "<%=color%>">
<h1>Online Fruit Stand Order Form</h1>
<h2>We're sure you'll enjoy our <%=fruit%>!</h2>
<blockquote>
    <h2>Please complete the order form:</h2>.
    <form method = "post" action = "orderFruit.asp">
        How many pounds would you like to order?
        <input type = "text" size = "5" name = "lbs"><br>

        Choose method of payment:
        <select name = "payment">
            <option SELECTED>Check
            <option>Charge
        </select><br>
```
Design   Source   Quick View

In this case, I've created two variables to hold the information that was sent in the query string. The process of getting the information from the query string is similar to getting information from a form. To get the value of a particular element from the query string you can refer to the element by name. In this case, the line `fruit = Request.QueryString("fruit")` gets the information from the "fruit" element and stuffs it into the "fruit" variable. Likewise, information from the "color" element is put in the "color" variable.

```
processPoint.asp
<BODY>
<font color = "<%=color%>">
<h1>Online Fruit Stand Order Form</h1>
<h2>We're sure you'll enjoy our <%=fruit%>!</h2>
<blockquote>
    <h2>Please complete the order form:</h2>
    <form method = "post" action = "orderFruit.asp">
        How many pounds would you like to order?
        <input type = "text" size = "5" name = "lbs"><br>

        Choose method of payment:
        <select name = "payment">
            <option SELECTED>Check
            <option>Charge
        </select><br>

        Choose shipping option:
        <input type = "radio" name = "shipping" CHECKED value = "fedex">
        Fed Ex
        <input type = "radio" name = "shipping" value = "ups">UPS
        <input type = "radio" name = "shipping" value = "air">
        Airborne Express
        <br><br>

        <input type = "hidden" name = "fruit" value = "<%=fruit%>">
        <input type = "submit" value = "Order">
        <input type = "reset" value = "Reset Form"><br>
    </form>
```
Design   Source   Quick View

Notice how the information we've gathered from the point and click page can now be used in this page. For one thing, I've taken the "color" element and used it to change the color of the text on the page. I also cajole my online customers by telling them that they will most certainly enjoy whatever type of fruit they selected (to boost their confidence, you know).

```
processPoint.asp
<BODY>
<font color = "<%=color%>">
<h1>Online Fruit Stand Order Form</h1>
<h2>We're sure you'll enjoy our <%=fruit%>!</h2>
<blockquote>
    <h2>Please complete the order form:</h2>
    <form method = "post" action = "orderFruit.asp">
        How many pounds would you like to order?
        <input type = "text" size = "5" name = "lbs"><br>

        Choose method of payment:
        <select name = "payment">
            <option SELECTED>Check
            <option>Charge
        </select><br>

        Choose shipping option:
        <input type = "radio" name = "shipping" CHECKED value = "fedex">
        Fed Ex
        <input type = "radio" name = "shipping" value = "ups">UPS
        <input type = "radio" name = "shipping" value = "air">
        Airborne Express
        <br><br>

        <input type = "hidden" name = "fruit" value = "<%=fruit%>">
        <input type = "submit" value = "Order">
        <input type = "reset" value = "Reset Form"><br>
    </form>
</blockquote>
```

Design   **Source**   Quick View

Lastly, notice that I set the value of the hidden "fruit" element to the value of the "fruit" variable. That way the type of fruit being purchased can be passed on along with the other order information to the orderFruit.asp page.

CAUTION

There is no orderFruit.asp page. If you click on the Order button you will get an error. This is the end of my example. If the customer was actually going to order the fruit then you would have an orderFruit.asp page in which all of the credit card info, customer address and so on would be retrieved.

Here is the output of processPoint.asp. Let me assure you that the color is "green" even though you're seeing it in black and white.

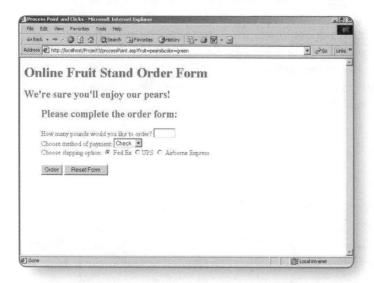

One last thing before we leave our introduction to query strings. The query strings I've created have had simple one-word values with only alpha-numeric characters. Often, however, the value of a query string might have spaces or special characters. In that case the query string has to be translated into the proper URL query string syntax. For example, a space will be translated to the "+" character, while a "/" will be translated to "%2F". Failure to properly encode complex query strings will confuse some Web browsers. The ASP Server object provides a means of encoding query strings.

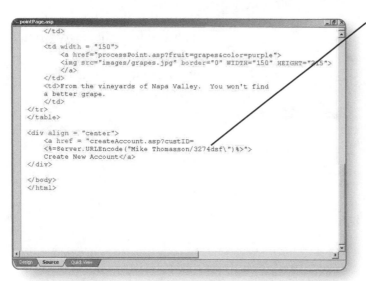

At the bottom of pointPage.asp you'll notice there's a hyperlink to createAccount.asp. Notice that the value of the custID element in the query string is passed to a function of the Server object called Server.URLEncode. Any string of characters passed to this function is translated into the proper URL query string syntax. I made up a customer ID with some special characters in it just to illustrate what the function does. Customers are often assigned a GUID (*globally unique identifier*) or some other complex ID that is passed by a query string from page to page. These IDs are good candidates for URL encoding.

NOTE

There is also a `Server.HTMLEncode` method that will "translate" text into the proper HTML encoding. For example, it will convert any "<" signs to `"&lt;"`. The ASP Server object is a "helper object." It provides many useful methods that aid in performing various other ASP tasks. Rather than having a section that explains the methods of the Server object I decided to explain the methods in the context of other examples. Look for examples that use the Server object throughout the book.

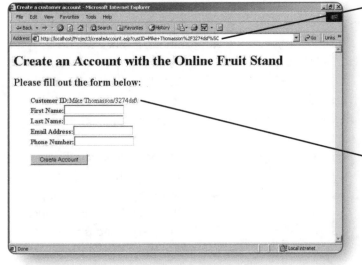

You can see from the address bar of createAccount.asp that the `Server.URLEncode` function has performed its duty. All special characters were translated into the correct URL syntax.

Notice that the information gathered from the query string using `Request.QueryString` is put back into the original "human" readable format.

Other Places to Request Information

Besides being used to retrieve information from forms and query strings the Request object can also be used to gather information from the ServerVariables, Cookies and ClientCertificate collections. In this section you'll learn about these collections as well as how to retrieve information from them using the Request object.

Server Variables

There's some valuable information that you can find using the `Request.ServerVariables` collection. This collection extracts information from the HTTP Headers that are sent between client and server. To find out about the available HTTP Headers, search for "server variables" or "http headers" in the online MSDN Library at http://msdn.microsoft.com .

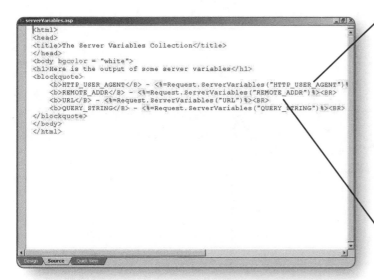

The `HTTP_USER_AGENT` header gives information about the Web browser and operating system a user is using. You can create a browser detection script that sends users different content depending on the browser used. This is also useful information to put in your own hit counter database.

The `REMOTE_ADDR` is the address of the server making the HTTP request (like the user's ISP). This can be useful information to put into a hit counter database as well. You could also grant or deny access to certain pages depending on which server IP address the user was coming from.

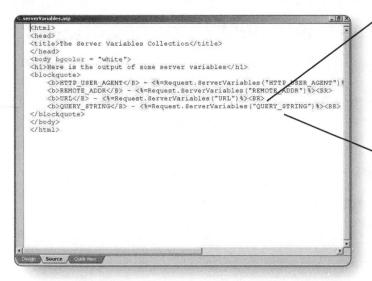

The URL shows the base URL of the current Web page. You can put this information in your hit counter database to find out how many hits a particular page is getting.

The QUERY_STRING header returns the query string appended to the URL (if there is one). You may want to put this in your hit counter database as well.

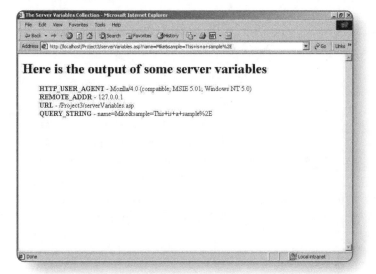

Here's the output of this page on my machine.

Cookies

Cookies are bits of information stored on a user's machine. Cookies are associated with a particular domain (Web site). Only the server from that domain can read cookies written by the domain. Examples of cookies might include a customer ID, a time of last visit, user preferences etc. To request the value of a cookie we use `Request.Cookies("name of cookie")`. Cookies can have sub values, called *keys*. These values can be accessed using `Request.Cookies("name of cookie")("name of key")`. For example, there might be a "customer" cookie that has two keys, one named "lastPurchaseDate" and another named "totalPurchases". These keys could be obtained using `Request.Cookies("customer")("lastPurchaseDate")` and `Request.Cookies("customer")("totalPurchases")` respectively. To find out if a particular cookie has keys, refer to `Request.Cookies("name of cookie").HasKeys`. If the cookie does have keys, then it will equal "true," otherwise it will be "false." I'll talk more about how to create and use cookies in Chapter 3, "Responding from the Server Using the Response Object."

Client Certificates

Most Web servers used in e-commerce have what's called a *server certificate*. The certificate is a unique "key" installed on the server. It allows visitors to Web sites on the server to authenticate that the Web site indeed belongs to a legitimate, verifiable company or organization. Certificates are issued by a *certificate authority* like Verisign (www.verisign.com), or Thawte (www.thawte.com). These authorities validate that a particular company is legitimate and that it has the right to use the domain name it's using. Web servers need to have such a certificate installed in order to host SSL encrypted Web sites. Individuals can also purchase a certificate from a certificate authority. An active server page can look for a client certificate on a client machine using the `Request.ClientCertificate` collection. To request various attributes of a client certificate, use `Request.ClientCertificate("name of attribute")`. For example, the issuer of the certificate can be obtained from `Request.ClientCertificate("Issuer")`. Information obtained from a client certificate can be used to grant or deny access, decide what content a user should see, forward a user to another page, etc. Among the information contained in a client certificate is the user's common name, initials, country, state or province, organization, title, and so on.

In this chapter you've learned how to request information from the five collections of the Request object. In addition to these collections, the Request object also has one property, TotalBytes, which specifies how many bytes of data the client is sending in the HTTP request. There is also one method, BinaryRead, which can be used in conjunction with the TotalBytes property to read in post data from a form. TotalBytes and BinaryRead are primarily used to upload files from the client to the server.

3

Responding from the Server Using the Response Object

In Chapter 2, "Requesting Information from a Client Using the Request Object," you learned about the ASP Request object. In this chapter, we'll learn about its counterpart, the ASP Response object. Whereas the Request object had to do with requesting information from the client (or HTTP headers), the Response object has to do with sending a response back to the client. These two objects work together to enable two-way communication between the client and the server.

The Response object has only one collection (the Cookies collection) as opposed to the Request object's five collections. The Response object makes up for this, however, with its many properties and methods, while the Request object only has one of each. In this chapter, you'll learn how to:

- Use the Response object's methods and properties
- Send Information back to the client browser
- Control when, how and what information is sent to the client

Keep in mind that while the Request object is used primarily to read information coming in from the client, the Response object is used to send information back to the client. Therefore, most of the time you will be setting the value of something to be sent back to the client. The syntax of the Response object usually looks something like this:

To set the value of a property:

```
Response[.SomeProperty] = Something
```

To use a method:

```
Response[.SomeMethod]("Some string of characters.")
```

You'll take a closer look at the exact syntax for the collection, properties, and methods of the Response object as you move through the chapter.

Sending Information Back to the Client

Okay, so you finally got the credit card number from your customer. Now what? Well, perhaps you ought to say, "thank you!" That's where the Response object comes in. Its main job is to send information out to the client. In this section, you'll learn about the two ways the ASP Response object can send information to a client. First, you'll consider the `Response.Write` method that allows ASP to add information directly into the HTTP stream along with other HTML. Second, you'll see how to use the `Response.Cookies` collection to create and send cookies to be stored on the client machine.

Response.Write

Response.Write is the most frequently used method of the Response object. All it does is add information into the HTTP response stream being sent to the client. Consider the following example.

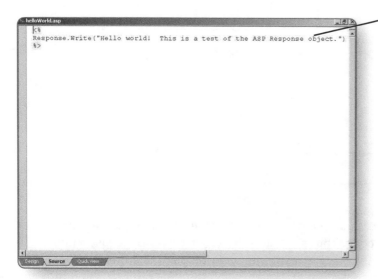

Notice that the text in quotes will simply be output to the HTTP stream as plain text.

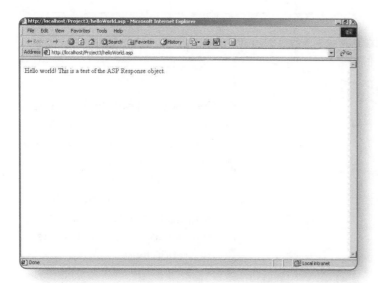

Since most browsers are set up to accept text or HTML by default, the browser will recognize that the stream contains text and display it. Usually, you'll want to display things in a Web browser as HTML (or XML or the like), rather than as text.

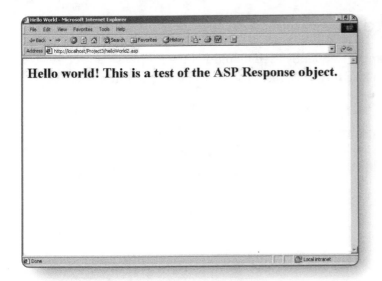

Here I've modified my "helloWorld.asp" page to output an entire HTML page.

NOTE

If you were to right-click on the page and select View Source, you would see a long line of HTML code. This is because the active server page just outputs the HTML code into the HTTP stream without adding any line breaks. Line breaks can be added to the output stream using the VBScript carriage return line feed command like this:

```
Response.Write("Something" & vbCrLf)
```

Here's the ASP that produced the page.

Notice that I put double quotes around the value "white". If you don't do this, the ASP processor sees the quotation mark and thinks that's the end of the information it's supposed to output. It then looks for the ")" that is supposed to follow the quotation mark.

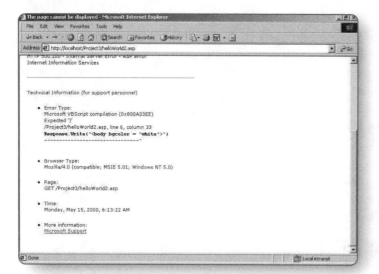

At that point you'll get the following error message.

At this point, you're probably not too impressed. In fact, you might even be muttering something about how it's a lot easier to write plain old HTML if you just want to output something like that. I couldn't agree with you more! Remember, I'm just trying to illustrate the basics of how the Response.Write method works. Actually, the Response.Write method is usually used to add HTML to a Web page based on the processing of user input or on information retrieved from a database. We saw a few examples of this in Chapter 2. Let's take a look at one of them again.

Remember that in my online fruit stand, users click on the fruit they want to purchase.

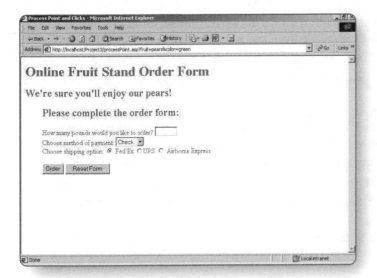

At that point, the choice of fruit, as well as the color of the fruit, is sent via query string to the processPoint.asp page, where the name of the fruit is placed into a marketing slogan and the color of the text is changed to the color of the fruit.

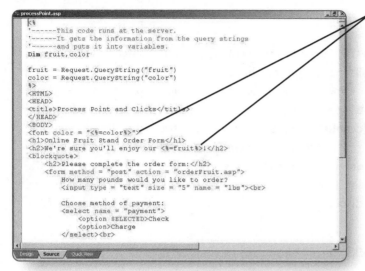

```
processPoint.asp
<%
'------This code runs at the server.
'------It gets the information from the query strings
'------and puts it into variables.
Dim fruit,color

fruit = Request.QueryString("fruit")
color = Request.QueryString("color")
%>
<HTML>
<HEAD>
<title>Process Point and Clicks</title>
</HEAD>
<BODY>
<font color = "<%=color%>">
<h1>Online Fruit Stand Order Form</h1>
<h2>We're sure you'll enjoy our <%=fruit%>!</h2>
<blockquote>
    <h2>Please complete the order form:</h2>
    <form method = "post" action = "orderFruit.asp">
        How many pounds would you like to order?
        <input type = "text" size = "5" name = "lbs"><br>

        Choose method of payment:
        <select name = "payment">
            <option SELECTED>Check
            <option>Charge
        </select><br>
```

In this example, the HTML displayed in processPoint.asp is changed based on the hyperlink the user clicks on in pointPage.asp. "But where's the `Response.Write` method?" you ask. Well...it's been there all along! The `<%= … %>` syntax is a shortcut way to put a `Response.Write` statement in the middle of some normal HTML code.

This statement:

```
<%= fruit %>
```

is equivalent to this code:

```
<%
Response.Write(fruit)
%>
```

NOTE

Don't get carried away with mixing HTML and ASP. I usually try to put most of my ASP script in a script block at the top of the ASP page. I place the HTML code with only essential pieces of ASP script after that. Mixing ASP and HTML code excessively can reduce performance.

Response.Cookies

In addition to sending HTML back to the client, you can use ASP to send *cookies* back to the client. Recall from Chapter 2 that cookies in the Web world are not made of gingerbread or chocolate chips, but information. Cookies are named pieces of information about a user's visits to a particular Web site. This information is stored on the user's (client's) computer and can be retrieved by the Web server any time the user visits the site that set the cookies. Cookies are a great way to store things (like a customer ID) that can be used to pull up information about the customer from a database. I'll talk more about how to use cookies to keep track of user sessions when we discuss different ways to "maintain state" in Chapter 7.

Creating Cookies

Here's how to use the ASP Response object to create cookies that will be stored on the client's machine.

Cookie Syntax

The general syntax for creating a cookie is as follows:

```
Response.Cookies("name of cookie") = "Whatever value you want"
```

As discussed earlier, cookies can also have subkeys.

```
Response.Cookies("name of cookie")("name of subkey") = "Whatever value you
want"
```

Besides keys and subkeys, there are several properties that can be set to determine the specific characteristics of the cookies you set: Expires, Path, Domain, and Secure. We'll examine these properties in the following example.

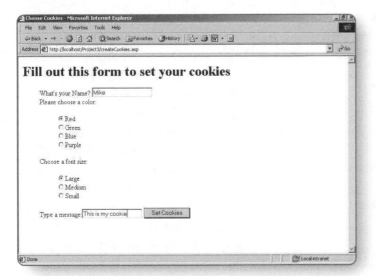

Nothing fancy here, this form called createCookies.asp simply gathers the information that will be stored in cookies on setCookies.asp.

NOTE

Notice that I made this page an active server page even though it only contains HTML. In IIS 4.0 or before, this would have decreased performance. However, in IIS 5.0, "scriptless" active server pages are processed just as quickly as standard HTML pages.

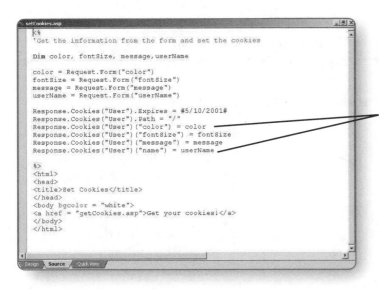

In this page we simply request the information sent in from the form and send it back to the client as cookies.

Notice that we are setting just one cookie on the client. The cookie's name is "User" and it is used to store information about the client user. The cookie has several subkeys.

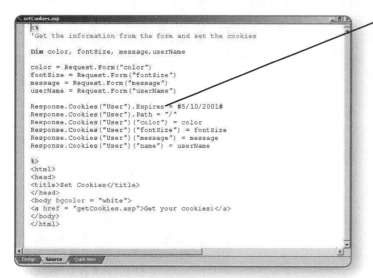

```
setCookies.asp
<%
'Get the information from the form and set the cookies

Dim color, fontSize, message,userName

color = Request.Form("color")
fontSize = Request.Form("fontSize")
message = Request.Form("message")
userName = Request.Form("userName")

Response.Cookies("User").Expires = #5/10/2001#
Response.Cookies("User").Path = "/"
Response.Cookies("User")("color") = color
Response.Cookies("User")("fontSize") = fontSize
Response.Cookies("User")("message") = message
Response.Cookies("User")("name") = userName

%>
<html>
<head>
<title>Set Cookies</title>
</head>
<body bgcolor = "white">
<a href = "getCookies.asp">Get your cookies!</a>
</body>
</html>

Design   Source   Quick View
```

The Expires property has been set to ensure that these cookies are valid until the date specified between the two hash signs (VBScript interprets information between hash signs as dates.) Several date formats are understood by VBScript. The Expires property has to be set for every cookie you create. One advantage to using cookies with subkeys is that the properties set for the cookie apply to all of the subkeys as well. If the subkeys were individual cookies then you would have to set the properties for each of them as well.

NOTE

If you don't set the Expires property, the cookies will be discarded when the user shuts down the browser.

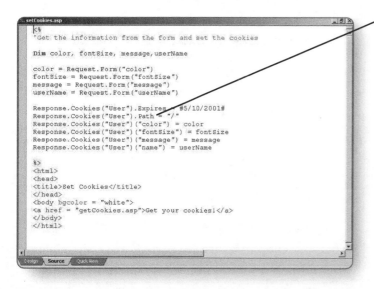

```
setCookies.asp
<%
'Get the information from the form and set the cookies

Dim color, fontSize, message,userName

color = Request.Form("color")
fontSize = Request.Form("fontSize")
message = Request.Form("message")
userName = Request.Form("userName")

Response.Cookies("User").Expires = #5/10/2001#
Response.Cookies("User").Path = "/"
Response.Cookies("User")("color") = color
Response.Cookies("User")("fontSize") = fontSize
Response.Cookies("User")("message") = message
Response.Cookies("User")("name") = userName

%>
<html>
<head>
<title>Set Cookies</title>
</head>
<body bgcolor = "white">
<a href = "getCookies.asp">Get your cookies!</a>
</body>
</html>

Design   Source   Quick View
```

The Path property sets the virtual path this cookie pertains to. A *virtual path* is the folder path starting from the root directory of your Web site. For example, if I set the Path property to, "/customers/ shopping", then the cookies would be retrieved from the customer's machine and sent to the server only when the user was looking at pages in the "shopping" directory.

Setting the Path property to the root directory, "/", causes the cookie to be sent to the server throughout the site.

NOTE

If you don't specify the path, it will be set to the directory the user is in when the cookie is created.

In this example, you didn't set the Domain or Secure properties. These properties often don't need to be set. The Domain property is the domain that the cookie is valid for (for example, www.microsoft.com). Only domains specified by the Domain property can access a particular cookie. When a cookie is created, the domain is set by default to the current domain. You need to change this property only if you want another Web site to be able to access a particular cookie. As for the Secure property, this refers to whether or not the cookie should be sent to the server using SSL encryption. If the Secure property is set to true, the cookie will be sent only if the user is currently in an encrypted session with the server. By default, this property is set to false.

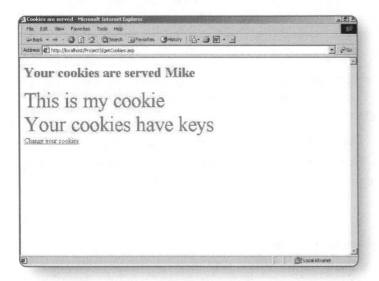

Just to prove that the cookies were actually set, I created the getCookies.asp page that reads the cookies set in setCookies.asp and does something with them.

Here's the code.

```
getCookies.asp

<html>
<head>
<title>Cookies are served</title>
</head>
<body bgcolor = "white">
<font color = "<%=Request.Cookies("User")("color")%>"
size = "<%=Request.Cookies("User")("fontSize")%>">
<h1>Your cookies are served <%=Request.Cookies("User")("name")%></h1>
<%=Request.Cookies("User")("message")%><br>

<%
If Request.Cookies("User").HasKeys = true then
    Response.Write("Your cookies have keys<br>")
Else
    Response.Write("Your cookies don't have keys</br>")
End If
%>
</font>
<a href = "createCookies.asp">Change your cookies</a>

</body>
</html>
```

Design | **Source** | Quick View

A FEW THINGS TO KEEP IN MIND ABOUT COOKIES

Changing any value or property of a multi-value cookie (a cookie with subkeys) causes all of the prior values of the cookie to be erased. If you want to keep those values, you must first collect them into variables using `Request.Cookies`. Then you can add them back in with any new values using `Response.Cookies`.

- Cookies must be written before any HTML content is written to the response stream. This is true of most of the methods and properties of the Response object.

- The official *cookie specification* places limits on how many cookies a particular domain can set and how big cookies can be. While Internet Explorer doesn't enforce the cookie limits, Netscape does. They are as follows:

1. 20 cookies per domain.
2. 4096 bytes per cookie description.
3. 300 cookies maximum

Controlling Information Sent Back to the Client

The ASP Response object has several methods and properties that can be used to specify the way in which information is sent back to the client. We'll consider these different control features built into the Response object in turn.

Specifying When Information Should be Sent Using Response.Buffer

One of the properties that can be set with the Response object is the `buffer` property. When this property is set to `true`, information is stored in a *buffer* on the server until all processing for the page is completed or until either the `flush` or the `end` method is called. Instead of opening and closing connections to the server multiple times as various sections of code are processed and sent out, it's much more efficient to do all the processing at one time and send the entire output in one output stream. Such buffering can increase performance on pages that have a lot of script to process.

> ### NOTE
>
> The statement `Response.Buffer = true` should be at the top of an active server page that is to be buffered. This line can be omitted in ASP 3.0 since page buffering is on by default (unless, of course, you turn it off). In earlier versions of ASP, buffering was off by default.

Alas, there is one dark secret to buffering information on the server. Nothing shows up on the client's browser until all processing is done. This might take several seconds if the script has to do a lot of database accesses. That's where the `Response.Flush` method comes in. The `Response.Flush` method sends all the information in the buffer out to the client. On scripts that will take a long time to process, `Response.Flush` can be used to send out data in segments. The main reason to flush something is to keep the user on the client machine from hitting the dreaded "Refresh" button and starting the whole process over. Using the flush method on long-loading pages keeps clients happy by giving them some indication that the page is loading, while keeping the server happy by limiting the number of connections it has to make to the client.

There are often times when you might want to stop processing an active server page at a particular point. This can be done using the `Response.End` method. `Response.End` simply outputs whatever is in the buffer and discontinues any further processing of the page. If you want to clear what's in the buffer before ending, use `Response.Clear` first, then `Response.End`. One reason for stopping an active server page's processing is if the client has moved on to another page. If your page takes a particularly long time to load, it's not a bad idea to see if there's still somebody out there periodically. This can be done using the `Response.IsClientConnected` property. This Boolean property will be `false` if the client is no longer connected. At that point, a `Response.End` could be used to stop processing.

NOTE

In IIS 5.0 the server will automatically check to see if the client is still connected if a client's request has been in the "queue" for longer than three seconds. However, it's still not a bad idea to explicitly check this property on long pages.

Specifying How Long Information is Valid

Web page caching by browsers or proxy servers can make Web pages load faster by pulling a frequently requested page out of cache rather than having to hunt it down again. While this can be great for static HTML pages, it could be disastrous for active server pages, where information changes often. For this reason, the Response object provides some properties that can be used to specify exactly how long a particular page is valid. The `CacheControl` property can be used to specify whether or not a proxy server is allowed to cache a certain page.

> ### NOTE
> Note that `"public"` or `"private"` needs to be in quotes.

The default setting is `"private"`. This specifies that a proxy should not cache the page. Only local machines may cache the page.

```
Response.CacheControl = "private"
```

The other option is:

```
Response.CacheControl = "public"
```

Proxy servers, or `"public"` caches, are allowed to cache the page.

To specify when a page expires (is no longer valid), use the `Response.Expires` property. `Response.Expires` determines the number of minutes an active server page is valid.

```
Response.Expires = 3
```

The preceding code means that the page expires in three minutes. Setting this property to 0 or a negative number means that the page should expire immediately (thus it will have to be reloaded from the host server every time it is requested).

`Response.Expires` can also be used to specify a particular date and time a page expires.

```
Response.Expires = #June 26, 2001 15:05:00#
```

This code specifies that the page should expire on June 26, 2001 at 3:05 PM GMT.

USING HTML TO CONTROL PAGE EXPIRATION

Expiration data can be built into the HTML code itself using META tags. Consider using the following tag when you want a page to refresh itself automatically after a certain amount of time:

```
<META HTTP-EQUIV="REFRESH" CONTENT="2">
```

The value of the content attribute (in this case "2") is the amount of time in seconds until the page is refreshed. This tag can be useful for updating content in pages that might be left open in a browser for a long time. An example of such a page might be an intranet page that has announcements or news that could change throughout the day.

Specifying the Type of Information Sent to the Client

Besides being able to specify when information should be sent to a client, and how long information is valid, the Response object also enables you to specify the type of information contained in an active server page. The Response.Charset property determines what character set should be used to display the text on the page. The Charset property goes along with the Response.ContentType property that specifies what type of information is on the page. The default ContentType is "text/html". Other content types include "text/xml", "text/plain", "image/gif", and so on. The Charset and ContentType information is translated into HTTP headers that tell the client Web browser how to display the information in the page.

You can use the Response.Pics property to set a rating for the page that tells the client browser whether the page contains violence, sexually explicit material, offensive language, and so on. For more information on how browsers and content selection software use PICS (*Platform for Internet Content Selection*) ratings and how to set the ratings for your site, check out http://www.ICRA.org. If you want to get a PICS rating, go to the ICRA site and register your Web site. They will assign a particular PICS label for you to use.

Finally, there is the `Response.Status` property that sets the HTTP status of the active server page. Of course, the status that we're all familiar with is "404 Page Not Found". While you probably wouldn't want to set the status of your .asp page to that, you might want to set it to something like "401 Unauthorized" if a user hasn't registered and had the appropriate cookies set to access certain pages in your site. The `Response.Status` property can be set to any valid HTTP status. To see a list of the various HTTP statuses that can be set, follow these steps (for IIS 5.0).

1. Click on Start, Settings, Control Panel.

2. Double-click on Administrative Tools, then Internet Service Manager.

3. Click on the + (plus) sign next to the name of your server.

4. Right-click on the Default Web Site, then click on Properties.

5. Click on the tab that reads Custom Errors.
   You'll see all of the various HTTP page statuses.

6. To find the meaning of a particular status, click on the status, then click on the Edit Properties button.

The following table shows the samples of how to set each of these properties.

Property	Syntax
Charset	Response.Charset = "ISO-LATIN-7"
ContentType	Response.ContentType = "text/XML"
Pics	Response.Pics("Put the PICS label assigned by the ICRA between the quotes")
Status	Response.Status = "401 Unauthorized"

Redirecting Clients to Another Page Using Response.Redirect

There are often times when you might want to send a client request to different active server pages, depending on the circumstances. The `Response.Redirect` method allows you to take a client request for a certain page and redirect it to another page. This page could be on your Web server or some other URL. The way `Response.Redirect` works is by sending an HTTP page moved status back to the browser with the new URL. The browser then sends a new HTTP request to the new URL. The syntax for `Response.Redirect` is as follows:

```
Response.Redirect "Some URL"
```

The URL can be an absolute or relative path.

ASP 3.0 introduces a new method of "redirecting" the client to a new page. The Server object now has the `Server.Transfer` method, which transfers the client request from one active server page to another. There are a few benefits to using this new method over the `Response.Redirect` method. One is that the `Response.Redirect` method requires a "round trip" to the server. The server has to send out an HTTP page moved response, then the client has to reconnect to the new active server page. With the `Server.Transfer` method, the request is shifted from one page to another without sending anything back to the client. Fewer round trips means better performance. A second advantage of `Server.Transfer` is that the .asp page that receives control has access to all of the intrinsic ASP objects that the first page had. This means, for example, that the new page could gather information submitted by a form using the `Request.Form` method even though the new page was not specified as the value of the `"action"` attribute in the form. One thing to keep in mind, however, is that `Server.Transfer` can only transfer control to active server pages on the **same server**. If you want to redirect the client to a page on another server, you'll have to use `Response.Redirect`.

Other Response Object Methods

The Response object has three other methods; `Response.BinaryWrite`, `Response.AppendToLog`, and `Response.AddHeader`. The `Response.BinaryWrite` method can be used to write binary information like files or pictures to the client. The `Response.AppendToLog` method allows you to write custom information to the IIS log. Finally, the `Response.AddHeader` method facilitates adding custom HTTP Headers to the HTTP stream. You'll look at the `Response.BinaryWrite` in Chapter 11 and `Response.AppendToLog` in Chapter 5.

4

VBScript Basics

There are two types of scripting involved in active server pages. *Client-side scripting* runs on the client machine. Client-side scripting is usually done using JavaScript (JScript, Microsoft's version of JavaScript). Web browsers are responsible for processing client-side scripts. There is also *server-side scripting* that is processed by the Web server. Scripting languages that can be used to do server-side scripting in ASP include VBScript, JavaScript, Perl Script, and so on. Most of the time, however, VBScript is the language used in ASP for server-side scripting. This chapter covers the main elements of VBScript that will be useful to you as an ASP developer. In this chapter, you'll learn how to:

- Work with VBScript data types
- Control the flow of data with VBScript
- Create loops with VBScript

> ### TIP
>
> If you're not using IIS 5.0 then I recommend that you download the latest version of VBScript from the Microsoft website (http://www.microsoft.com/msdownload/vbscript/scripting.asp). There are several useful new features in VBScript 5. Version 5 has also been optimized to provide greater performance than earlier versions.

VBScript Data Types

VBScript is a subset of the Visual Basic programming language. Although there are many similarities between VBScript and Visual Basic, there are also some big differences. One of the differences is that Visual Basic is a *strongly typed* language, while VBScript is *weakly typed*. In a strongly typed language, there are several different data types. For example, Integer, Long, Double, Boolean, String, Date, Currency, and so on, are all examples of different *types* of data that can be declared as variables in Visual Basic. In VBScript there is only one data type, the Variant.

Declarations in VBScript

Variables are pieces of the computer's memory that are assigned a name by a programmer. After a name has been assigned to the memory location, the programmer can send and retrieve information to and from that memory by referencing its name. The process of assigning a name to a piece of memory is called *declaration*.

In VBScript, declarations of variables are made using the keyword `Dim`, which stands for dimension. The following example declares a variable in VBScript.

```
Dim myVariable
```

Pretty simple, huh? Since there is only one data type in VBScript, `Variant`, there is no need to "declare" what data type your variable is. You simply use the `Dim` keyword followed by the name of the variable. Keep in mind when declaring variables that VBScript is not case sensitive. That means that a variable named "myVariable" would refer to the same memory as a variable named "myvariable," or "MyVariable," or "MYVARIABLE." Got the idea?

NOTE

If you're used to programming in Visual Basic then you're probably used to declaring the variables and assigning them a data type using the `As` keyword. You will get an error if you try to assign a data type to a VB Script variable.

If you want to declare several variables at the same time, you can use the `Dim` keyword just once and separate the variables by commas.

```
Dim myApples, myOranges, myNectarines, myPears
```

Sometimes it's helpful to create a variable that has a set value. This type of variable is not a variable at all, but a *constant*. To create a constant, use the `Const` keyword.

```
Const myConstant = 5
```

The value of a constant can't be changed while the script is running.

Naming your Variables

So what should you name your variables? There are several different naming conventions used by programmers. Many of them designate the type of data in the name of the variable. You could do this with your VBScript variables as well, even though there is "officially" only one data type. For example, if you have a *boolean* variable (meaning that it will be only true or false), you could name the variable something like "blnCompleted." Another common practice is to vary the case of the first letter in each word of a variable's name (if a variable has many words). For example:

```
Dim strCustomerFirstName
```

> ### NOTE
>
> In case you missed it, a variable name can't have spaces in it. Additionally, variables must begin with an alphabetic character, can't contain a period or other special character (%,&,!,*,$, and so on), and can be no longer than 255 characters. You can use an underscore (_) in your variable names instead of spaces.

The bottom line on variable naming is to use descriptive names. The name of the variable should somehow describe what it's used for. If it has to be a couple words, so be it. The real value of descriptive naming arises when you, or someone else, has to come back and do something to your code several months after you wrote it.

Arrays

Arrays are variables that can hold several values each. Consider the following:

```
Dim myArray(3)
```

The variable `myArray` can actually hold four different values. Each value is referred to by its position in the array. We could assign values to each element in the array like this:

```
myArray(1) = "Hello"
myArray(2) = "Good Bye"
myArray(3) = "Good Afternoon"
```

If you wanted to, you could also assign a value to `myArray(0)`.

> ### NOTE
>
> Every array in VBScript has a *lower bound* of 0. That means that if you declare an array of three elements, as I did in this example, you actually get a fourth element for free! I know, this doesn't make much sense. I think the reason it's set up this way is for the sake of programmers of other languages (like C) who are used to arrays starting at 0.

You can also create *multi-dimensional* arrays in VBScript. In fact, you can have up to sixty dimensions. Here's how to declare a multi-dimensional array.

```
Dim myMultiDimensionalArray(5,5)
```

You put the upper bound of each dimension between the parentheses. Consider for a moment the two-dimensional array just declared. If you think of this array as having five rows and five columns, you can see how the array works. You can assign a value to a particular element in the array by referring to the coordinates of the element.

```
MyMultiDimensionalArray(3,2)= "This is fun"
```

ReDim

Often it's not initially apparent how large an array needs to be. You can declare a dynamic array using the following syntax:

```
Dim myDynamicArray()
```

When you figure out how big you want the array to be, use the `ReDim` statement to re-dimension the array.

```
ReDim myDynamicArray(5)
```

It turns out that you can re-dimension any array using the `ReDim` keyword. However, when you re-dimension an array, any information that was stored in the array is lost—that is, unless you also use the keyword `Preserve`. `Preserve` keeps all the data and adds new dimensions. (If you decrease the number of dimensions, you lose the data that was in those dimensions.) We could re-dimension the above array and preserve the data in it using the following line:

```
ReDim Preserve myDynamicArray(10)
```

TIP

Re-dimensioning an array is a very processor intensive exercise. Make sure that you don't do it frequently.

Option Explicit

Well, I've given all this instruction about declaring variables, and now I have to break the news to you—in VBScript you don't have to declare variables! That's right, you can just start using variables without ever using the Dim statement at all! This practice, however, can quickly lead to some real debugging problems. All you have to do is misspell a variable somewhere deep down in your code and you could have hours of fun trying to figure out why it's not working right. That's why I recommend that you force yourself to declare all the variables you use by putting the Option Explicit statement at the top of your active server pages. This statement enforces variable declaration. If you don't declare a variable, it will produce an error for you.

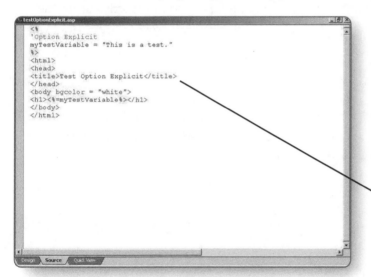

Notice that I did not declare the variable myTestVariable. Option Explicit is not on (it's commented out), so the page works fine.

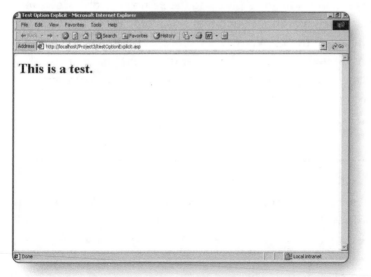

Here's the output.

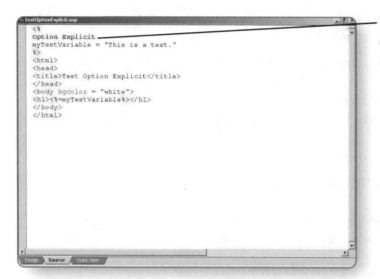

Now I've uncommented the
Option Explicit statement
at the top of the screen.

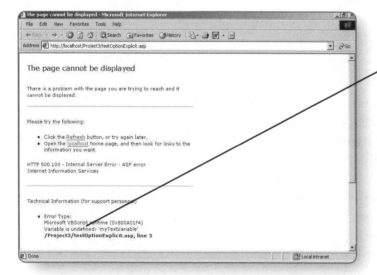

Here's the output when I run the
page again.

The VBScript processor has
returned a "Variable is
undefined" error. Again, it might
seem like extra work to declare
your variables. But let me assure
you that as your ASP pages get
more complex, you'll save lots
of debugging time by allowing
Option Explicit to catch
misspelled variable names
up front.

Controlling Data Flow

Every programming language makes use of *conditional* or *control-of-flow* statements. Conditional statements are used to determine what code should run in a given situation. In VBScript there are two types of conditional constructs: the If…Then…Else construct and the Select Case construct. We'll consider both of them in turn.

If…Then…Else Statements

Perhaps the most commonly used conditional statement is the If…Then…End If statement. Here's how to use it.

```
If [Some expression that can be evaluated] Then
        [Do this code]
ElseIf [Some expression(s)] Then
        [Do this code]
ElseIf [Some other expression(s)] Then
        [Do this code]
Else
        [Do this code]
End If
```

The preceding example is the full implementation of the If…Then…Else statement. Not every If statement has to include all these parts. You might, for example, have just an If…Then…End If statement. The best way to understand how to use these statements is to look at them in action.

Let's cut to the code…

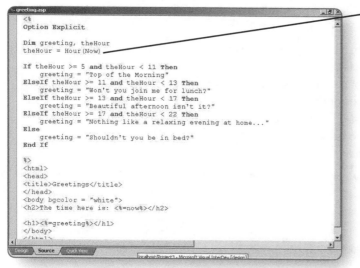

At the top of this script I've declared two variables, `greeting` and `theHour`. Notice that I set `theHour = Hour(Now)`. `Now` is a VBScript function that returns the computer's system date and time. The `Hour` function is another built-in function that returns the hour portion of a date/time as a number between 0 and 23 (military time).

TIP

There are several useful "built-in" VBScript functions. I use several of them in the various examples in this book. However a full explanation of all of the functions is beyond the scope of this book. I recommend that you look at the VBScript Language Reference that can be found at the Microsoft Windows Script Technologies site (http://msdn.microsoft.com/scripting/).

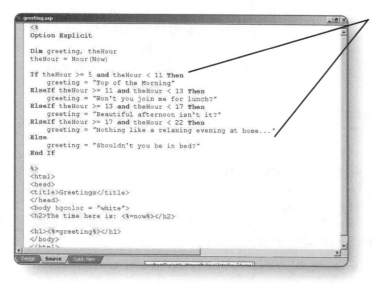

All I've done in the rest of the code is check to see in which time period the current hour falls. Each `If...Then` and `ElseIf...Then` expression is evaluated in turn. When one of them evaluates to `True`, the statement following that expression is executed. In this case, if one of the expressions is `True`, the `greeting` variable is changed to the appropriate greeting. If none of the expressions evaluate to `True`, the statement after `Else` will execute.

NOTE

Although in this example I have only one line of code that executes if a particular expression is True, you can have multiple lines of code, including additional conditional statements, that execute when an expression is True. Also, you may be wondering where the word "True" is in these conditional statements. All conditional statements evaluate to True, but the keyword True does not have to be written explicitly. For example the expression If x < 5 Then is the same as If (x < 5) = True Then.

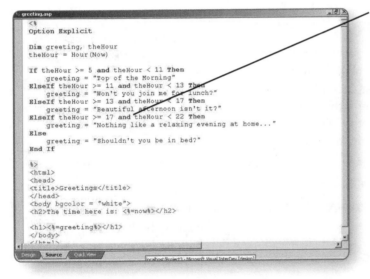

```
<%
Option Explicit

Dim greeting, theHour
theHour = Hour(Now)

If theHour >= 5 and theHour < 11 Then
    greeting = "Top of the Morning"
ElseIf theHour >= 11 and theHour < 13 Then
    greeting = "Won't you join me for lunch?"
ElseIf theHour >= 13 and theHour < 17 Then
    greeting = "Beautiful afternoon isn't it?"
ElseIf theHour >= 17 and theHour < 22 Then
    greeting = "Nothing like a relaxing evening at home..."
Else
    greeting = "Shouldn't you be in bed?"
End If

%>
<html>
<head>
<title>Greetings</title>
</head>
<body bgcolor = "white">
<h2>The time here is: <%=now%></h2>

<h1><%=greeting%></h1>
</body>
</html>
```

You'll also see that the expression to be evaluated can have multiple conditions in it. Each one of the conditions can be compared to the other conditions using the *logical* operators (And, Or, Xor, Not). In these examples, the And operator is used, which means that both of the conditions have to be True if the expression is going to evaluate to True. You can also use parentheses around conditions that you want to have evaluated first.

NOTE

The And, Or, and Not logical operators are self-explanatory. The Xor operator (also known as the "exclusion" operator) can use some explanation. The Xor operator will return True if one and only one of the two statements being compared is True. If both of the statements are True then the expression will return False, likewise if both expressions are False.

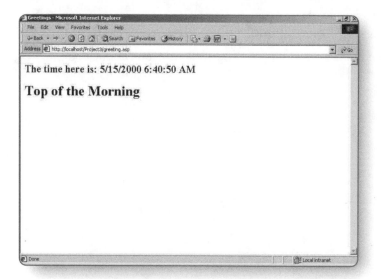

Here's the output. Of course, I did test it at different times of the day to see if the message changes.

Select Case Statements

The other type of conditional construction in VBScript is the Select Case statement.

```
Select Case [A numeric or string expression to test]
      Case [Some expression(s)]
            [Do this code]
      Case [Some expression(s)]
            [Do this code]
      Case [Some expression(s)]
            [Do this code]
      Case Else
            [Do this code]
End Select
```

A value to be tested is placed at the end of the Select Case statement. If the "test value" matches the first Case statement, the code after that expression is executed. Otherwise, the next Case is evaluated. The process continues until the test value matches one of the Case expressions. If no match is found, the code following the Case Else expression is executed.

This is the starting form for this example. The form has a set of radio buttons about one's weather preferences.

The output from the weather.htm page is sent to interests.asp for processing. Notice the "choice" query string parameter passed in from weather.htm is requested and put in the choice variable on interests.asp using the Request.Form method. This variable then becomes the "test expression" for the Select Case statement.

```
  interests.asp
         Response.Write("</form></body></html>")
         Response.End
End If
'----------If coming from weather page do this----------
Dim choice
choice = Request.Form("choice")

If choice <> "" then
    Select Case choice
        Case "sunny"
            offer = "Can I offer you a trip to Hawaii?"
            picture = "beach.jpg"
        Case "fog"
            offer = "Can I offer you a trip to San Francisco?"
            picture = "sanfran.jpg"
        Case "snow"
            offer = "Can I offer you a trip to the Swiss Alps?"
            picture = "snow.jpg"
        Case "rain"
            offer = "Can I offer you a trip to Portland, Oregon?"
            picture = "portland.jpg"
        Case Else
            offer = "Can I offer you a psychiatrist?"
            picture = "psychologist.jpg"
    End Select
End If
%>
<html>
<head>
  Design  Source  Quick View
```

Each `Case` is evaluated to see whether it matches the value of the `choice` variable. If it does match, the code following (indented from) the `Case` statement is executed. In this series, the code after the `Case` statements sets the values of the `offer` and `picture` variables. At the bottom of the series of `Case` statements is a `Case Else`. If none of the other cases match the "test expression," the code after the `Case Else` statement executes.

```
  interests.asp
            offer = "Can I offer you a trip to the Swiss Alps?"
            picture = "snow.jpg"
        Case "rain"
            offer = "Can I offer you a trip to Portland, Oregon?"
            picture = "portland.jpg"
        Case Else
            offer = "Can I offer you a psychiatrist?"
            picture = "psychologist.jpg"
        'End Select
End If
%>
<html>
<head>
<title>Make Offer</title>
</head>
<body bgcolor = "white">
<h1>Mike's Online Travel</h1>
<blockquote>
    <div align = "center">
        <img src = "images/<%=picture%>" alt = "<%=picture%>"><br><br>
        <h2><%=offer%></h2>
        <br>
        <a href = "interests.asp?purchase=<%=choice%>">[YES]</a> 
        <a href = "weather.htm">[NO]</a>
    </div>
</blockquote>
</body>
</html>
  Design  Source  Quick View
```

At the bottom of the page is the actual HTML code to be executed. In this simple example, an offer is made to the client based on the particular weather preferences expressed in the weather.htm page.

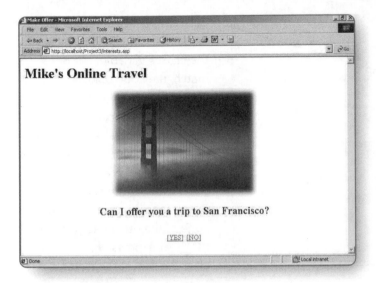

Perhaps you noticed that in the previous code shot, the `choice` variable was appended to a URL that points back to the same active server page (interests.asp). If the user clicks on the hyperlink that reads [YES], the same .asp page will be used to process that request.

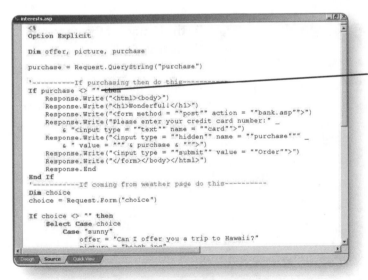

Here's the code at the top of the interests.asp page.

If the "purchase" query string contains a value, the code in the `If` block is executed. All the code does is produce a short HTML page that asks interested customers to enter their credit card number. The `Response.End` method stops processing the active server page at the end of the HTML.

NOTE

Notice that a few of these lines of code have an "_" at the end. This syntax allows you to break up long lines of code into multiple lines. To break up a long line, put a space followed by a "_" where you want to break the line of code then press the Enter key and start typing again. If you're breaking up a string (as in these lines of code) then you will also have to use the string concatenation operator "&". The ampersand concatenates the strings together. The concatenation operator also has to be used when inserting a VBScript variable into a string. You must also add an extra quote mark on either side of the variable (see the "purchase" variable, for example). This type of notation can take some getting used to. You'll just have to try it a few times.

This method of posting information multiple times to the same active server page can help keep a Web application from becoming cluttered with lots of small pages. It can also make Web site maintenance easier if it's done properly. Be careful however, because such pages can become very difficult to interpret if you get carried away with using the same page over and over. Make sure you put comments in the code that indicate what each section does.

CLEANING UP THE CODE

Server-side scripting code can quickly get ugly. As the book progresses, you'll see that active server pages are really a conglomeration of ASP, HTML, VBScript, JavaScript, SQL, ADO, and so on. Therefore, it's essential that you make the code as readable as possible. Follow these guidelines:

- Try to keep your ASP (server-side script) separate from your HTML as much as possible. I try to keep the server-side scripts at the top of the page and the HTML at the bottom.

- Practice indenting your code. Indent wherever it makes sense to indent.

- Comment your code well. Discuss what each section does. Not only will this help others who might have to work on your pages, it will help you too!

- Keep your ASP pages short. If they're more than about 300 lines, they're probably too long. You should consider putting the logic from complex pages into a COM+ component. We'll see how to do that in Chapter 11.

Looping

Another common feature of programming languages is the ability to set up loops that iterate through a section of code a prescribed number of times (hopefully not infinitely) or until a certain condition is reached. In VBScript there are two different types of looping mechanisms: For loops and While loops. Each type of loop has a few "flavors." We'll consider each of them in this section.

For Loops

There are two "flavors" of For loop. A general For loop can be used to loop through a section of code a specified number of times. A For Each loop is used to iterate through the elements of a collection or an array.

The syntax for a standard For...Next loop is as follows:

```
For [counter variable] = [starting number] to [ending number] [Step Number]
        [Code to run]
        Exit For
        [Code to run]
Next
```

According to this syntax, the code between the For and Next will be executed each time the loop is run. The Step is an optional expression that can be used to specify how much to increment the counter with each iteration of the loop. The Step is 1 by default. You can make the starting number larger than the ending number and specify the Step as a negative number if you want to loop backwards. The Exit For statement is another optional expression that can be used to exit out of a For loop. The Exit statement is usually put within a conditional statement (like an If...Then). Upon exiting a loop, the first line of code following the Next statement is executed. Loops can be nested (one loop can contain another loop.) If exiting from a nested loop, the control returns to the outer loop.

The syntax for a `For Each...Next` loop is as follows:

```
For Each [element variable] in [array or collection]
        [Code to run]
        Exit For
        [Code to run]
Next
```

This type of `For` loop is tailored to arrays and collections of information. This type of loop iterates through each element of an array or collection. Any code between the `For` and `Next` statements is run with each iteration. If an `Exit For` is encountered, control is returned to an outer loop (if in a nested loop) or to the line of code following the `Next`.

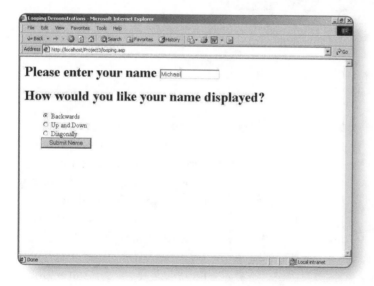

Here is a page (looping.asp) that demonstrates how to do just about all the different kinds of looping. This page consists of a simple form with a text box element and a radio button series. Users are instructed to enter their name in the text box and to select how the name should be displayed. I'll start by putting my name in and selecting the first radio button, "Backwards."

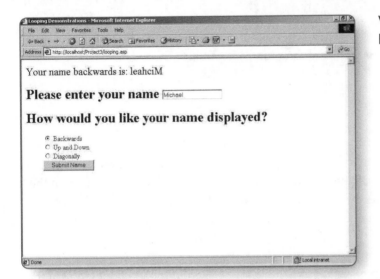

Voilà! There you have it! But how...?

Let's analyze what this code does.

At the top of the page you'll notice that I've declared three variables. Two capture the information from the form using the Request.Form method. The other variable, nameArray(), is a dynamic array.

I then use the ReDim statement to size the array to the size of the name passed in from the form. The Len() function is a built-in function that returns the length of a string.

```
looping.asp
<%
Option Explicit

Dim yourname, nameArray(), display

yourname = Request.Form("yourname")
display = Request.Form("display")

If yourname <> "" then
    '--------First Make an Array of the Letters in the Name--------
    Redim nameArray(Len(yourname)) 'Resize Array to size of yourname
    Dim i
    'populate the array
    For i = 1 to UBound(nameArray)
        nameArray(i) = Mid(yourname,i,1)
    Next

    Select Case display
        Case "backwards" 'show the name backwards
            Response.Write("<font size = ""+2"">Your name backwards is: ")
            For i = UBound(nameArray) to 1 Step -1
                Response.Write(nameArray(i))
            Next
            Response.Write("</font")
        Case "upanddown" 'show the name up and down
            Response.Write("<h2>Your name up and down is:</h2>")
            Dim letter
            For Each letter in nameArray
                Response.Write("<h2>" & letter & "</h2>")
```

Next, I populate the array using a `For Next` loop that iterates from 1 to the upper bound of the array called `nameArray`. (Note that the `UBound()` function returns the upper bound of an array.) With every iteration of the loop I assign a single character from the variable `yourname` to the element of the array specified by the counter variable (`i`). So if it's the second time going through the loop (`i = 2`), I am assigning the second character of the value of `yourname` to the array element `nameArray(2)`. Don't get confused by the `Mid()` function syntax. It is another built-in function that returns a specified part of a string. I'm using it to return one character from the name that is passed in.

```
looping.asp
    'populate the array
    For i = 1 to UBound(nameArray)
        nameArray(i) = Mid(yourname,i,1)|
    Next

    Select Case display
        Case "backwards" 'show the name backwards
            Response.Write("<font size = ""+2"">Your name backwards is: ")
            For i = UBound(nameArray) to 1 Step -1
                Response.Write(nameArray(i))
            Next
            Response.Write("</font")
        Case "upanddown" 'show the name up and down
            Response.Write("<h2>Your name up and down is:</h2>")
            Dim letter
            For Each letter in nameArray
                Response.Write("<h2>" & letter & "</h2>")
            Next
        Case "diagonal" 'show the name diagonally
            Response.Write("<h2>Your name diagonally is:</h2>")
            Dim loopCounter, someSpaces
            loopCounter = 1 'Initialize counter
            someSpaces = "" 'Start this as a blank
            Response.Write("<h2>")
            Do While loopCounter < (UBound(nameArray) + 1)
                Response.Write(someSpaces)
                Response.Write(nameArray(loopCounter) & "<br>")
                loopCounter = loopCounter + 1 'Increment counter
                someSpaces = someSpaces & "    "
```

Now we have the array of individual letters we can play with. Notice that the `display` variable is used as the test expression for a `Select Case` statement. If the user selected "Backwards," the first case is run. This code loops through the array backwards and prints out one character at a time. The `For` loop starts with the upper bound of the array and counts down to the first element.

```
looping.asp                                                       _ & X
    'populate the array
    For i = 1 to UBound(nameArray)
        nameArray(i) = Mid(yourname,i,1)|
    Next

    Select Case display
        Case "backwards" 'show the name backwards
            Response.Write("<font size = ""+2"">Your name backwards is: ")
            For i = UBound(nameArray) to 1 Step -1
                Response.Write(nameArray(i))
            Next
            Response.Write("</font")
        Case "upanddown" 'show the name up and down
            Response.Write("<h2>Your name up and down is:</h2>")
            Dim letter
            For Each letter in nameArray
                Response.Write("<h2>" & letter & "</h2>")
            Next
        Case "diagonal" 'show the name diagonally
            Response.Write("<h2>Your name diagonally is:</h2>")
            Dim loopCounter, someSpaces
            loopCounter = 1 'Initialize counter
            someSpaces = "" 'Start this as a blank
            Response.Write("<h2>")
            Do While loopCounter < (UBound(nameArray) + 1)
                Response.Write(someSpaces)
                Response.Write(nameArray(loopCounter) & "<br>")
                loopCounter = loopCounter + 1 'Increment counter
                someSpaces = someSpaces & "<nbsp:<nbsp:<nbsp:<nbsp:" 'Add
Design   Source   Quick View
```

Note that the Step -1 decrements the counter by one with each iteration.

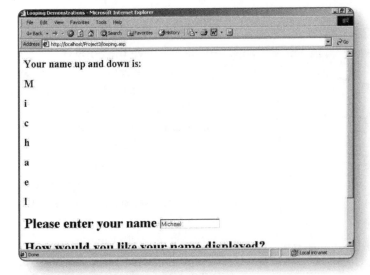

Here's the output when the user selects "Up and Down."

```
                                                             _|_|X|
% looping.asp
'populate the array
For i = 1 to UBound(nameArray)
    nameArray(i) = Mid(yourname,i,1)|
Next

Select Case display
    Case "backwards" 'show the name backwards
        Response.Write("<font size = ""+2"">Your name backwards is: ")
        For i = UBound(nameArray) to 1 Step -1
            Response.Write(nameArray(i))
        Next
        Response.Write("</font")
    Case "upanddown" 'show the name up and down
        Response.Write("<h2>Your name up and down is:</h2>")
        Dim letter
        For Each letter in nameArray
            Response.Write("<h2>" & letter & "</h2>")
        Next
    Case "diagonal" 'show the name diagonally
        Response.Write("<h2>Your name diagonally is:</h2>")
        Dim loopCounter, someSpaces
        loopCounter = 1 'Initialize counter
        someSpaces = "" 'Start this as a blank
        Response.Write("<h2>")
        Do While loopCounter < (UBound(nameArray) + 1)
            Response.Write(someSpaces)
            Response.Write(nameArray(loopCounter) & "<br>")
            loopCounter = loopCounter + 1 'Increment counter
            someSpaces = someSpaces & "<nbsp><nbsp><nbsp><nbsp>" 'Add
```

`Design` | **Source** | `Quick View`

This code uses the `For Each` statement to loop through each element of the array. Notice that I created a variable `letter` that holds the value of the array element for each iteration. I simply output the element between the `<h2>…</h2>` tags to get the letters to print out vertically rather than horizontally on the screen.

While Loops

The other variety of loop in VBScript is the `While` loop. There are a few flavors of `While` loop as well.

The `While` loop that I use most often is the `Do While` flavor.

```
Do While(or Until) [Some Condition]
        [Code to run]
        Exit Do
        [Code to run]
Loop
```

This type of loop checks to see whether some condition is met in the first line. If it is met, the code between the `Do` and `Loop` statements is run. An `Exit Do` statement can be used within the loop (usually inside of a conditional statement) to leave the loop. The loop will continue until the condition is no longer `True`. The `Until` syntax is usually used to loop through the code "until" something (like a variable) equals a certain value.

This type of loop can also be used with the following syntax:

```
Do
        [Code to run]
        Exit Do
        [Code to run]
Loop While (or Until) [Some Condition]
```

This does the same thing as the first Do Loop except that the code runs before the condition is checked. If the condition is still true, the code runs again. This continues until the condition is no longer True.

One more variety of While loop is the While…Wend loop.

```
While [Some condition]
        [Code to run]
Wend
```

This simple loop runs the code between the While and Wend statements as long as the condition is met. Note that there is no Exit statement for this type of loop.

Using the While Loop

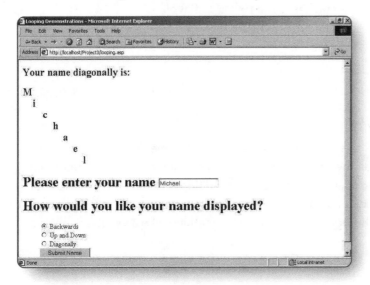

It's back to the name game for an example of a While loop.

This is the Grand Finale; a user's name printed diagonally!

```
                    Response.Write(nameArray(i))
            Next
            Response.Write("</font")
        Case "upanddown" 'show the name up and down
            Response.Write("<h2>Your name up and down is:</h2>")
            Dim letter
            For Each letter in nameArray
                Response.Write("<h2>" & letter & "</h2>")
            Next
        Case "diagonal" 'show the name diagonally
            Response.Write("<h2>Your name diagonally is:</h2>")
            Dim loopCounter, someSpaces
            loopCounter = 1 'Initialize counter
            someSpaces = "" 'Start this as a blank
            Response.Write("<h2>")
            Do While loopCounter <= UBound(nameArray)
                Response.Write(someSpaces)
                Response.Write(nameArray(loopCounter) & "<br>")
                loopCounter = loopCounter + 1 'Increment counter
                'Add spaces
                someSpaces = someSpaces & "    "
            Loop
            Response.Write("</h2>")
        End Select
    End If
%>
<html>
<head>
<title>Looping Demonstrations</title>
```

This "amazing" feature was implemented with a Do While loop.

I've created two variables to help with the task. The loopCounter variable is used to keep track of how many times the loop has run. The someSpaces variable is used to add the "tabbing" affect that will make the characters print out diagonally.

```
                    Response.Write(nameArray(i))
            Next
            Response.Write("</font")
        Case "upanddown" 'show the name up and down
            Response.Write("<h2>Your name up and down is:</h2>")
            Dim letter
            For Each letter in nameArray
                Response.Write("<h2>" & letter & "</h2>")
            Next
        Case "diagonal" 'show the name diagonally
            Response.Write("<h2>Your name diagonally is:</h2>")
            Dim loopCounter, someSpaces
            loopCounter = 1 'Initialize counter
            someSpaces = "" 'Start this as a blank
            Response.Write("<h2>")
            Do While loopCounter <= UBound(nameArray)
                Response.Write(someSpaces)
                Response.Write(nameArray(loopCounter) & "<br>")
                loopCounter = loopCounter + 1 'Increment counter
                'Add spaces
                someSpaces = someSpaces & "    "
            Loop
            Response.Write("</h2>")
        End Select
    End If
%>
<html>
<head>
<title>Looping Demonstrations</title>
```

With each iteration of the loop, the someSpaces variable is output. Then the particular element of nameArray specified by the loopCounter variable is output. After that, the loopCounter variable is incremented by one, and four spaces ( ) are added to the someSpaces variable. By the time this loop is done, the user's name is printed out diagonally at the top of the HTML page.

5

ASP Error Handling

Errors just happen! It's just a fact of programming life. But it's your attitude about errors that's important! Actually, it's how you handle them that's important. This chapter covers where errors in your ASP pages can come from and what to do about them. In this chapter, you'll learn how to:

- Handle VBScript errors
- Create custom IIS error pages
- Debug ASP projects using Visual InterDev

Understanding Errors

Errors in active server pages can come from many places. They can come from server-side script in your ASP page. There might be errors in client-side script that you put into your page. If you're connecting to a database or using some COM or COM+ components in your page, they too can raise errors. There are ways of handling errors in all of these arenas. In this chapter, you'll be looking at errors caused by your server-side scripts.

In ASP scripts, there are two basic categories of errors that can occur. First, a script can have some type of "syntax" or "compilation" error. This type of error results from something not being quite right in your script when you try to run it. Perhaps you misspelled a keyword or tried to use a function that a particular object doesn't support. When you try to view the page in a browser, it never even gets off the ground. Instead, you get the all too familiar, "The page cannot be displayed" message. You've already seen an example of one compilation error in Chapter 4, "VBScript Basics," in the section introducing Option Explicit. If Option Explicit is on and you try to use a variable without declaring it, you get a "Variable is undefined" error.

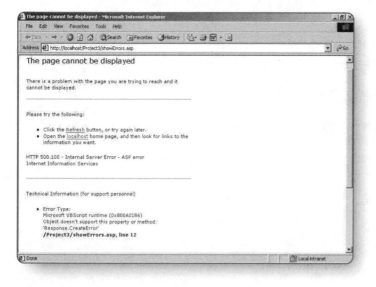

This is what you get if you try to use a method that doesn't exist. In this case I used a Response. CreateError method that does just what it's supposed to do—create an error. Often you'll get this error when you misspell a method.

The other category of error is a *runtime* error. These occur when something causes an error while the page is running. These are usually the hardest errors to track down. Runtime errors are the type we try to *handle*. Handling errors involves determining where errors are likely to occur in your code and building in some sort of *error handler* that catches the error and does something about it. Typical things that an error handler might do include displaying a friendly error message to the user, logging the error in an error log or database, emailing the developer about the error, keeping the program from crashing, and so on.

VBScript Error Handling

Error handling is not a particularly strong point of VBScript. JavaScript actually provides cleaner mechanisms for trapping errors. Be that as it may, we can still do the job of handling errors using the VBScript Err object and the `On Error` statement.

The On Error Statement

The statement used to implement error handling in VBScript is the `On Error Resume Next` statement. Without this line in your VBScript, any runtime error will cause your script to crash and the default error message to appear. However, if you use the `On Error Resume Next` statement, execution of the code will continue at the next line after the code that caused an error. Just as you can turn on custom error handling using `On Error Resume Next`, you can go back to default error handling using `On Error Goto 0`. I haven't talked about procedures (functions and subroutines) yet, but each procedure must have it's own `On Error Resume Next` statement if you want to handle errors in the procedure. The idea behind this statement is not to just ignore errors. Rather, it is to keep the error from crashing the page until the error can be discovered and remedied or reported. The error can be caught using the VBScript Err object.

The Err Object

Three properties of the Err object are useful in VBScript. Each is automatically set when an error occurs. The programmer can also set them to send a custom error message to the user. The Err object's default property is the `Err.Number` property. This is the VBScript error number assigned to a particular error. Next, the `Err.Description` property contains a description of the error. Finally, the `Err.Source` property contains the name of the object that caused the error. After you have caught an error and handled it, call the `Err.Clear` method to reset the Err object properties to empty strings. The Err object has one other method, the `Err.Raise` method. This method can be used to set the properties of the Err object manually, causing a runtime error to occur. It can be useful to send a user-friendly error message back to the client. The syntax for the `Err.Raise` method is as follows:

```
Err.Raise Number,Source,Description
```

If you've already set the properties, you can just call `Err.Raise` without any arguments to make a runtime error occur.

Using the Err Object

To demonstrate custom error handling using VBScript, I created a sample (primitive) calculator program. In this simple program, the user enters two numbers and selects the type of arithmetic to perform on the numbers. When this form is submitted, the arithmetic occurs and the result is displayed. If an error occurs while performing the arithmetic, my custom error handler displays a user-friendly error message.

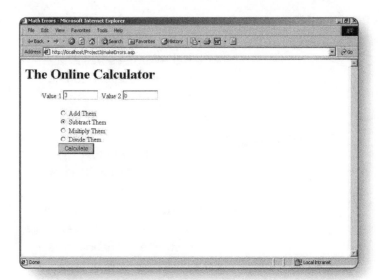

I will try to subtract a letter "b" from the number "3".

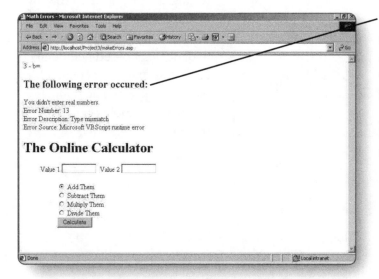

Notice that my custom error message was displayed. If I had allowed the default error handler to display a message, it would have said "Type Mismatch."

Now let's see how the custom error handler works.

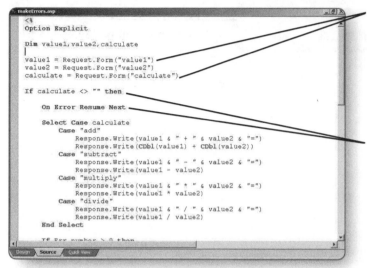

Notice that I've created variables to get the two values from the form, as well as a `calculate` variable to find out what type of computation is to be performed.

I check to see whether the form has been submitted by evaluating whether the `calculate` variable contains any information. If it does, I turn on custom error handling using the `On Error Resume Next` statement.

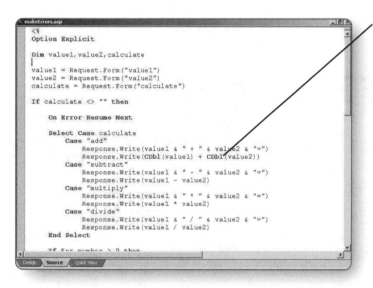

A `Select Case` statement causes the chosen arithmetic operation to take place. I had to explicitly convert the "value1" and "value2" variables to doubles (big, decimal-based numbers) using the `CDbl()` function. If I didn't do that, the addition operator (+)simply concatenates the numbers together.

```
makeErrors.asp
            Response.Write(value1 & " * " & value2 & "=")
            Response.Write(value1 * value2)
        Case "divide"
            Response.Write(value1 & " / " & value2 & "=")
            Response.Write(value1 / value2)
    End Select

    If Err.number > 0 then
        Response.Write("<h2>The following error occured:</h2>")
        Select Case Err.number
            Case 11
                Response.Write("You tried to divide by zero.")
            Case 13
                Response.Write("You didn't enter real numbers.")
            Case Else
                Response.Write Err.description
        End Select
        Response.Write("<br>")
        Response.Write("Error Number: " & Err.number & "<br>")
        Response.Write("Error Description: " & Err.description & "<br>")
        Response.Write("Error Source: " & Err.source & "<br>")
        Err.Clear
    End If
    Response.Write("<br>")
End If

%>
<html>
<head>
Design   Source   Quick View
```

If an error does occur while performing the arithmetic, the `Err.Number` property will be greater than 0. The `If…Then` statement checks for this condition.

If an error has occurred, the `Select Case` statement prints out a user-friendly error message based on which error occurred. In this case, likely errors would be "Type Mismatch," error number 13, or "Divide by Zero," error number 11. Since the arithmetic operators work only on numbers, the "Type Mismatch" error would be created if the user entered something other than a number in one or both of the text boxes.

```
makeErrors.asp
            Response.Write(value1 & " * " & value2 & "=")
            Response.Write(value1 * value2)
        Case "divide"
            Response.Write(value1 & " / " & value2 & "=")
            Response.Write(value1 / value2)
    End Select

    If Err.number > 0 then
        Response.Write("<h2>The following error occured:</h2>")
        Select Case Err.number
            Case 11
                Response.Write("You tried to divide by zero.")
            Case 13
                Response.Write("You didn't enter real numbers.")
            Case Else
                Response.Write Err.description
        End Select
        Response.Write("<br>")
        Response.Write("Error Number: " & Err.number & "<br>")
        Response.Write("Error Description: " & Err.description & "<br>")
        Response.Write("Error Source: " & Err.source & "<br>")
        Err.Clear
    End If
    Response.Write("<br>")
End If

%>
<html>
<head>
Design   Source   Quick View
```

If an error has occurred, I also print out the standard error information just so you can see what it would be. Lastly, I clear the properties of the Err object using the `Err.Clear` method.

NOTE

You should put code to check the Err object after any code that you think might cause an error. This is because the VBScript Err object only contains information about the last error that occurred. If you only check the Err object once in a long listing of code then you would only find out about the last error that occurred even though many errors may have occurred between the `On Error Resume Next` statement and the `If Err.Number > 0` statement. The Err object's properties are reset to zero-length strings after an `On Error Resume Next` statement or when the `Err.Clear` method is called.

Creating Custom IIS Error Pages

Try as we might, we just don't catch all the errors in our programs. Even with custom error handlers in our scripts, somewhere, at some time one of our pages will crash for some reason. When that happens, a page like this will show up:

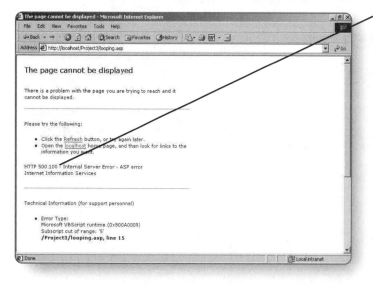

Notice that the HTTP error number is HTTP 500.100. This is the error number that nearly all ASP related errors will generate. IIS provides a way for us to change the error page that is shown to the user for any of the various HTTP errors that might occur. There are a couple reasons for designing your own ASP error page. For one thing, it would be nice to output a simple user-friendly error message when something goes terribly wrong. Secondly, it would be good to build in some method of logging the error or of notifying you, the developer, of the details of the error. In this section I'll go over the details of creating your own ASP error pages.

The ASPError Object

The ubiquitous ASP Server object provides yet another useful method, `Server.GetLastError`. This method returns an ASPError object that contains all kinds of useful information about the last ASP error that occurred. By the way, the ASPError object will contain useful information only if it's used on an active server page that has been designated by IIS as an error page (I'll go over how to do that in the next section.) The ASPError object contains the following properties:

ASPError Object Properties

Property	Description
ASPCode	This is the error code assigned by IIS.
Number	The normal error code. For example, a VBScript error number.
Source	The source code of the line that caused the error.
File	The name of the ASP page that had the error on it.
Line	The line number of the error.
Column	The column number in the line where the error occurred.
Category	The type of error that occurred.
ASPDescription	The ASP Error description assigned by IIS.
Description	The normal description of the error. For example, a VBScript error description.

Not all these properties will necessarily contain values for every error that occurs in an active server page. If you are displaying this information on your error page, you might want to use an `If…Then` statement to check whether a particular property contains any information before displaying it to the user.

NOTE

The ASPError object is new to ASP 3. If you are using IIS 4.0 or PWS then the examples in this section won't work on your machine.

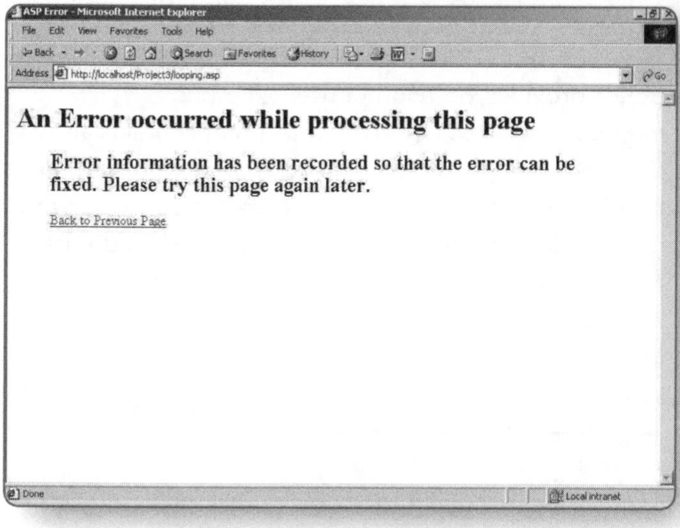

Using the ASPError Object

Here is a sample custom error page that I created. All this page does is write out a generic message to the user that an error occurred on the page. It also records the error in the IIS log.

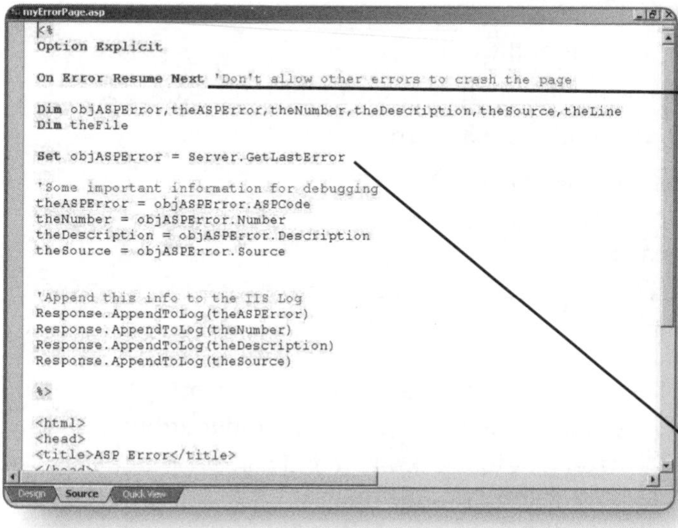

```
<%
Option Explicit

On Error Resume Next 'Don't allow other errors to crash the page

Dim objASPError,theASPError,theNumber,theDescription,theSource,theLine
Dim theFile

Set objASPError = Server.GetLastError

'Some important information for debugging
theASPError = objASPError.ASPCode
theNumber = objASPError.Number
theDescription = objASPError.Description
theSource = objASPError.Source


'Append this info to the IIS Log
Response.AppendToLog(theASPError)
Response.AppendToLog(theNumber)
Response.AppendToLog(theDescription)
Response.AppendToLog(theSource)

%>

<html>
<head>
<title>ASP Error</title>
```

Here's the code.

First, I turn on custom error handling using the `On Error Resume Next` statement. I do this so any errors that happen on this page will not be displayed. If you don't do this and an error occurs, IIS uses another error page instead of the one you assigned.

After declaring a bunch of variables I create a reference to the ASPError object.

> **NOTE**
>
> I haven't talked about declaring object variables yet. If a variable is going to be used to hold an object, you must use the `Set` keyword to assign the object to the variable.

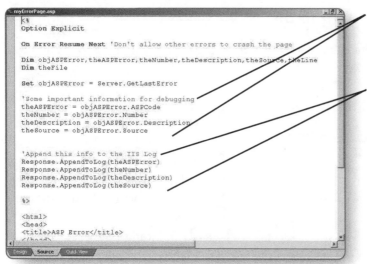

```
myErrorPage.asp                                              _ |e|X
<%
Option Explicit

On Error Resume Next 'Don't allow other errors to crash the page

Dim objASPError,theASPError,theNumber,theDescription,theSource,theLine
Dim theFile

Set objASPError = Server.GetLastError

'Some important information for debugging
theASPError = objASPError.ASPCode
theNumber = objASPError.Number
theDescription = objASPError.Description
theSource = objASPError.Source


'Append this info to the IIS Log
Response.AppendToLog(theASPError)
Response.AppendToLog(theNumber)
Response.AppendToLog(theDescription)
Response.AppendToLog(theSource)

%>

<html>
<head>
<title>ASP Error</title>
</head>
```

I then assign various properties of the ASPError object to the variables I created.

Finally, I use the `Response.AppendToLog` method to add the information to the IIS log.

There are many other things you might want to record when an error occurs. From your custom error page, you have access to all the information that the active server page that caused the error had. For example, you could gather information from the `Request.Form` or `Request.QueryString` collection to see what, if any, form input might have triggered an error. You might also record information from the `Request.Cookies` or `Request.ServerVariables` collections. All this information will be helpful as you begin debugging runtime errors.

In this example I used the IIS log to record the error information. There are other things to do with this information that would probably be more helpful. The IIS log records information about every page that is hit in your Web site (not just pages with errors). That means that you would have to page through the logs to find the pages with errors. Here are some other things you might consider doing in your custom error pages:

● Use the "Logging Utility Component" to create an error log that only logs errors.

● Record error information in an error table in a database.

● Use CDO, CDONTS or a COM component like ASPMail to have an e-mail message with error information sent to you whenever an error occurs.

Using the IIS Log in IIS 5.0

If you do decide to write custom information to the IIS log, you need to set up IIS appropriately. Here's how:

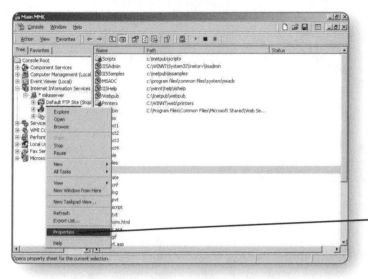

1. Click on Start, Settings, Control Panel.

2. In Control Panel, click on Administrative Tools, then Internet Services Manager.

3. In Internet Services Manager, expand the + next to your server.

4. Right-click on the Web site or virtual directory for which you want to log errors and click on Properties.

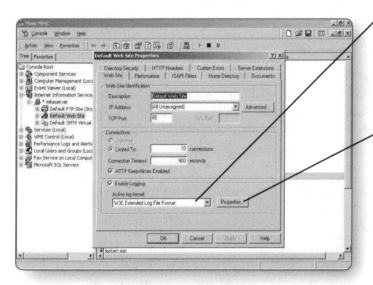

5. Under the Web Site tab, make sure that Enable logging is checked and that the type of logging is W3C Extended Log File Format.

6. Click on the Properties button.

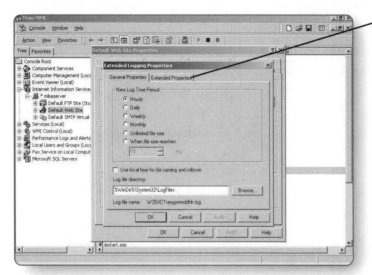

7. On the window that opens, click on the Extended Properties tab.

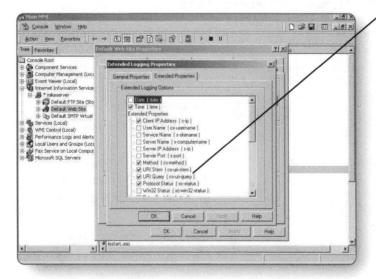

8. On the Extended Properties page, make sure that both URI Stem and URI Query are checked.

Log files are saved as comma delimited text files. The default location of log files for the Default Web Site in Windows NT and Windows 2000 is C:\WINNT\System32\LogFiles\ W3SVC1.

Here's a sample of what one of my log files looks like.

Note that pages with a status of 500 contain the error information I logged in my custom error page.

Assigning Custom Error Pages in IIS

After you've created your custom ASP error page, you'll need to go in to IIS and establish that it is the page that should be displayed when an active server page error occurs. Here are the steps to do that:

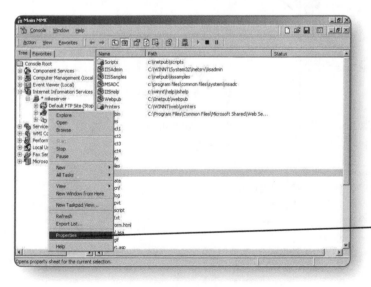

1. Click on Start, Settings, Control Panel.

2. In Control Panel, click on Administrative Tools, then Internet Services Manager.

3. In Internet Services Manager, expand the + next to your server.

4. Right-click on the Web site or virtual directory for which you set up the custom error page and click on Properties.

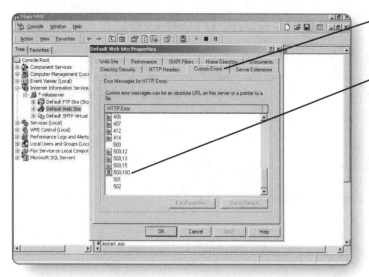

5. Click on the Custom Errors tab.

6. Scroll down the list of errors until you find 500;100.

7. Double-click on the error number.

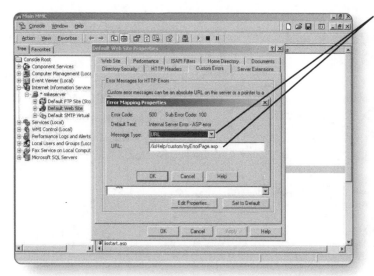

8. Make sure that the Message Type is URL. Then put the URL of your error page in the URL text box. The default location is /IISHelp/common/500-100.asp. I created a new directory called /IISHelp/custom/ in which to put my custom error pages.

After you've completed these steps, IIS will use your custom error pages for active server page errors that occur. You can create custom error pages for any of the HTTP errors by following the same steps.

Debugging Using Visual InterDev

Visual InterDev has extensive debugging functionality built in. If you don't have Visual InterDev, you can use the Microsoft Script Debugger that comes with IIS to do the same things. I'm not going to go into all the details of debugging with Visual InterDev, but I will show you how to get it up and running.

Configuring IIS for ASP Debugging

First you have to set up your Web site to allow server-side script debugging. Here are the steps to take:

1. Click on Start, Settings, Control Panel.

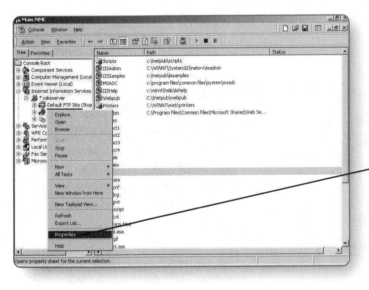

2. In Control Panel, click on Administrative Tools, then Internet Services Manager.

3. In Internet Services Manager, expand the + next to your server.

4. Right-click on the Web site or virtual directory you want to enable for debugging and click on Properties.

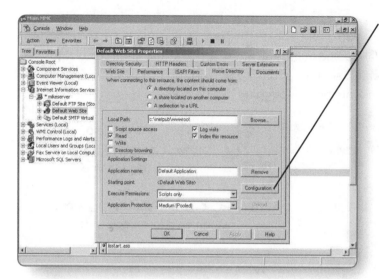

5. Click on the Home Directory tab, then the Configuration button.

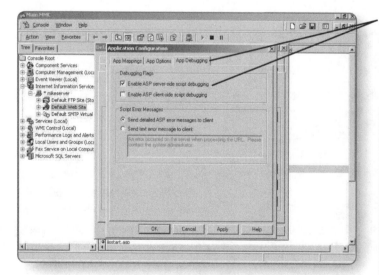

6. Click on the App Debugging tab, then check the box next to Enable ASP server-side script debugging.

CAUTION

Enabling server-side script debugging will have a negative effect on your Web application's performance. It will also cause pages with errors on them to "hang" in the client's browser. For these reasons you should enable server-side script debugging on your development servers only. Never enable it on a production Web server!

Using the Debugger

After you've enabled debugging in IIS, you are ready to begin debugging with Visual InterDev. I've created an error in the looping.asp page that we looked at earlier so I could demonstrate how debugging can be done.

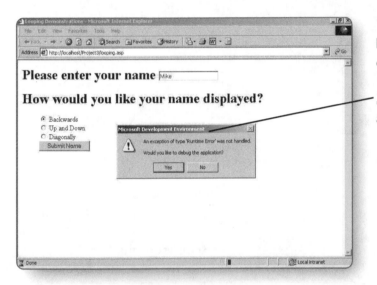

1. First, I open the page in a browser, enter my name, and click on Submit Name.

2. Since debugging is enabled, an error message is displayed.

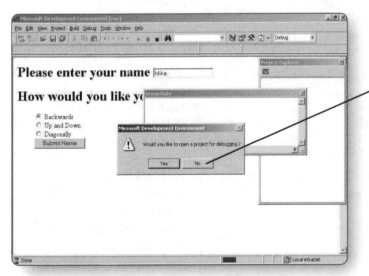

3. After clicking on the Yes button, I face yet another message box.

4. This box asks whether I would like to open a project for debugging. Since I already have the project open, I'll click on No. Otherwise, I would get an error about the project already being in use.

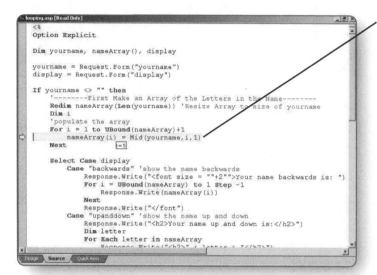

5. The debugger then opens another instance of Visual InterDev and displays the page that has the error. Notice that it highlights the line that caused the error.

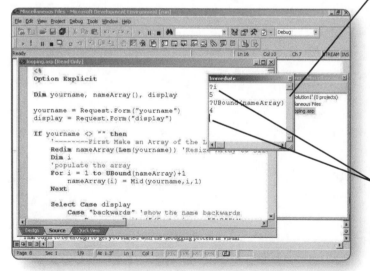

6. The Immediate window is a helpful feature. To view the Immediate window, select View, Debug Windows, Immediate. You can also open it by clicking on the appropriate button on the Debug toolbar. Move your mouse slowly over the buttons to find it.

7. Notice that I have printed out the value of the loop counter variable i and the value of the upper bound of nameArray. You can see that the error was caused because the program was trying to assign a value to nameArray(5) while the upper bound of the array was only 4. This error was caused because I changed the For loop to go to one beyond the upper bound of the array.

That ought to be enough to get you started with the debugging process in Visual InterDev. You can learn more by reading the Visual InterDev documentation or, of course, by experimentation.

6

Procedures, Classes and Server-Side Includes

In Chapters 4 and 5 you learned about the basics of scripting with VBScript. In this chapter, you learn to take those basics and put them together in packages that provide reusable functionality. Reusable code can be anything from a subroutine or function that can be used repeatedly in a single script, to a class that can be used in several scripts, to a COM/COM+ component that can be used by programmers around the world. In this chapter, you'll learn how to:

- Create and use VBScript procedures
- Create and use VBScript classes
- Use server-side includes and the `Server.Execute` method

Understanding Procedures

You'll start your journey into reusable code by considering procedures. In VBScript there are essentially two types of procedures: subroutines and functions. We'll consider both of them in turn.

Subroutines

Subroutines are perhaps the simplest form of code packaging. A *subroutine* is a section of code that has a name. When you want to use the code, you just "call" its name. Subroutines can also accept *arguments* or *parameters*, which are variables that are passed to the subroutine. These variables can then be used in the section of code between the Sub and End Sub statements.

Here is the syntax of a subroutine:

```
Sub [Name of Subroutine] ([list of arguments])
       [Some code]
       Exit Sub
       [Some code]
End Sub
```

The subroutine name should be descriptive (like a variable name is). Also, it can't start with a number or special character. Subroutines do not have to accept arguments. If you don't want your sub to contain arguments, don't put anything between the parentheses after the name of the sub. If you do pass in variables as arguments, you can use those arguments in the code within the sub as if they were variables that you declared in the sub.

As you can with For loops and Do While loops, you can use an Exit statement to exit out of a sub. You might want to put an Exit Sub statement in a conditional expression within the sub. An Exit Sub statement causes the control to return to the code that "called" the sub.

Calling a Subroutine

To use a subroutine, you need to call it from some code. There are two ways of doing this, as follows:

```
MySub firstArgument,secondArgument
```

Or

```
Call MySub (firstArgument,secondArgument)
```

When a subroutine is called, the code in the sub is executed and control returns to the line of code that called the subroutine.

ByRef versus ByVal

At this point I had better explain a little more about the arguments that are passed to a subroutine or function. There are two keywords that can be placed in front of an argument: `ByRef` and `ByVal`. Here is an example of what I mean.

```
Sub MyExampleSub (ByVal myVariable,ByRef yourVariable)
```

I can call this sub from within my script like this:

```
MyExampleSub custID, neighborID
```

First, assume that I've already declared `custID` and `neighborID` elsewhere in my script. Next, notice that I don't have to call the variable I'm passing in by the same name as the argument in the subroutine. In this case, I'm passing in a variable named `custID` to the sub. In the subroutine, the variable will be referred to as `myVariable`. Because the `myVariable` argument is specified as `ByVal` (meaning "By Value"), the value of `myVariable` is set equal to the value of `custID`. The argument `myVariable` becomes, essentially, a copy of the `custID` variable. Changes made to `myVariable` within the subroutine will not affect the value of `custID`. This is not the case, however, with the `neighborID` variable. Since the subroutine specifies that the second argument, `yourVariable`, should be passed `ByRef` (meaning "By Reference"), the actual `neighborID` variable is passed to the subroutine rather than just the value of `neighborID`. That means that `yourVariable` is now the same as `neighborID`. If the value of `yourVariable` is changed within the subroutine, so is the value of `neighborID`.

In general, it's safest to pass variables into subroutines and functions by value (`ByVal`) unless you actually want the variable to be changed by the sub or function. It is not advisable to pass large objects to functions or subroutines in a VBScript environment.

> ### NOTE
>
> In earlier versions of VBScript you could not specify that arguments be passed `ByRef` or `ByVal`. All arguments were passed `ByVal`. In VBScript version 5 however, all arguments are passed `ByRef` by default. This means that if you don't put either keyword in front of the argument, it will be passed `ByRef`. Also, if you are not using at least VBScript 5.0 then all of the examples that use the `ByVal` and `ByRef` keywords will not work. You can download the latest version of VBScript from the Microsoft site as mentioned in Chapter 4.

Using Subroutines

If you've never worked with procedures before, you might be fairly confused at this point. These concepts should make more sense to you if you see them in action.

I've created an online Age Calculator. The application consists of two active server pages, ageCalculator.asp and calculateAge.asp. First, you'll look at what the pages do, then you'll see how they use procedures to do it.

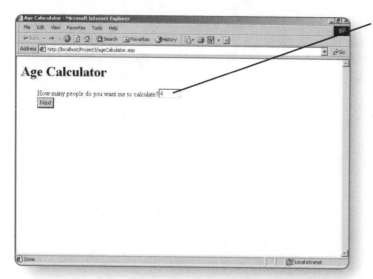

Initially, the ageCalulator.asp page loads and prompts the user to enter the number of people to "calculate" ages for. The user clicks on Next to go to the next screen of the wizard.

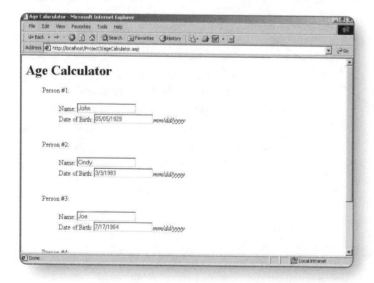

The same page, ageCalculator.asp, receives the number of people from the previous form and prompts for a name and date of birth for each of the people.

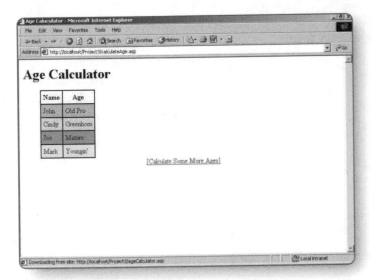

Upon submitting the form, the information is sent to calculateAge.asp where a table is built. The table contains each person's name and a "statement" about their age. Although this example doesn't do anything really useful, the code behind these pages illustrates how to use procedures in VBScript.

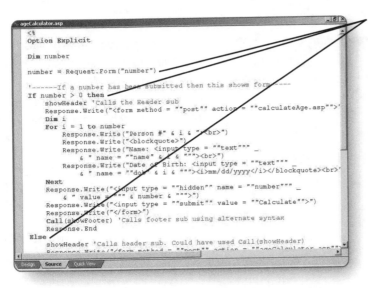

First, notice that the page has one variable, number, which is assigned the value of the "number" form element. If this number is not greater than zero, the form has not been submitted. In that case, the code after the Else statement is run. This code builds the initial input screen.

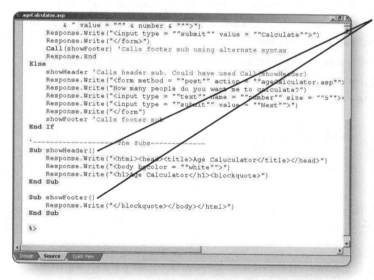

```
                & " value = """ & number & """>")
        Response.Write("<input type = ""submit"" value = ""Calculate"">")
        Response.Write("</form>")
        Call(showFooter) 'Calls footer sub using alternate syntax
        Response.End
    Else
        showHeader 'Calls header sub. Could have used Call(showHeader)
        Response.Write("<form method = ""post"" action = ""ageCalculator.asp"">")
        Response.Write("How many people do you want me to calculate?")
        Response.Write("<input type = ""text"" name = ""number"" size = ""5"">
        Response.Write("<input type = ""submit"" value = ""Next"">")
        Response.Write("</form>")
        showFooter 'Calls footer sub
    End If

    '--------------------The Subs-------------
    Sub showHeader()
        Response.Write("<html><head><title>Age Calculator</title></head>")
        Response.Write("<body bgcolor = ""white"">")
        Response.Write("<h1>Age Calculator</h1><blockquote>")
    End Sub

    Sub showFooter()
        Response.Write("</blockquote></body></html>")
    End Sub

%>
```

This section of code begins with a call to a subroutine named `showHeader()`. I could have called the sub using the alternate syntax, `Call(showHeader())`. This syntax would probably be clearer since the word `showHeader()` by itself could be mistaken for a variable. Notice that at the end of the code that builds the initial form, there is another subroutine call to the sub `showFooter()`.

All the `showHeader()` sub does is write out the first few lines of an HTML page. Likewise, the `showFooter()` sub writes out the last few lines. Using these subs we can easily build multiple Web pages from this one active server page. In this example we build only two. Obviously, you don't need to use procedures to do this, but using procedures makes the code easier to read and reduces duplication of code that does the same thing.

These two simple subs don't have any input parameters. In the next page of this application, calculateAge.asp, you'll see an example of a sub that does take input parameters. Before going on to calculateAge.asp, you need to learn a little more about functions.

Functions

Functions are very similar to subroutines. They can accept parameters and use those parameters to do some work. Functions, however, have one additional feature. They have the ability to *return* something back to the code that called it. You might call them "socially responsible" procedures. They give back to their code community.

```
Function [Name of function] (list of arguments)
      [Some code]
      [Name of function] = something
      Exit Function
      [Some code]
      [Name of function] = something2
End Function
```

As you can see, the syntax of a function is nearly the same as that of a subroutine. They have a name, they can have arguments, there can be code between the `Function...End Function` statements, and you can use the `Exit Function` statement to exit out of the procedure. The only real difference between the syntax for a function and that for a sub is that the function can return a value (or object) to the calling code by setting the name of the function equal to something. The *something* is what will be returned to the calling code.

As with subroutines, a function may or may not accept arguments. You can also specify how the individual arguments should be passed by using the `ByRef` or `ByVal` keywords.

Calling a Function

You can call a function using the `Call(Name of Function(list of arguments))` syntax. In this case, the function is essentially the same thing as a subroutine.

The code in the function is executed, but any return value would be discarded. Here is the normal syntax for using functions:

```
Dim theFirstInitial
theFirstInitial = GetFirstInitial("Mike")
```

In this example there is a variable named `theFirstInitial` that is set equal to the return value of the `GetFirstInitial()` function. When this code is executed, the function statement, `GetFirstInitial("Mike")` will magically be replaced by the return value of the function, which should be "M". Thus the variable `theFirstInitial` will equal "M". Let's continue with the Age Calculator example to see VBScript functions in action.

Using Functions

I've already discussed the code that takes place on the ageCalculator.asp page. The user fills out a form that asks how many people to calculate ages for. After clicking on Next, the user fills out another form in which the name and date of birth is specified for each of the persons. At that point, the information is sent to the calculateAge.asp page for processing. Here's the code for that page.

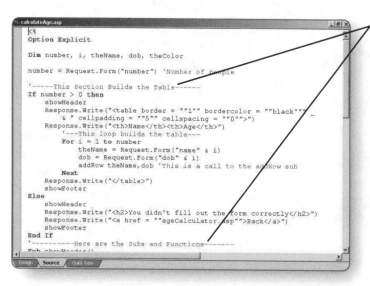

All this page does is build a table that lists each person's name and a "calculated" expression about their age. The page is divided into two sections. The top of the page has an If...End If statement that builds the HTML page with the table on it. The rest of the page is made up of the subs and functions that do the work.

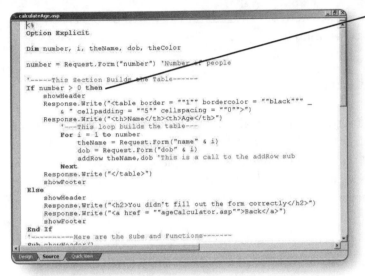

The `If` statement checks to see if the number of people submitted from the previous form is greater than zero. If it is, then there is work to be done; if not, then the user needs to go back and fill out the form. Assuming the number is greater than zero, the `showHeader()` sub is executed, building the header of the HTML page. Next, the opening tags and headers of the table are created.

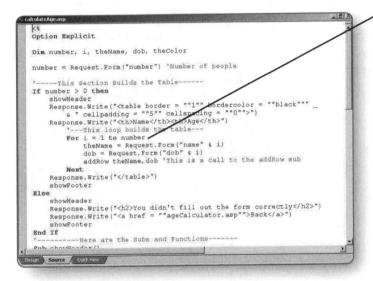

The `For…Next` loop creates a row in the table for each person. Notice that I simply concatenate "name" or "dob" with the variable i to request the name and date of birth of the individual persons. I can do this since I created the form elements using the same technique in the ageCalculator.asp page. I did it that way because the number of people is dynamic—it is not a fixed number. The values of the form elements are placed into the variables `theName` and `dob`.

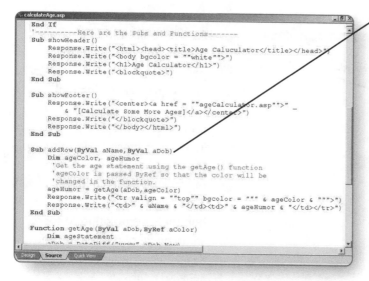

```
calculateAge.asp
<%
Option Explicit

Dim number, i, theName, dob, theColor

number = Request.Form("number") 'Number of people

'-----This Section Builds the Table------
If number > 0 then
    showHeader
    Response.Write("<table border = ""1"" bordercolor = ""black""" _
        & " cellpadding = ""5"" cellspacing = ""0"">")
    Response.Write("<th>Name</th><th>Age</th>")
        '---This loop builds the table---
        For i = 1 to number
            theName = Request.Form("name" & i)
            dob = Request.Form("dob" & i)
            addRow theName,dob 'This is a call to the addRow sub
        Next
    Response.Write("</table>")
    showFooter
Else
    showHeader
    Response.Write("<h2>You didn't fill out the form correctly</h2>")
    Response.Write("<a href = ""ageCalculator.asp"">Back</a>")
    showFooter
End If
'----------Here are the Subs and Functions-------
Sub showHeader()
```

The two variables become the input parameters of the addRow() subroutine. With each iteration of the loop, the addRow() subroutine is executed with new input parameters. The addRow() sub is responsible for constructing a row of the table. I'll consider it next.

```
calculateAge.asp
End If
'----------Here are the Subs and Functions-------
Sub showHeader()
    Response.Write("<html><head><title>Age Caluculator</title></head>")
    Response.Write("<body bgcolor = ""white"">")
    Response.Write("<h1>Age Calculator</h1>")
    Response.Write("<blockquote>")
End Sub

Sub showFooter()
    Response.Write("<center><a href = ""ageCalculator.asp"">" _
        & "[Calculate Some More Ages]</a></center>")
    Response.Write("</blockquote>")
    Response.Write("</body></html>")
End Sub

Sub addRow(ByVal aName,ByVal aDob)
    Dim ageColor, ageHumor
    'Get the age statement using the getAge() function
    'ageColor is passed ByRef so that the color will be
    'changed in the function.
    ageHumor = getAge(aDob,ageColor)
    Response.Write("<tr valign = ""top"" bgcolor = """ & ageColor & """>")
    Response.Write("<td>" & aName & "</td><td>" & ageHumor & "</td></tr>")
End Sub

Function getAge(ByVal aDob, ByRef aColor)
    Dim ageStatement
    aDob = DateDiff("yyyy", aDob, Now)
```

Notice that the addRow() subroutine accepts the two input parameters ByVal. This is because I don't need to have the values of the theName and dob variables changed by the sub. I simply want the sub to be able to use the values of the parameters to calculate the age and write out a row of the table.

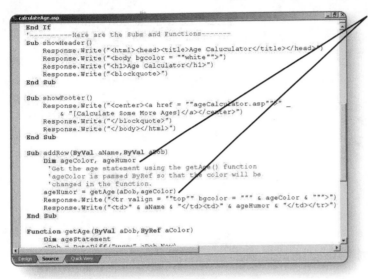

```
        End If
        '----------Here are the Subs and Functions-------
        Sub showHeader()
            Response.Write("<html><head><title>Age Caluculator</title></head>")
            Response.Write("<body bgcolor = ""white"">")
            Response.Write("<h1>Age Calculator</h1>")
            Response.Write("<blockquote>")
        End Sub

        Sub showFooter()
            Response.Write("<center><a href = ""ageCalculator.asp""" _
                & "[Calculate Some More Ages]</a></center>")
            Response.Write("</blockquote>")
            Response.Write("</body></html>")
        End Sub

        Sub addRow(ByVal aName, ByVal aDob)
            Dim ageColor, ageHumor
            'Get the age statement using the getAge() function
            'ageColor is passed ByRef so that the color will be
            'changed in the function.
            ageHumor = getAge(aDob, ageColor)
            Response.Write("<tr valign = ""top"" bgcolor = """ & ageColor & """>")
            Response.Write("<td>" & aName & "</td><td>" & ageHumor & "</td></tr>")
        End Sub

        Function getAge(ByVal aDob, ByRef aColor)
            Dim ageStatement
            aDob = DateDiff("yyyy", aDob, Now)
```

Inside the subroutine I declare two variables, ageColor and ageHumor. Notice in the last two lines of the sub that the ageColor variable is used to set the background color of the row and the ageHumor variable is the calculated statement of age that is presented in the row. The values of these two variables are set in the preceding statement, ageHumor = getAge(aDob, ageColor). The ageHumor variable is set equal to the return value of the getAge() function. So "how is the ageColor variable set?" you ask. Well, it is passed ByRef, which means that its value can be changed in the getAge() function. Let's take a look at the function to see what it does.

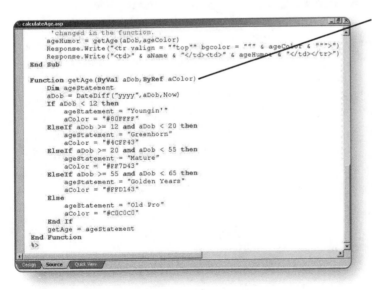

```
            'changed in the function.
            ageHumor = getAge(aDob, ageColor)
            Response.Write("<tr valign = ""top"" bgcolor = """ & ageColor & """>")
            Response.Write("<td>" & aName & "</td><td>" & ageHumor & "</td></tr>")
        End Sub

        Function getAge(ByVal aDob, ByRef aColor)
            Dim ageStatement
            aDob = DateDiff("yyyy", aDob, Now)
            If aDob < 12 then
                ageStatement = "Youngin'"
                aColor = "#80FFFF"
            ElseIf aDob >= 12 and aDob < 20 then
                ageStatement = "Greenhorn"
                aColor = "#4CFF43"
            ElseIf aDob >= 20 and aDob < 55 then
                ageStatement = "Mature"
                aColor = "#FF7D43"
            ElseIf aDob >= 55 and aDob < 65 then
                ageStatement = "Golden Years"
                aColor = "#FFFD143"
            Else
                ageStatement = "Old Pro"
                aColor = "#C0C0C0"
            End If
            getAge = ageStatement
        End Function
    %>
```

As you can see, the function accepts the date of birth parameter ByVal and the color parameter ByRef. Remember that I can call the input parameters whatever I want to in a sub or function. In this case the aDob parameter is a copy of the aDob variable in the addRow() sub, and the aColor parameter is pointing to the same piece of memory as the ageColor variable in the addRow() sub.

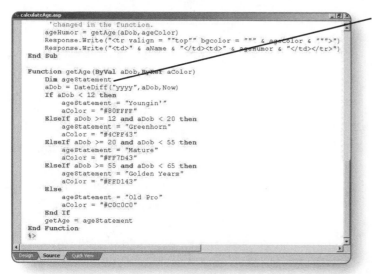

```
- calculateAge.asp
        'changed in the function.
    ageHumor = getAge(aDob,ageColor)
    Response.Write("<tr valign = ""top"" bgcolor = """ & ageColor & """>")
    Response.Write("<td>" & aName & "</td><td>" & ageHumor & "</td></tr>")
End Sub

Function getAge(ByVal aDob, ByRef aColor)
    Dim ageStatement
    aDob = DateDiff("yyyy",aDob,Now)
    If aDob < 12 then
        ageStatement = "Youngin'"
        aColor = "#80FFFF"
    ElseIf aDob >= 12 and aDob < 20 then
        ageStatement = "Greenhorn"
        aColor = "#4CFF43"
    ElseIf aDob >= 20 and aDob < 55 then
        ageStatement = "Mature"
        aColor = "#FF7D43"
    ElseIf aDob >= 55 and aDob < 65 then
        ageStatement = "Golden Years"
        aColor = "#FFD143"
    Else
        ageStatement = "Old Pro"
        aColor = "#C0C0C0"
    End If
    getAge = ageStatement
End Function
%>
```

I next declare a variable named ageStatement, then I set the aDob variable equal to the return value of the DateDiff() function. DateDiff() is a VBScript built-in function that calculates the difference between two dates. The first parameter of the function is the aspect of the date you want returned. In this case I want to know how many years old the person is, so I use "yyyy", which is the constant used when you want to know the difference in years between two dates. You can also find the difference in months, hours, minutes, and so on. The second parameter is the first date, and the third parameter is the second date. Remember that the Now() function returns the current system date and time. All that this line does is set the aDob variable equal to the difference between the person's year of birth and the present year.

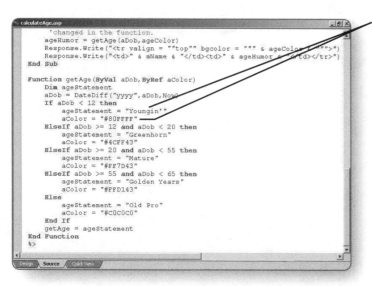

```
- calculateAge.asp
        'changed in the function.
    ageHumor = getAge(aDob,ageColor)
    Response.Write("<tr valign = ""top"" bgcolor = """ & ageColor & """>")
    Response.Write("<td>" & aName & "</td><td>" & ageHumor & "</td></tr>")
End Sub

Function getAge(ByVal aDob, ByRef aColor)
    Dim ageStatement
    aDob = DateDiff("yyyy",aDob,Now)
    If aDob < 12 then
        ageStatement = "Youngin'"
        aColor = "#80FFFF"
    ElseIf aDob >= 12 and aDob < 20 then
        ageStatement = "Greenhorn"
        aColor = "#4CFF43"
    ElseIf aDob >= 20 and aDob < 55 then
        ageStatement = "Mature"
        aColor = "#FF7D43"
    ElseIf aDob >= 55 and aDob < 65 then
        ageStatement = "Golden Years"
        aColor = "#FFD143"
    Else
        ageStatement = "Old Pro"
        aColor = "#C0C0C0"
    End If
    getAge = ageStatement
End Function
%>
```

Next comes a big If…ElseIf…End If statement that evaluates which range the person's age fits in. When the correct range is determined, the ageStatement variable is set to some "age appropriate" statement and the aColor variable is set equal to a hexadecimal color value.

```
'changed in the function.
    ageHumor = getAge(aDob,ageColor)
    Response.Write("<tr valign = ""top"" bgcolor = """ & ageColor & """>")
    Response.Write("<td>" & aName & "</td><td>" & ageHumor & "</td></tr>")
End Sub

Function getAge(ByVal aDob,ByRef aColor)
    Dim ageStatement
    aDob = DateDiff("yyyy",aDob,Now)
    If aDob < 12 then
        ageStatement = "Youngin'"
        aColor = "#80FFFF"
    ElseIf aDob >= 12 and aDob < 20 then
        ageStatement = "Greenhorn"
        aColor = "#4CFF43"
    ElseIf aDob >= 20 and aDob < 55 then
        ageStatement = "Mature"
        aColor = "#FF7D43"
    ElseIf aDob >= 55 and aDob < 65 then
        ageStatement = "Golden Years"
        aColor = "#FFD143"
    Else
        ageStatement = "Old Pro"
        aColor = "#C0C0C0"
    End If
    getAge = ageStatement
End Function
%>
```

At the end of the conditional statement the name of the function, getAge() is set equal to the ageStatement variable. This sets the return value for the function. This return value will be sent back to the calling code and become the value of the ageHumor variable. If you're not familiar with procedures, you might need to look at this example carefully, then try creating some of your own subs and functions.

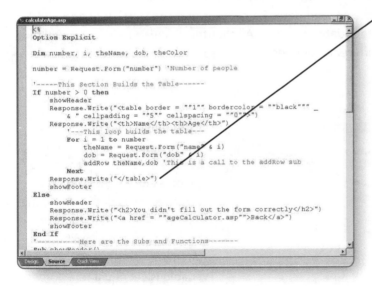

```
<%
Option Explicit

Dim number, i, theName, dob, theColor

number = Request.Form("number") 'Number of people

'-----This Section Builds the Table------
If number > 0 then
    showHeader
    Response.Write("<table border = ""1"" bordercolor = ""black""" _
        & " cellpadding = ""5"" cellspacing = ""0"">")
    Response.Write("<th>Name</th><th>Age</th>")
        '---This loop builds the table---
        For i = 1 to number
            theName = Request.Form("name" & i)
            dob = Request.Form("dob" & i)
            addRow theName,dob 'This is a call to the addRow sub
        Next
    Response.Write("</table>")
    showFooter
Else
    showHeader
    Response.Write("<h2>You didn't fill out the form correctly</h2>")
    Response.Write("<a href = ""ageCalculator.asp"">Back</a>")
    showFooter
End If
'----------Here are the Subs and Functions--------
Sub showHeader()
```

After all of the rows have been added, the closing </table> tag is written and the showFooter() sub closes out the HTML page.

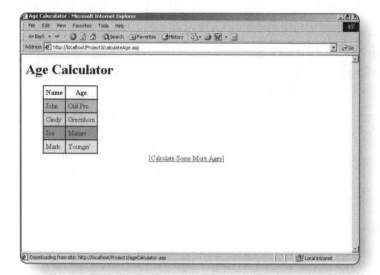

Here's a screen shot to refresh your memory as to what the code actually does.

That's the basics of VBScript procedures. You'll find that using procedures will make your code more readable as well as more efficient. In the next section you'll consider how to take groups of procedures and package them together into *classes*.

Classes

When we start talking *classes*, we're talking *objects*. When we're talking objects, we're starting to talk about object-oriented programming. While VBScript does not implement all the concepts of a true object-oriented programming language like C++ or Java, it does point in the object-oriented direction. I'm not going to explain all that object-oriented programming is. However, I'll do my best to give a brief description of an object. *Objects* in VBScript are made up of three things: properties, methods and events. *Properties* are attributes of an object. *Methods* are things that an object can do. Finally, *events* are things that can happen to an object.

We'll briefly consider a dog as an object. A dog object has several properties. It has eye color, hair color, hair length, weight, height, length, breed, and so on. Likewise, a dog has many methods. A dog can sit, stand, heel (at least some can), run, eat, bark, and so on. Finally, there are many events that can happen to a dog. A dog can be told to sit, told to heel, told to sic 'em, and so on. If we were going to "program" a dog, we would need to define all the properties, methods, and events of a dog object. Such a definition would serve as a prototype for creating dogs. This is essentially what a class is. It is a prototype for an object. To use some object-oriented programming terminology, an object is an *instance* of a class. The process of creating a new object from a class is called *instantiation*. Next we'll consider the syntax of a VBScript class.

> **NOTE**
>
> Classes are new to VBScript 5.0. If you have an older version of VBScript then you will need to download the latest version from the Microsoft site in order for the examples in this section to work.

The general syntax for a class is as follows:

```
Class [Name of class]
        Private variables
        Properties
        Methods
        Events
End Class
```

I'll explain these elements of a class in turn. They don't need to be in any particular order, but it makes your code easier to read if you put like elements together.

Private Variables

You can declare variables in classes the same way that you declare variables in any other VBScript code:

```
Dim myVariable
```

However, at this point I need to bring up another object-oriented programming concept called *encapsulation*. One goal of object-oriented programming is to encapsulate or hide the logic inside a class. A class is supposed to be like a black box. A class has particular ways it will accept input, and given that input it will always give a prescribed output. Exactly how it comes up with the output is supposed to be kept secret. One reason for this is that object-oriented code is usually used by several programmers. One programmer might create one class and another programmer might create another class that "interfaces" with it. The purpose of encapsulation is to try to keep one class from interfering with the inner workings of another class.

When you're designing a class you need to decide which methods and properties are seen by the outside world and which will be for "internal use only." Those that will be used by others should be made *public* using the `Public` keyword. Those for internal use only should be made `Private`. Variables in your classes should be made private using this syntax:

```
Private myVariable
```

The default setting for variables is `Public`. That means that a variable declared using the `Dim` keyword is the same as a variable declared using the `Public` keyword. Such a variable would be able to be seen and changed by code outside of the class.

Properties

Properties are a means by which outside code can retrieve or set the values of private variables. There are three types of property statements: `Property Let`, `Property Get`, and `Property Set`.

Property Let

`Property Let` statements are just like subroutines. They can accept arguments, but they don't return a value. `Property Let` statements are used to set the value of a variable within the class. Here is the syntax:

```
[Public or Private] Property Let [Name of Property] (arguments and value)
        [Some code]
        Exit Property
        [Some code]
End Property
```

Properties can be `Public` or `Private`. If they are private, they can be used only by procedures within the class. Arguments are not required, but a value is. The value is used to set the value of a private variable within the `Property…End Property` code. Usually, code inside the Property block is used to verify that the value is of the correct type. If it is, the value of some private variable is set equal to the value that was passed in. Otherwise the value is set to some default value. You'll see how this works when you get to the example.

Property Get

The `Property Get` statement is essentially a function that returns the value of a class variable. Here is the syntax:

```
[Public [Default] or Private] Property Get [Name of property](arguments)
     [Some code]
     [Set]Name of Property = some value or object
     Exit Property
     [Some code]
     [Set]Name of Property = some value or object
End Property
```

`Property Get` statements can be either `Public` or `Private`. If the property is `Public`, you can also use the `Default` keyword to make this the default property for the class. That means that if someone references the class without specifying the name of a property, this property will be used to return a value. There can be only one `Default` property in a class. The name of the property is set equal to the value of some class variable. This value is returned to the code that called the property. If the `Property Get` statement is to return an object, the `Set` keyword must be used before the name of the property.

Property Set

The `Property Set` statement is just like a `Property Let` statement, except that instead of setting a private class variable equal to some value, it sets the class variable equal to an object. Don't get too confused over the concept of an object right now. You'll get lots of practice working with objects in future chapters. Basically, instead of setting a variable equal to a number or a string of characters (like "Hello"), the `Property Set` statement can set a variable equal to an object like a Dog object. The object is not simply a number or string of characters; it is an object with its own methods, properties and events.

Methods

So, what exactly are methods? Well, the good news is you already know what methods are. They are simply procedures—good old subroutines and functions. These procedures define what a class can do. You can use the `Public` and `Private` keywords to expose or hide your methods. If you have some procedures that are used internally only, they should be made `Private`.

Events

In a VBScript class there are only two events that can be fired. One is the
Class_Initialize() event and the other is the Class_Terminate() event. The
initialize event is fired when an object is instantiated from the class; the *terminate*
event is fired when an object is destroyed. The initialize event is a good place to
initialize any of the private variables in your class. The terminate event can be used
to do any necessary cleanup.

These two events are essentially subroutines that are automatically called when an
object is either created or destroyed. If you want to put some code in these subs,
you can do so using the following syntax:

```
Private Sub Class_Initiate()
      [Some Code]
End Sub

Private Sub Class_Terminate()
      [Some Code]
End Sub
```

Using Classes

After you've created your class you'll want to be able to create objects from it.
To create a reference to an object, you have to use the Set keyword. Assume that
I have a class called "Dog". The New keyword allocates memory for a Dog object
and creates the Dog object. Here's how I could create a Dog object:

```
Dim MyDog
Set MyDog = New Dog
```

If I want to set some of the dog's properties, I can use the following syntax.

```
MyDog.HairColor = "Black"
MyDog.EyeColor = "Brown"
MyDog.Name = "Rex"
```

In the class, the corresponding Property Let statements are called and passed the
value that's on the right side of the equals sign.

If I wanted to retrieve the value of one of the Dog properties, I could do so like this:

```
Dim theBreed
theBreed = MyDog.Breed
```

In this case, the corresponding `Property Get` statement is called and the value of the breed is returned.

Here's how to use an object's method. I'll pretend to call the Dog class's "Jump" method.

```
Dim howFar, howHigh
howFar = 5ft
howHigh = 2ft
MyDog.Jump howFar,howHigh
```

When you're done with your object, you can explicitly release the memory used to store the object by setting it equal to `Nothing`.

```
Set MyDog = Nothing
```

By now you ought to have a good idea of what a class is and how to create an object from a class. Now we'll take a look at an example.

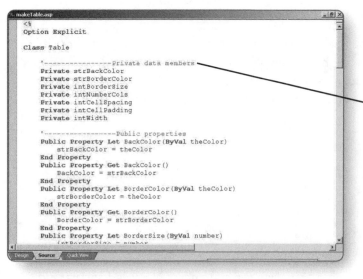

I've created a class called "Table" that can be used to construct HTML tables on the fly. Let's walk through the code.

I've broken up the class code into sections. The first section is the "private data members" section in which I declare all of my private variables. Remember that private variables can only be seen by procedures within the class. There are seven private data members, each of which has to do with some attribute of an HTML table.

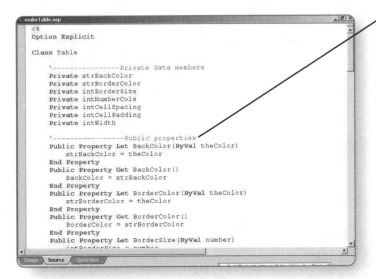

The next section contains the "Public properties." This series of Property Let and Property Get statements enable code outside of the class to access and change the values of the private data members. In this case I've created Public Property Lets and Gets for six of the seven private data members. The only private data member that cannot be set or read directly from outside of the class is the intNumberCols variable. I didn't do anything fancy with these properties, the Property Let statements simply set the private data member equal to the value sent in from the external code. Likewise, the Property Get statements simply return the value of the private data member.

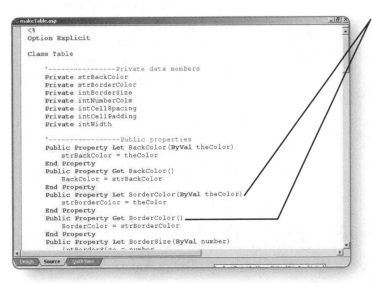

Notice that the Property Get and Property Let statements for each of the data members have the same name. This is the way that Properties are supposed to be set up. Remember, from the perspective of the outside code that references your object, there is only one property that is either being read or changed. A read-only property would have only a Public Property Let, while a write only property would have only a Public Property Get statement. If you are using arguments in a Property Let statement, you must use the same arguments with the same names in the corresponding Property Get statement (if there is one) and vice-versa.

```
makeTable.asp
    Public Property Get Width()
        Width = intWidth
    End Property

    '-------------------------Public Methods
    Public Sub StartTable(ByVal headingArray)
        'Check to see if array was passed in
        If Not isArray(headingArray) then
            Err.Raise ,"TableClass","Need to pass in an array to " _
            & "startTable sub"
            Exit Sub
        End If
        'Write out the table tag
        Response.Write("<table border = """ & intBorderSize & """" _
            & " bordercolor = """ & strBorderColor & """" _
            & " cellpadding = """ & intCellPadding & """" _
            & " cellspacing = """ & intCellSpacing & """" _
            & " width = """ & intWidth & """" _
            & " bgcolor = """ & strBackColor & """>")
        'Write out table headings
        Dim heading
        For Each heading in headingArray
            Response.Write("<th>" & heading & "</th>")
        Next
        intNumberCols = UBound(headingArray)
    End Sub
    Public Sub AddRow(ByVal colArray)
        '---Must pass in correct number of columns, otherwise
Design   Source   Quick View
```

The next section of code contains the Public methods of the class. (There aren't any Private methods in this class.) There are three Public methods: StartTable(), AddRow() and EndTable(). I'll consider each in turn.

```
makeTable.asp
    Public Property Get Width()
        Width = intWidth
    End Property

    '-------------------------Public Methods
    Public Sub StartTable(ByVal headingArray)
        'Check to see if array was passed in
        If Not isArray(headingArray) then
            Err.Raise ,"TableClass","Need to pass in an array to " _
            & "startTable sub"
            Exit Sub
        End If
        'Write out the table tag
        Response.Write("<table border = """ & intBorderSize & """" _
            & " bordercolor = """ & strBorderColor & """" _
            & " cellpadding = """ & intCellPadding & """" _
            & " cellspacing = """ & intCellSpacing & """" _
            & " width = """ & intWidth & """" _
            & " bgcolor = """ & strBackColor & """>")
        'Write out table headings
        Dim heading
        For Each heading in headingArray
            Response.Write("<th>" & heading & "</th>")
        Next
        intNumberCols = UBound(headingArray)
    End Sub
    Public Sub AddRow(ByVal colArray)
        '---Must pass in correct number of columns, otherwise
Design   Source   Quick View
```

Notice that the StartTable() sub expects one parameter, named headingArray. As the name indicates, this parameter ought to be an array. In the If...End If statement, I check to see that the parameter passed in is indeed an array. isArray() is a built-in function that returns True if the value passed to it is an array. I use the Not operator to see if it is true that headingArray is not an array. If it's not, I raise an error using the Err.Raise method of the

VBScript Err object. I didn't pass in a number, so the first parameter is blank. The next parameter is the source of the error, in this case the "Table Class". Finally, I send in a description of the error. After throwing the error, the sub is exited. It is up to the code that called the subroutine to handle the error.

```
makeTable.asp
    Public Property Get Width()
        Width = intWidth
    End Property

    '------------------------------Public Methods
    Public Sub StartTable(ByVal headingArray)
        'Check to see if array was passed in
        If Not isArray(headingArray) then
            Err.Raise ,"TableClass","Need to pass in an array to " _
                & "startTable sub"
            Exit Sub
        End If
        'Write out the table tag
        Response.Write("<table border = """ & intBorderSize & """" _
            & " bordercolor = """ & strBorderColor & """" _
            & " cellpadding = """ & intCellPadding & """" _
            & " cellspacing = """ & intCellSpacing & """" _
            & " width = """ & intWidth & """" _
            & " bgcolor = """ & strBackColor & """>")
        'Write out table headings
        Dim heading
        For Each heading in headingArray
            Response.Write("<th>" & heading & "</th>")
        Next
        intNumberCols = UBound(headingArray)
    End Sub
    Public Sub AddRow(ByVal colArray)
        '---Must pass in correct number of columns, otherwise
        '___raise an error

Design   Source   Quick View
```

If the parameter is an array, the next statement in the sub is executed. This statement builds the <table> tag. Notice that the sub can refer to the private data members directly. The procedure can read or write to the private data members since it is in the class. All the statement does is set the attributes of the table tag to whatever values are contained in the private data members.

```
makeTable.asp
    Public Property Get Width()
        Width = intWidth
    End Property

    '------------------------------Public Methods
    Public Sub StartTable(ByVal headingArray)
        'Check to see if array was passed in
        If Not isArray(headingArray) then
            Err.Raise ,"TableClass","Need to pass in an array to " _
                & "startTable sub"
            Exit Sub
        End If
        'Write out the table tag
        Response.Write("<table border = """ & intBorderSize & """" _
            & " bordercolor = """ & strBorderColor & """" _
            & " cellpadding = """ & intCellPadding & """" _
            & " cellspacing = """ & intCellSpacing & """" _
            & " width = """ & intWidth & """" _
            & " bgcolor = """ & strBackColor & """>")
        'Write out table headings
        Dim heading
        For Each heading in headingArray
            Response.Write("<th>" & heading & "</th>")
        Next
        intNumberCols = UBound(headingArray)
    End Sub
    Public Sub AddRow(ByVal colArray)
        '---Must pass in correct number of columns, otherwise
        '___raise an error

Design   Source   Quick View
```

Next comes a For Each...Next loop that loops through each element of the headingArray. Each element becomes one of the headings in the table. Finally, the intNumberCols variable is set equal to the upper bound of the heading array. This variable contains the number of columns that the table will have.

```
makeTable.asp
        Next
        intNumberCols = UBound(headingArray)
    End Sub
    Public Sub AddRow(ByVal colArray)
        '---Must pass in correct number of columns, otherwise
        '---raise an error.
        If Not isArray(colArray) then
            Err.Raise ,"Table Class","Need to pass in an array."
            Exit Sub
        End If
        If UBound(colArray) <> intNumberCols Then
            Err.Raise ,"Table Class","Need to pass in " & intNumberCols _
                & " columns to this Sub."
            Exit Sub
        End If
        'Start the Row
        Response.Write("<tr valign = ""top"">")
        Dim column
        For Each column in colArray
            Response.Write("<td>" & column & "</td>")
        Next
        'End the Row
        Response.Write("</tr>")
    End Sub
    Public Sub EndTable()
        'Closing table tag
        Response.Write("</table>")
    End Sub
Design   Source   Quick View
```

The next method is the AddRow() method. As the name implies, this method adds a row to the table. First, you need to check that the input parameter matches the criteria the sub expects. The first If…End If statement checks to see whether the input parameter is an array. The second checks whether the array has the correct number of elements.

```
makeTable.asp
        Next
        intNumberCols = UBound(headingArray)
    End Sub
    Public Sub AddRow(ByVal colArray)
        '---Must pass in correct number of columns, otherwise
        '---raise an error.
        If Not isArray(colArray) then
            Err.Raise ,"Table Class","Need to pass in an array."
            Exit Sub
        End If
        If UBound(colArray) <> intNumberCols Then
            Err.Raise ,"Table Class","Need to pass in " & intNumberCols _
                & " columns to this Sub."
            Exit Sub
        End If
        'Start the Row
        Response.Write("<tr valign = ""top"">")
        Dim column
        For Each column in colArray
            Response.Write("<td>" & column & "</td>")
        Next
        'End the Row
        Response.Write("</tr>")
    End Sub
    Public Sub EndTable()
        'Closing table tag
        Response.Write("</table>")
    End Sub
Design   Source   Quick View
```

The <tr> tag is written out first. Next, a For Each…Next loop iterates through the array and writes out a <td></td> statement for each column in the row. The sub ends by writing out the closing </tr> tag.

The EndTable() method simply writes out the closing </table> tag.

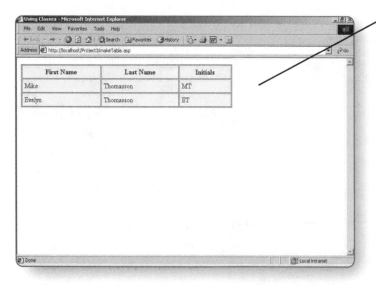

```
                Next
                'End the Row
                Response.Write("</tr>")
        End Sub
        Public Sub EndTable()
                'Closing table tag
                Response.Write("</table>")
        End Sub
        '----------------------------Events
        Private Sub Class_Initialize()
                strBorderColor = "black"
                strBackColor = "white"
                intBorderSize = 1
                intCellPadding = 2
                intCellSpacing = 2
                intNumberCols = 1
                intWidth = "300"
        End Sub
End Class
%>

<html>
<head>
<title>Using Classes</title>
</head>
<body bgcolor = "white">
<%
Dim myTable,myHeadings(2),myRow1(2),myRow2(2)
Set myTable = New Table 'Instantiate a Table object
```

I've only written code for the Class_Initialize() event in this class. All I do in the sub is initialize the value of the private data members of the class. These are the default values of the table.

To show you that it works, I've attached a short HTML page to the end of the makeTable.asp page that uses the Table class.

First Name	Last Name	Initials
Mike	Thomasson	MT
Evelyn	Thomasson	ET

This page uses the Table class to create a table with two rows. I'll use the Table class to do more impressive things in the next section.

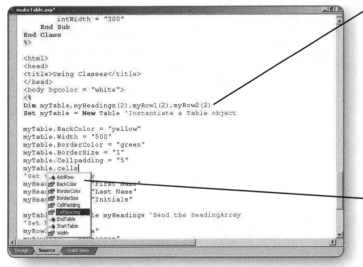

First, I declare the necessary variables, then I instantiate a new Table object named "myTable". Next, I set the properties of myTable I want to change. Any property that I don't set will simply have the default setting set in the Class_Initialize() event.

Notice that the intellisense (Auto complete) list shows all of the public properties and methods of my class. As I type, the property or method that most closely matches what I'm typing is highlighted. To select the highlighted value I can simply hit the Tab key and save myself some typing. Intellisense is one of my favorite features in Visual InterDev.

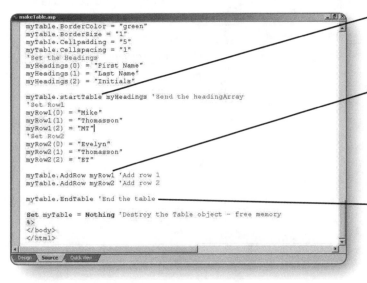

I then set the heading array elements and call the StartTable() method.

Next, I set the values of each of the two row arrays. I create the rows by calling the AddRow() method twice, sending in one of the arrays with each call.

Finally, I call the EndTable() method to finish off the table.

```
makeTable.asp
myTable.BorderColor = "green"
myTable.BorderSize = "1"
myTable.Cellpadding = "5"
myTable.Cellspacing = "1"
'Set the Headings
myHeadings(0) = "First Name"
myHeadings(1) = "Last Name"
myHeadings(2) = "Initials"

myTable.startTable myHeadings 'Send the headingArray
'Set Row1
myRow1(0) = "Mike"
myRow1(1) = "Thomasson"
myRow1(2) = "MT"
'Set Row2
myRow2(0) = "Evelyn"
myRow2(1) = "Thomasson"
myRow2(2) = "ET"

myTable.AddRow myRow1 'Add row 1
myTable.AddRow myRow2 'Add row 2

myTable.EndTable 'End the table

Set myTable = Nothing 'Destroy the Table object - free memory
%>
</body>
</html>
```

Design **Source** Quick View

Finally, I set `myTable` equal to `Nothing` to explicitly destroy the object and release the memory. If I don't explicitly destroy the object, then it will be destroyed automatically once the processing of the page is complete.

Server-Side Includes

If you've created some classes or procedures with functionality that could be used in several active server pages, you can make that script into an *include* file that can be used in other active server pages. Using an include file is kind of like copying and pasting code from one active server page into another. The included file is inserted into the active server page before the ASP interpreter processes the page. The active server page is then executed as if all of the code was in the same page. Even though server-side includes are not really part of VBScript, they do fit in with the concept of code-packaging which is what procedures and classes are all about. I thought this would be an appropriate place to talk about them.

The #include directive is the primary means of including script files in your active server pages. Here is the syntax for a #include statement:

```
<!-#include file="myFile.inc"->
```

or you can use this syntax:

```
<!-#include virtual="/mySite/myFile.inc" ->
```

The #include directive cannot be within a server-side script block. For example, this will not work:

```
<% 'This causes an error
Dim myVariable
<!-#include file="myFile.inc" ->
%>
```

Instead, the #include statement must be outside of the server-side script as if it were part of the client-side HTML.

```
<!-#include file = "myFile.inc"->
<% 'This code will work
Dim myVariable
%>
```

When this page is processed, the #include statement will be replaced with the code in "myFile.inc".

Notice the keywords file and virtual. If you use the file keyword, you need to specify the relative physical path to your include file between the quotation marks. If you use the virtual keyword, you need to specify the virtual path to your include file. Here are some examples:

```
<!-#include file = "..\includes\myFile.inc"->
<!-#include virtual = "/mySite/includes/myFile.inc"->
```

In the first case, the file keyword is used, so the include file path is the physical path to the file relative to the active server page. In the second case, the include file is in the virtual directory called mySite, in the folder called includes.

> ## CAUTION
>
> I've used the traditional .inc notation for these include files. It's better to use .asp extensions on your include files. The reason for this is that if someone knows the name and location of your include file they could point their browser directly at the file. If the file has the .inc extension, they could download the file and look at your code (this could be bad if you have something like a database connection string with passwords in the include file.) If you put the .asp extension on your include files, the ASP interpreter will process the script in the include file and send out only HTML to the browser.

Using #include

I've created an example that uses the `#include` directive. I took my Table class code and put it into its own page, called clsTable.asp. I then created two active server pages, one called tablizer.asp and the other called createTable.asp, which use the Table class to build a user defined table. The createTable.asp page includes the clsTable.asp page. I'm not going to go through all of the code. You can examine it yourself in the code samples on the CD-ROM. Here is what the pages do.

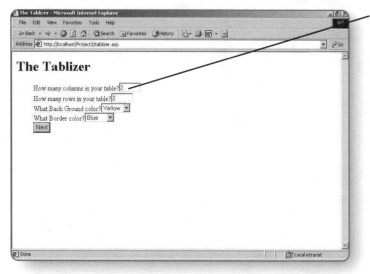

First, users are asked to choose the number of rows and columns they would like in the table. They also choose a background color and border color.

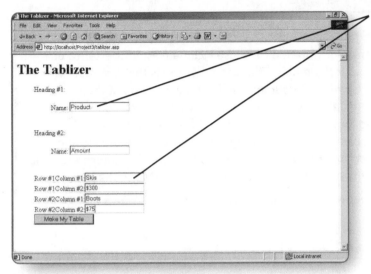

Upon clicking on Next, they supply the appropriate heading and row information.

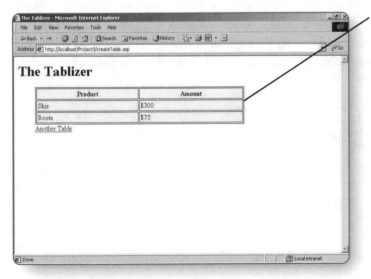

Finally, a table is created according to the user's specifications. The table is created using an object instantiated from the Table class.

```
createTable.asp                                              _ 8 X
<%Option Explicit%>
<!--#include file = "clsTable.asp"-->
<%

Dim backColor,borderColor,numberCols,numberRows

numberCols = Request.Form("numberCols")
numberRows = Request.Form("numberRows")
backColor = Request.Form("backColor")
borderColor = Request.Form("borderColor")

'Check to see if numbers were entered for rows and cols
If Not isNumeric(numberCols) Or Not isNumeric(numberRows) Then
    Response.Write("You didn't enter numbers.")
    Response.End
End If

Dim myTable
Set myTable = New Table

myTable.BackColor = backColor
myTable.BorderColor = borderColor
myTable.Width = "500"

'Get the headings
Dim heading, theHeadings()
Redim theHeadings(numberCols - 1)
For heading = 1 to numberCols
Design   Source   Quick view
```

Here is the #include statement that incorporates all of the code from the clsTable.asp page into the createTable.asp page.

> **NOTE**
>
> If you want to see what the page looks like after the include file has been incorporated into the active server page but before the page has been processed, you can rename the createTable.asp page to createTable.stm. When you view the page in a browser you will not see anything, but if you view the source code for the page you will see all the ASP code for the page. This can be helpful if your page is getting too long with all the #includes. Notice that all of the code in the #include statements is "expanded" so that you can see all of the code that actually makes up the page.

Using <Script> Tags

You can also use a <Script> tag to include script from another page. The tag should be used within the HTML page code, not in a section of server-side script. Here is the syntax:

```
<script runat = "server" src = "myFile.asp" language = "VBScript"></script>
```

If you use this method, you can't have an opening <% at the beginning of the file to be included, nor can you have a closing %>. You should also not put any other code between the <script></script> tags.

Server.Execute

The `Server.Execute` method doesn't do exactly the same thing as a server-side include. I've included it here, however, because it is similar. `Server.Execute` is similar to the `Server.Transfer` method discussed in an earlier chapter. Like the `Server.Transfer` method, control is transferred from the current active server page to the page specified in the `Server.Execute` call. The new active server page then has access to all of the collections available to the calling active server page (like Form, QueryString, ServerVariables, Cookies, and so on). The only difference between `Server.Transfer` and `Server.Execute` is that with the `Server.Execute` method, the control returns to the original active server page as soon as the called active server page finishes executing. Once control has returned to the original active server page, processing of that page continues where it left off. If you encapsulate frequently used code into "mini active server pages," you can use the `Server.Execute` method to run the "mini pages" in the context of one active server page. You could use the `Server.Execute` method to insert code that creates headers or footers, add "page hit" information to a database, send out an e-mail, or the like. You'll see an example of the `Server.Execute` method in Chapter 10. Here is the syntax:

```
<%
Response.Write("Thank you for placing your order")
Server.Execute ("SendCustomerThankYou.asp")
Response.Write("You will soon receive an email with the purchase details.")
Response.End
%>
```

In this sample code, the `Server.Execute` method is used to call the SendCustomerThankYou.asp page that would send an e-mail to the customer detailing their purchase and thanking them for their business.

7

Application and Session Objects

One of the harsh realities of the HTTP protocol is that it is stateless. A *stateless* protocol doesn't "remember" things from one moment to the next. When a client machine requests some information from a Web server, the server processes the request and sends back the appropriate response. At that point all communication between the client and the server ceases. Most Web applications rely on things being remembered from one page of the application to the next. For example, if a user is browsing your online catalog, adding items to a shopping cart along the way, you want the application to remember whom the user is and what has been added to the cart (called the user's "state"). Here is the dilemma: how do we implement state in a stateless world? Well, fortunately ASP provides a simple way to maintain state by using the ASP Application and Session objects. In this chapter, you'll learn to:

- Use the ASP Session object to store user "state" information
- Use other methods to maintain "state"
- Use the ASP Application object to store "global" information

The Session Object

The Session object is an ASP object that allows a Web application to remember information about a particular user's session. You can think of a *session* as the time that a user spends at your Web site during a particular visit. During a visit, a user might go to many different pages within your Web application. Using the Session object, you can keep track of who the user is and what they have done during the visit.

The Session object is easy to use. Here is the syntax:

```
Session("Name of Session Variable") = some value
```

Information is stored in the Session object by using *session variables*. You create a session variable on any page of your application by putting the name of the session variable between the parentheses after the Session keyword. You can then set the variable equal to whatever value you want to store in the variable. Here is an example:

```
<%
Dim userID
userID = Request.Form("userID")
Session("user") = userID
%>
```

In this example, a variable called userID is used to get the "userID" element from a form. A session variable named "user" is then created and assigned the value of the userID variable. After creating a session variable, you can use it anywhere in your Web application by simply referring to its name. Here is an example:

```
<h1>Your userID is <%=Session("user")%>.</h1>
```

You can assign a new value to the session variable at any time by simply referring to the variable by name and setting it equal to something else.

You are not limited to simply saving strings, numbers, dates, and the like to the Session Object. You can also save objects to the Session object. We introduced the concept of objects in Chapter 6, "Procedures, Classes, and Server-Side Includes."

Recall that if you are going to set a variable equal to an object, you must use the Set keyword. The same rule applies to session variables. Here is the syntax that must be used if a session variable will be used to reference an object:

```
Set Session("Name of session variable") = an object
```

I'll look at objects in more detail in later chapters. Here is an example of setting a session variable equal to an object:

```
<%
Dim myDBConnection
Set Session("myDBConnection") = Server.CreateObject("ADODB.Connection")
%>
```

In this case I am using session variable named myDBConnection to reference an ADO Connection object. Don't worry about ADO yet—I discuss it in detail in Chapters 8,9 and 10. Simply recognize that the Server.CreateObject method is used to create an ADO Connection object. Here's how you could use the variable in an active server page somewhere else in your application:

```
<%
Dim dbConnection
Set dbConnection = Session("myDBConnection")
%>
```

Session Object Collections, Methods, Properties, and Events

Here is everything you need to know about the Session object's collections, methods, properties and events.

Collections of the Session Object

The Session Object has two collections, the Contents collection and the StaticObjects collection.

Contents

The Contents collection contains all the session variables that do not reference objects created with the <Object> tag (see StaticObjects discussion later in this section). It does contain variables that reference objects created with the `Server.CreateObject` method. As with any collection, you can refer to an element of the collection by referencing its name or number in the collection. Consider the following:

```
<%
Dim username
username = Session.Contents("username")
%>
```

This example simply extracts the value of a session variable named `username` and puts the information in the local variable named "username". The `Contents` collection also has two methods, the `Remove` method and the `RemoveAll` method. The `Remove` method can be used to remove a specific session variable.

```
Session.Contents.Remove("username")
```

This code would remove the session variable named "username" from the `Contents` collection. The `RemoveAll` method removes all of the items in the `Contents` collection.

```
Session.Contents.RemoveAll
```

StaticObjects

The `StaticObjects` collection contains all of the session variables that reference objects that were created using the `<Object>` tag. The `<Object>` tag is an HTML tag that can be used to create client-side or server-side objects. To create a server-side object with this tag you would use the following syntax:

```
<Object id = "objConnection" progId = "ADODB.Connection" runat =
"server"></Object>
```

In this example the name of the object I'm creating is "objConnection." The type of object is an ADO Connection object (`ADODB.Connection`). This method of creating objects is similar to using the `Server.CreateObject` method. However, the `Server.CreateObject` method creates an "instance" of the object immediately while the `<Object>` tag method doesn't create an instance of the object until some code references the object. We'll discuss both of these methods more in Chapter 11.

The `StaticObjects` collection can be used just like the `Contents` collection except that it doesn't support the `Remove` and `RemoveAll` methods.

NOTE

You can find out how many session variables are in the Contents collection or the StaticObjects collection by referencing the respective collection's Count property. The syntax is Collection.Count.

Methods of the Session Object

The Session object has one method. The Abandon method can be used to "abandon" a session. When the Abandon method is called, all session variables contained in both the Contents and StaticObjects collections are destroyed and the memory that held them is released. Here is the syntax:

```
Session.Abandon
```

Properties of the Session Object

The Session Object has four properties: CodePage, LCID, SessionID, and Timeout. The CodePage and LCID properties both have to do with setting the language and locality information for the application. The SessionID property returns the value of a cookie that identifies the current user session. This value is determined automatically whenever a new session is started. The Timeout property contains or sets the number of minutes that are allowed to elapse before a session is automatically abandoned. The default Session.Timeout is twenty minutes. This value can be changed in an active server page as follows:

```
Session.Timeout = 10
```

This sets the session to time out in ten minutes if no user activity has been detected.

NOTE

The Session.Timeout property does not mean that a user will have only X number of minutes to browse your site before the session ends. It means that the session will end when no user activity has been detected for X number of minutes.

You can also set the default session timeout in IIS by following these steps:

1. Click on Start, Settings, Control Panel. Then double-click on Administrative Tools.

2. Double-click on Internet Services Manager.

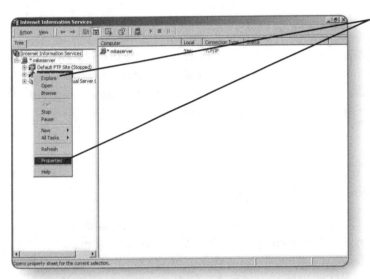

3. Click on the + to expand your Web server. Right-click on your Web site and click on Properties.

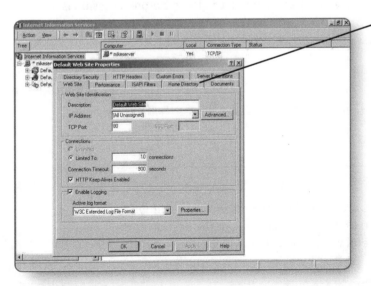

4. Click on the Home Directory tab.

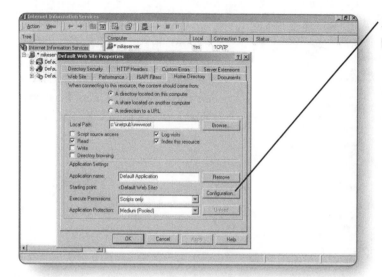

5. Click on the Configuration button.

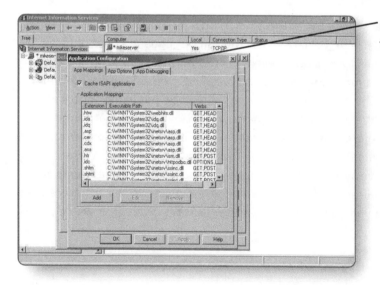

6. Click on the App Options tab.

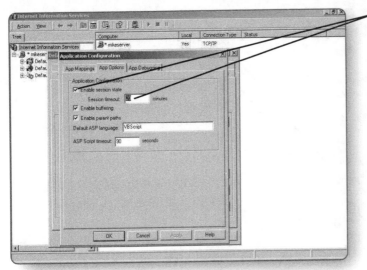

7. Put the desired number of minutes in the Session Timeout text box. Notice also that you can disable the Session object by clearing the check mark from the Enable session state check box.

Session Object Events

There are two events associated with the Session object. They are the Session_OnStart and Session_OnEnd events. You can put code in either of these events. Obviously the Session_OnStart event is fired when a session starts. The Session_OnEnd event is fired when the Session.Abandon method is called or when the session times out. The code for these events should be put in the Global.asa file. An active server page application can have one Global.asa file that can be used to create global references as well as contain the code for the Session and Application object events. The Global.asa file cannot be viewed in a browser; it is used only by other active server pages in your Web application. These events can be used to do any initialization or clean-up when a session starts or ends. Here is an example of some code you could put in a Session_OnStart event (this would be in your Global.asa file).

```
Sub Session_OnStart
        Session("pagesVisited") = 0
End Sub
```

You could increment the Session("pagesVisited") variable on each page like this:

```
Session("pagesVisited") = Session("pagesVisited") + 1
```

> **NOTE**
>
> You must use `<Script>` tags at the beginning and end of your Global.asa file rather than `<% …%>`. The opening tag should look like this: `<Script language = "VBScript" Runat = "server">`. At the end of the file close the server-side script with `</Script>`.

On your `Session_OnEnd` event you could record in a database the number of pages a user visited.

```
Sub Session_OnEnd
        Dim objConnection 'A database connection
        Set objConnection = Server.CreateObject("ADODB.Connection")
        objConnection.Open "DSN=myDatabase"
        Dim sqlPagesVisited
sqlPagesVisited = "insert into UserSessions(userHits) values
(Session("pagesVisited"));"
        objConnection.Execute sqlPagesVisited
        objConnection.Close
        Set objConnection = Nothing
End Sub
```

This code inserts the number of pages the user visited into a database table called `UserSessions`. Don't worry about all the database code right now. You'll look at similar code in detail in Chapters 8,9 and 10. Just note that the `Session("pagesVisited")` session variable is being recorded in the database when the session ends. Such code might be useful if you want to know how many pages in your site users were hitting in a session.

The Dark Side of Session Objects

There are just a few more things to know about the Session object. One is that the Session object creates a cookie on users' machines whenever a session starts. It uses this cookie to keep track of users as they move from page to page. Thus, the Session object won't work for users who don't have a cookie-enabled browser, or for users that have disabled cookies in their browsers.

Another thing to be aware of is that Session variables are stored in the Web server's memory. Every user who visits your site will have their own set of session variables, and the memory holding those variables won't be released until you call the `Session.Abandon` method or until the user's session times out (which by default is twenty minutes after the user leaves your site). If you are placing lots of information (like objects) into session variables, the Web server's memory will be used up rapidly as the number of users hitting your site increases. Therefore, use session variables conservatively.

CAUTION

Placing objects in session variables seriously diminishes the scalability (traffic capacity) of your Web application because server resources are used up rapidly as more users hit your site. For this reason I recommend that you don't put object references in session variables.

Alternatives To Session State

Using session variables to maintain state is extremely easy. Unfortunately, it is not the most scalable means of storing state (as already discussed). There are several other ways that you can maintain state in a Web application. The following sections present a few ideas.

Cookies and a Database

One alternative is to use cookies in conjunction with a database to store information pertaining to a user session. Of course, cookies, like session variables, require that the client have a cookie-enabled browser. If you want just to store information on the client machine, you can use cookies by themselves. You can also create a cookie on the client that uniquely identifies the user. This same identifier could also be used in a database table to keep track of a user's session information. Information can then be written to and retrieved from the database rather than using the Session object. Other database solutions I've seen use the user's IP address as an identifier (remember that `Request.ServerVariables("REMOTE_ADDR")` will return the IP address of the client.) In that case you wouldn't have to rely on cookies to keep track of Sessions. In most cases the IP address will be a temporary address assigned by the user's ISP, so you would not want to use it as a user's permanent identifier. You should make sure that your database automatically removes old sessions on an ongoing basis.

Query Strings and HIDDEN Form Elements

We've already seen how information can be passed from page to page by appending it to query strings or by placing it in hidden form elements (using `<input type = "hidden"...>`). You can use these techniques to manage state as well. This technique doesn't require the client to have a cookie-enabled browser either. Unfortunately, passing information in this way can become very burdensome because you must put code that passes along session information on every page in your Web site.

NOTE

If you don't plan to use the Session object at all, you should disable session state in IIS. You can also disable the Session object for an individual active server page by putting the following directive at the top of the page: `<%@ EnableSessionState=False %>`. Disabling the Session object will result in faster loading pages.

The Application Object

The ASP Application object is similar to the Session object. The main difference is that the Application object is used to store global information while the Session object is used to store information about an individual user. One Application object variable can be used for all user sessions throughout a Web application, while each individual user session has it's own copies of session variables. The Application object is a great place to store information like database connection strings that you want to be able to use from any page in your Web application.

The syntax used to save information to an Application object variable is very similar to that for saving information to a Session object variable.

```
Application("Name of application variable") = some value
```

Likewise, to make an application variable reference an object, use the Set keyword.

```
Set Application("Name of application variable") = an object
```

You can create an application variable in any web page in the application.

Here is an example that creates some application variables in the Global.asa file.

```
<Script language = "VBScript" runat = "server">

Application("dbConnectionString") = "Provider=sqloledb; data source=MYSERVER;
initial catalog=PUBS; user id=fast; password=easy"

Sub Application_OnStart
        Application("overallHits") = 0
End Sub
Sub Application_OnEnd
        Some code
End Sub
Sub Session_OnStart
        Some code
End Sub
Sub Session_OnEnd
        Some code
End Sub
</Script>
```

I created two variables Application("overallHits") and
Application("dbConnectionString") in this Global.asa file. These variables
could be used from any page in the Web application by referencing them as
an application variable. For example:

```
<%
Dim myConnection
Set myConnection = Server.CreateObject("ADODB.Connection")
myConnection.Open Application("dbConnectionString")
%>
```

In this example an ADO Connection object is created. The connection is then opened using the information stored in the application variable named `Application("dbConnectionString")`.

You'll also notice that the Application object has `On_Start` and `On_End` events just like the Session object. These can be used to take care of any initialization or clean up that needs to be done when the application starts or when it ends. Only the Application and Server objects can be used within the Application Events. Attempts to use the Response, Request, or Session objects will result in an error. The `Application_OnStart` event is called when the first user hits your site after the Web site has been started. It is fired before the user's `Session_OnStart` event. The `Application_OnEnd` event is fired when the Web site is stopped in IIS or after the last `Session_OnEnd` event is fired.

Application Object Collections and Methods

The Application object doesn't have any special properties other than those of its collections. I've already discussed the two events associated with the Application object. All that remains is to discuss its collections and methods.

Application Object Collections

The Application object has the same two collections as the Session object. The `Contents` collection contains all of the variables that don't reference objects created with the `<Object>` tag. It has `Remove` and `RemoveAll` methods. The `StaticObjects` collection contains all of the variables that reference objects that were created with the `<Object>` tag.

Application Object Methods

The Application object has two methods. Remember that the variables in the Application object are available to any Web page in the application as well as for any user session. To prevent users from trying to change the same application variable at the same time, there are the `Application.Lock` and `Application.Unlock` methods. Calling the `Application.Lock` method prevents any other user from changing any application variables until the `Application.Unlock` method is called.

If the `Application.Unlock` method is not explicitly called, it is called automatically when the active server page that locked the application finishes processing or times out. Here is an example:

```
<Script language = "VBScript" runat = "server">
Option Explicit
Dim numberUsers
Sub Session_OnStart
Application.Lock
Application("numberUsers") = Application("numberUsers") + 1
Application.Unlock
End Sub
Sub Session_OnEnd
        Application.Lock
        Application("numberUsers") = Application("numberUsers") - 1
        Application.Unlock
End Sub
</Script>
```

This code would be put in the Global.asa file. Notice that the application is locked before the `Application("numberUsers")` variable is changed and unlocked after the change has been made. Using such code you could let the users know how many people are currently browsing your Web site by putting something like this on your home page:

```
<%
Response.Write("There are currently " & Application("numberUsers") & "
browsing this web site.")
%>
```

Facts About the Application Object

The variables in the Application object, like Session object variables, are stored in the Web server's memory. Application variables are not as much of a threat to the performance of your Web site as session variables because there is only one copy of each application variable for the whole application, while every user has their own copy of session variables. There are, however, a few things to keep in mind about the Application object. One is that any information stored in application variables will be lost when the Web application is stopped. If you are using application variables to store information that you want to keep, you should use the `Application_OnEnd` event to write the values of the variables to a database or a file. Also, both the Application object and Session objects are associated with one and only one server. If your Web site grows in popularity to the point that you need other servers to handle the traffic (this is known as a *Web farm*), you must realize that changing the value of an application variable on one server does not automatically change the value on the other servers in your cluster.

Using Session and Application Objects

I've put together a few pages that demonstrate the basics of the Session and Application objects. There are three active server pages: sessionPage1.asp, sessionPage2.asp, and sessionPage3.asp. There is also the Global.asa file. We'll start with that.

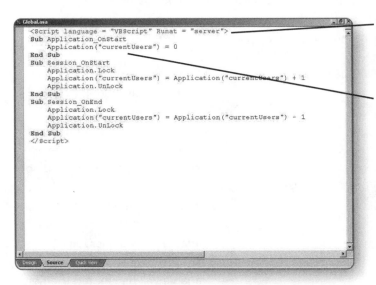

Script in the Global.asa file must be enclosed by <script> tags rather than <%…%> tags.

I've created one application variable named `Application ("currentUsers.")` If I didn't declare the variable here it would have been created automatically the first time I referred to `Application ("currentUsers")` in an active server page.

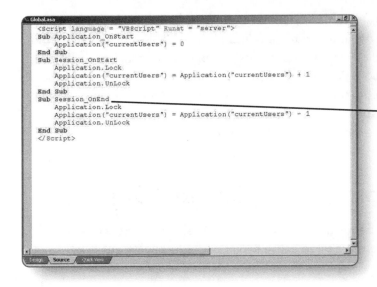

```
GlobalLasa
<Script language = "VBScript" Runat = "server">
Sub Application_OnStart
    Application("currentUsers") = 0
End Sub
Sub Session_OnStart
    Application.Lock
    Application("currentUsers") = Application("currentUsers") + 1
    Application.UnLock
End Sub
Sub Session_OnEnd
    Application.Lock
    Application("currentUsers") = Application("currentUsers") - 1
    Application.UnLock
End Sub
</Script>

Design   Source   Quick View
```

In the `Application_OnStart` event I simply initialize the `Application("currentUsers")` variable by setting it to zero.

In the `Session_OnStart` event, the application is locked while the application variable, "currentUsers" is increased by one. Likewise, in the `Session_OnEnd` event, the variable is decreased by one. Because I left the `Session.Timeout` property at the default setting of twenty minutes, the `Application("currentUsers")` variable will not be totally accurate. Users will not be subtracted from the `Application ("currentUsers")` variable until twenty minutes after they leave.

```
sessionPage1.asp
<%
Option Explicit

Session("pagesVisited") = Session("pagesVisited") _
& Request.ServerVariables("SCRIPT_NAME") & "<br>"
%>
<html>
<head>
<title>SessionPage 1</title>
</head>
<body bgcolor = "white">
<h1>This is Session Page 1</h1>
<blockquote>
    <h2>There are currently <%=Application("currentUsers")%> people
    browsing this website</h2>

    <h2>Your SessionID is <%=Session.SessionID%></h2>

    <h2>Here is your cookie string:
    <%=Request.ServerVariables("HTTP_COOKIE")%></h2>

    <h2>So far you have visited the following pages:</h2>
    <blockquote>
        <%=Session("pagesVisited")%>
    </blockquote>
</blockquote>
<div align = "center">
    <a href = "sessionPage1.asp">Page 1</a><br>

Design   Source   Quick View
```

Here is sessionPage1.asp. The other two pages look exactly like this one except that their titles and header statements reflect whichever page they are. I start each page by appending the name of the current page (supplied by the server variable "SCRIPT_NAME") to the session variable named `Session ("pagesVisited")` The session variable will be created the first time it is called. Remember, because this is a session variable, users each have their own copy of it that reflects the pages that they have visited.

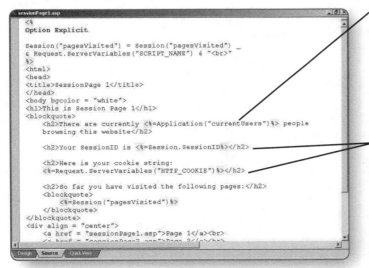

The number of people currently browsing the site is displayed by referencing the application variable named `Application ("currentUsers")` that I created in my Global.asa file.

Next, the user's `SessionID` is displayed. This `SessionID` will not change for the duration of the user's session. I also show the cookies that are being shipped with the page (server variable `"HTTP_COOKIE"`). Since I haven't set any other cookies, the only cookie that shows is the single `"ASPSESSIONID"` cookie that was created when the user's session began.

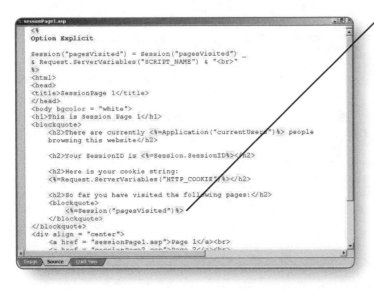

Finally, I show the information contained in the session variable named `Session("pagesVisited")`. This variable will grow each time the user visits another page because the current page will be concatenated onto the existing pages in the variable as the page is processed.

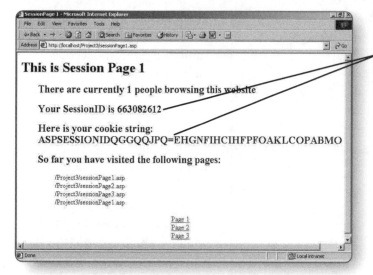

Here is the page in action.

I've opened the page in Internet Explorer first. Notice that I've viewed several pages. Also notice that the SessionID and "ASPSESSIONID" cookie are unique to this user session. They remain the same across all the pages for this user.

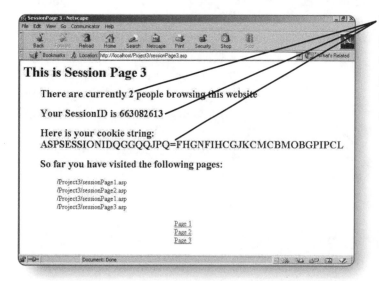

Now I've opened one of the pages in Netscape. The number of users currently browsing has gone up by one. Notice that this user has a different SessionID and cookie.

If I refresh the page in Internet Explorer, you can see that it too reflects the fact that there are now two visitors browsing the site.

8

The ADO Connection Object

Most online applications interface with one or more databases. Consider a typical online storefront application. People are searching for products to purchase. Those products are in a product database. When someone decides that they want to purchase something, the customer purchase information is to be stored in a customer database, and the product inventory has to be adjusted in the product database. An active server page developer needs some way to hook up the active server page front end to a database or multi-database back end. ActiveX Data Objects (ADO) provides just such a service. ADO is a simple yet powerful way to hook up front end applications (including, but not limited to, ASP applications) to data sources. The reason I say "data sources" rather than "databases" is that ADO provides the ability to access and manipulate data from active directories, Exchange information stores, Web servers, and so on, in addition to accessing and manipulating data in databases. In this and the next two chapters you'll learn the essentials of using ADO to begin developing powerful, data-driven Web applications. In this chapter, you'll learn how to:

- Connect to a database using the ADO Connection object
- Create database connection strings use OLE DB or ODBC
- Execute SQL Insert, Update and Delete statements with the Execute Method

Connecting to a Database with the ADO Connection Object

I won't be able to go into a full explanation of database design and the Structured Query Language(SQL) that is used to define and manipulate data in databases. If you're not familiar with SQL, you would do well to read Prima Tech's *SQL Server 7 Administrator's Guide* since it is an essential element of ASP development.

After considering how to connect to a database with ADO, you will briefly take a look at the major data-manipulation methods of SQL.

The ADO Connection object has two primary methods: Open and Execute. The Open method is used to open a connection to a data source. The Execute method is used to execute SQL statements. You'll look at both of these methods in the following sections.

Referencing the ADO Type Library

ADO has a library of parameters that can be used with various ADO methods. You can use ADO without referencing the type library, but you will have to pass numbers to the ADO methods rather than passing ADO constants. The following sections cover two common ways of referencing the ADO type library.

adovbs.inc

You can `include` the file adovbs.inc. The easiest thing to do is search for the file, copy it, and paste it into the root directory of your Web application. Then you can use a `#include` statement to reference the file. Here is the syntax if your Web page is in the same directory as the adovbs.inc file.

```
<!-#include file = "adovbs.inc"->
```

You simply include this file in every page in which you want to use ADO. The adovbs.inc file comes with ADO (which is installed with IIS). You can find the file in the following directory: C:\Program Files\Common Files\System\ado.

msado15.dll

At the time this book was printed, the latest version of ADO was version 2.5. The .dll that houses the ADO type library for this version is msado15.dll. You can put the following statement at the top of a page that will contain ADO:

```
<!—METADATA TYPE = "typelib" FILE = "C:\Program Files\Common
Files\System\ado\msado15.dll" —>
```

According to the IIS 5.0 documentation, using this method to reference type libraries (as opposed to using an `include` file) might increase the performance of your Web application. If you put this statement in your global.asa file, the library will be available for all the pages in your application. You can use the <Metadata> method of referencing type libraries in IIS 4.0 or IIS 5.0. You can put a copy of the file in the root directory of your application if you want to.

Creating a Connection Object

The first step to opening a database connection is creating a database object. This entails creating a variable and assigning it a reference to an ADO Connection object. Here's an example:

```
<%
Option Explicit
Dim myConn
Set myConn = Server.CreateObject("ADODB.Connection")
%>
```

Remember that if a variable is to reference an object, the reference must be *set* using the Set keyword. In this case I've declared a variable called myConn and set the variable equal to an ADO Connection object. The Server object provides the CreateObject method that creates an object of the type specified by its input parameter. The ADO Connection object is referred to as "ADODB.Connection". After you've created the object you can use its methods and properties.

Opening a Connection

The first method you'll use is the Open method. As the name implies, the method opens a connection to a data source. Here is the syntax:

```
Connection.Open ConnectionString, UserID, Password, Options
```

All these arguments are actually optional. However, if you don't specify the connection string in the `Open` statement, you have to set the connection string earlier. The `ConnectionString` parameter specifies where the data "lives." It is the information detailing the server, database name, DSN name, and so on. I'll discuss this important parameter in more detail shortly. Depending on how you're connecting to the database and what kind of security is being implemented on the database, you may have to specify a `userID` and `password`. I'll consider the `Options` parameter more in Chapter 10, "The Command object," because the same options are available.

You may also want to set the `ConnectionTimeout` property prior to opening a database connection. This property determines how long, in seconds, ADO will attempt to make the database connection before generating an error. The default is 15 seconds. Here is the syntax:

```
Connection.ConnectionTimeout = 30
```

This statement would set the `ConnectionTimeout` property to 30 seconds.

OLE DB versus ODBC

OLE DB(*Object Linking and Embedding Database*) and ODBC (*Open Database Connectivity*) are two existing technologies for accessing information in data sources. They are complex technologies that, for direct use, require programming in languages like C++ or Java. ADO is a *wrapper* for OLE DB that hides much of the complexity but still provides plenty of functionality. ODBC is another technology that's commonly used to access data sources. I'll discuss how to connect to a database using either technology.

Connecting with ODBC

There are two ways of connecting to a database using ODBC. One way involves using a DSN (*Data Source Name*), and the other consists of writing a connection string that uses an ODBC Driver.

Creating and Using a DSN

To create a DSN, follow these steps:

1. Go to the Administrative Tools folder by clicking on Start, Settings, Control Panel. Then, double-click on Administrative Tools.

2. Next double-click on Data Sources (ODBC).

3. The ODBC Administrator will open up. Click on the System DSN tab.

4. Click on Add.

5. Next, you pick a driver. Click on the SQL Server Driver, then click on Finish.

6. After that, a wizard starts. The wizard will be different depending on the data source driver you choose. The data source name is the name you want for your DSN. Type a description if you want to. Type the name of the server where the database is, then click on Next.

7. With SQL Server, I recommend creating a SQL Server login for your Web site and logging in using "SQL Server Authentication." NT Authentication won't work if your database is on a different server from your Web server. Create a login and click on Next.

8. Choose the default database to connect to. Click on Next.

9. Accept the defaults and click on Finish.

10. The machine will crank away and create your DSN. When it's done you can click on the Test Data Source button to see whether it works. Then Click on OK.

11. Your new DSN will now show up under the System DSN tab. Later you can choose Configure if you want to change a setting. You're now ready to use the DSN.

To connect to the database using a DSN, simply use the name of the DSN as the `ConnectionString` and use the `UserID` and `Password` if they're needed. To connect to the database using the DSN you just created, you would use the following syntax where "Pubs" is the name of the database with a login of "fast" and a password of "easy."

```
<%
Dim myConn
Set myConn = Server.CreateObject("ADODB.Connection")
myConn.Open "DSN=Pubs","fast","easy"
%>
```

DSN-less Connections

You can also connect using ODBC without creating a DSN. Here's how to create a DSN-less connection string for an Access database and a SQL Server database.

```
<%
'Using ODBC drivers
Dim myAccessConn,mySQLConn,strAccess,strSQL
strAccess = "Driver={Microsoft Access Driver (*.mdb)};DBQ=C:\Program
Files\Microsoft Office\Office\Samples\Northwind.mdb"
strSQL = "Driver={SQL Server}; Server=MIKESERVER; Database=pubs; UID=fast;
PWD=easy"
Set myAccessConn = Server.CreateObject ("ADODB.Connection")
Set mySQLConn = Server.CreateObject ("ADODB.Connection")
myAccessConn.Open strAccess
mySQLConn.Open strSQL
%>
```

The `strAccess` variable contains the `ConnectionString` used to connect to the sample Northwind database that ships with Microsoft Access.

NOTE

Make sure that you put your Access database files in a directory that is not a Web directory. If you put them in a published Web directory, anyone could download your database simply by pointing to it with a browser.

The syntax for the connection string is self-explanatory: The Driver is the ODBC driver for the specific type of database you're connecting to, the DBQ is the path to the database. If your Access database has a userID and password, you can specify those as well.

The strSQL variable is the ConnectionString for the SQL Server database "pubs". Notice that a driver, database, user ID, and password are specified.

Connecting with OLE DB

The alternative to ODBC is OLE DB. There are currently many more data sources that have ODBC drivers than OLE DB. However OLE DB supplies a *provider* (the OLE DB version of a driver) for ODBC that can be used to connect to an ODBC data source. OLE DB providers are often referred to as *native providers*. If a native provider exists for a particular data source, it will probably be marginally faster than using an ODBC connection. Here is the syntax for building OLE DB connection strings for the same two databases I used before.

```
<%
'Using OLE DB providers
Dim myAccessConn,mySQLConn,strAccess,strSQL
strAccess = "Provider=Microsoft.Jet.OLEDB.4.0; Data Source = C:\Program
Files\Microsoft Office\Office\Samples\Northwind.mdb"
strSQL = "Provider=SQLOLEDB; Data Source=MIKESERVER; Initial Catalog=pubs;
User ID=fast; Password=easy"
Set myAccessConn = Server.CreateObject ("ADODB.Connection")
Set mySQLConn = Server.CreateObject ("ADODB.Connection")
myAccessConn.Open strAccess
mySQLConn.Open strSQL
%>
```

The parameters are slightly different than the ODBC connection parameters. Provider is the OLE DB equivalent of a driver. Data Source is the name of the database server in the case of SQL Server (or other enterprise type databases), whereas it is the path to the database file in the case of an Access database. Initial Catalog is the name of the SQL Server (or Oracle, DB2, and so on) database you're trying to connect to.

Executing SQL Statements with the Connection Object's Execute Method

Another useful method of the Connection object is the `Execute` method. The `Execute` method provides the ability to execute SQL statements. The Recordset and Command objects also provide the ability to execute SQL statements, and they provide a little more control than the Connection object. Still, there are times when the `Execute` method comes in handy.

The syntax for the `Execute` method is simple:

```
Connection.Execute [SQL String],[Records Affected],[Options]
```

The SQL String can be either an SQL statement or the name of a stored procedure. You can pass in a variable as the `Records Affected` parameter if you want to retrieve the number of rows affected by an insert, update, or delete statement. I'll consider the `Options` parameter more in the Chapter 10.

Database Basics

At this point I'll digress into an overview of relational databases. I'll then give a brief explanation of the three *action* SQL statements. These statements are used to add, update, or delete information in a database. Finally, I'll consider some examples that use the `Execute` method to execute SQL statements.

Database Schema

Relational databases store information in tables. A *table* is made up of rows and columns. Each column in a database table has a name and a data-type. Tables in a database often have a *primary key*: a column that must have a unique value in every row of the table. Tables can be *related* to each other by having a foreign key column in one table reference a primary key column in another table. A *schema* is the name for the relationships among tables in a database. You'll see a sample database schema in the example later in this chapter.

SQL Action Statements

These statements are all you need to manipulate SQL.

Insert

The Insert statement is used to add rows to a database table. Here is the syntax:

```
Insert Into [table name] ([list of columns]) values ([list of values])
```

The list of columns is a comma-separated list of column names corresponding to the columns in the table into which you want to insert a row. If not all of the columns are required, you can specify just those columns into which you want to insert information. The list of values is the information you want to insert into the table. The values should be separated by commas and should correspond to the list of columns specified.

Update

The Update statement is used to update existing information in a database table. Here is the syntax:

```
Update [table name] Set [column name] = [some value],[column name = [some value] where [some expression]
```

You can update one table per update statement. However, you can update multiple columns in the table by specifying the column names and values after the Set keyword. Separate the column name/value pairs by commas. The where statement is an optional SQL expression that can be used to limit the rows of the table that are updated. For example, to update only those authors in the authors table who have a last name of "Smith," you could specify the following in the where statement:

```
Where au_lname = 'Smith'
```

au_lname is the name of a column in the authors table. Notice that character data is by default enclosed in *single quotes* rather than double quotes in SQL.

Delete

The `delete` statement can be used to delete information from a database table. Here is the syntax:

```
Delete From [table name] Where [some expression]
```

This is a simple but dangerous statement. You don't have to include the `where` part if you want to delete all rows from the specified table. If you do use the `where` expression, you can specify which rows you want to delete.

NOTE

SQL is not case sensitive by default.

Using SQL Action Statements

All right, now you're ready for some SQL action! I've created a small online application that serves as a front end for the Access 2000 sample database Northwind.mdb. If you have Office 2000, you should be able to use these examples as long as you set up your connection strings correctly. (I'll comment on that at the appropriate time.) The Northwind database is the database for a fictitious trading company. Here is the database schema:

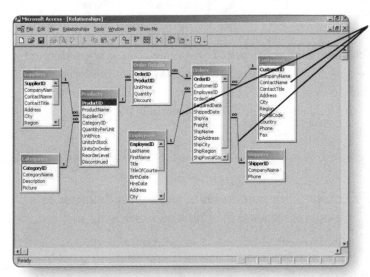

The database has eight tables. Notice how the tables are *related* to one another by primary key and foreign key relationships.

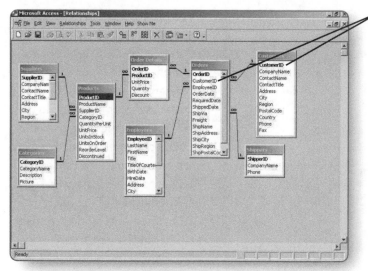

These relationships are all *one-to-many* relationships with the exception of the `Order Details` table that defines a *many-to-many* relationship between the `Orders` table and the `Products` table. Notice that the `Customers` table has a primary key named `CustomerID`. The `CustomerID` column also shows up in the `Orders` table. The `Orders` table has a foreign key that references the primary key in the `Customers` table. Such a relationship means that a customer can place *many* orders but an order can have only *one* customer.

Here it is! OK, so it's not that impressive. This page is just a simple form that adds new customers to the Northwind database using an SQL insert statement and an ADO Connection object. We'll look first at the code, then we'll see if it works.

```
 newCustomer.asp
<%Option Explicit%>
<!--METADATA TYPE= "TypeLib"
     FILE="C:\Program Files\Common Files\System\ado\msado15.dll" -->
<%
Dim company, custID, contact, title, address, city, state, zipcode
company = Request.Form("company")
custID = Request.Form("custID")
contact = Request.Form("contact")
title = Request.Form("title")
address = Request.Form("address")
city = Request.Form("city")
state = Request.Form("state")
zipcode = Request.Form("zipcode")

If company <> "" and custID <> "" then 'Add the customer

    Dim strSQL 'This is the SQL string that inserts the customer

    strSQL = "Insert into customers(CustomerID,CompanyName,ContactName," _
    & "ContactTitle,Address,City,Region,PostalCode) " _
    & "Values('" & FixIt(custID) & "','" & FixIt(company) & "','" _
    & FixIt(contact) & "','" & FixIt(title) & "','" & FixIt(address) _
    & "','" & FixIt(city) & "','" & FixIt(state) & "','" _
    & FixIt(zipcode) & "');"

    On Error Resume Next
    'Open the connection
```

First, I've included the <METADATA> tag at the top of the page to reference the ADO type library. Referencing the type library allows me to use the ADO constants rather than having to look up the numeric equivalents in ADO documentation. Creating such a reference also causes the ADO constants to show up by intellisense while I'm typing my ADO statements, and I like that! I could put the <METADATA> statement in the global.asa file. I put it in the local active server page so you can see that it's there. Remember that you could also use the adovbs.inc file to do the same thing (although not as efficiently).

```
 newCustomer.asp
    End Function
%>
<html>
<head>
<title>Add a Customer</title>
<link rel = "stylesheet" type = "text/css" href = "myStyle.css">
</head>
<body bgcolor = white onload="document.forms[0].elements[0].focus();">
<h1>Northwind Traders</h1>
<blockquote>
    <h2>New Customer Form</h2>
    <form method = "post" action = "newCustomer.asp">
        Company:<input type = "text" name = "company"><br>
        CustomerID:<input type = "text" name = "custID" maxlength = "5">
        <i>5 Characters</i><br>
        Contact Name:<input type = "text" name = "contact"><br>
        Contact Title:<input type = "text" name = "title"><br>
        Address:<input type = "text" name = "address"><br>
        City:<input type = "text" name = "city"><br>
        State:<input type = "text" name = "state"><br>
        Zipcode:<input type = "text" name = "zipcode" maxlength = "10"><br>
        <br>
        <input type = "submit" value = "Add Customer"> 
        <input type = "reset" value = "Clear">
    </form>
</blockquote>
</body>
</html>
```

At this point I'm going to skip to the bottom of the page to consider the data entry form. This form posts the data to the same active server page, newCustomer.asp, so we'll return to the top in a moment to see how the form is processed.

This is a simple HTML form that uses the POST method to send the form information back to the same .asp page for processing. Notice that I'm making use of a style sheet for the first time in this book.

```
newCustomer.asp
End Function
%>
<html>
<head>
<title>Add a Customer</title>
<link rel = "stylesheet" type = "text/css" href = "myStyle.css">
</head>
<body bgcolor = white onload="document.forms[0].elements[0].focus();">
<h1>Northwind Traders</h1>
<blockquote>
    <h2>New Customer Form</h2>
    <form method = "post" action = "newCustomer.asp">
        Company:<input type = "text" name = "company"><br>
        CustomerID:<input type = "text" name = "custID" maxlength = "5">
        <i>5 Characters</i><br>
        Contact Name:<input type = "text" name = "contact"><br>
        Contact Title:<input type = "text" name = "title"><br>
        Address:<input type = "text" name = "address"><br>
        City:<input type = "text" name = "city"><br>
        State:<input type = "text" name = "state"><br>
        Zipcode:<input type = "text" name = "zipcode" maxlength = "10"><br>
        <br>
        <input type = "submit" value = "Add Customer"> 
        <input type = "reset" value = "Clear">
    </form>
</blockquote>
</body>
</html>
Design   Source   Quick View
```

Here's a little JavaScript trick that sets the focus to the first element in the form. Just put this statement in the <body> tag on the onload event.

```
newCustomer.asp
<%Option Explicit%>
<!--METADATA TYPE="TypeLib"
    FILE="C:\Program Files\Common Files\System\ado\msado15.dll" -->
<%
Dim company,custID,contact,title,address,city,state,zipcode
company = Request.Form("company")
custID = Request.Form("custID")
contact = Request.Form("contact")
title = Request.Form("title")
address = Request.Form("address")
city = Request.Form("city")
state = Request.Form("state")
zipcode = Request.Form("zipcode")

If company <> "" and custID <> "" then 'Add the customer

    Dim strSQL 'This is the SQL string that inserts the customer

    strSQL = "Insert into customers(CustomerID,CompanyName,ContactName," _
    & "ContactTitle,Address,City,Region,PostalCode) " _
    & "Values('" & FixIt(custID) & "','" & FixIt(company) & "','" _
    & FixIt(contact) & "','" & FixIt(title) & "','" & FixIt(address) _
    & "','" & FixIt(city) & "','" & FixIt(state) & "','" _
    & FixIt(zipcode) & "');"

    On Error Resume Next
    'Open the connection
Design   Source   Quick View
```

OK, back to the top. First we need to get all the information from the form and stuff it into some variables.

The CustomerID and CompanyName fields of the Customers table are required. The values of the variables custID and company will be inserted into these fields. The If…End If statement checks to see if these variables contain data. If they do, I assume that the form has been filled out and begin processing the form.

NOTE

I haven't really built much form validation into this form processing section. In practice, you would want to make sure that the user filled in all of the appropriate fields with appropriate data. You can do this either on the server, using VBScript, or on the client, using JavaScript. If you're targeting newer browsers (IE 4.0 or Netscape 4.0 or later) then consider validating forms on the client to reduce server workload.

Ahh...the SQL string. Building SQL strings in your ASP page can be an ugly thing. I prefer to use the ADO Command Object and stored procedures to do SQL (you'll see how in Chapter 10). However, there are times when it's useful or necessary to build SQL strings and execute them with a Connection object.

```
newCustomer.asp                                                    _ 8 x
<%Option Explicit%>
<!--METADATA TYPE="TypeLib"
     FILE="C:\Program Files\Common Files\System\ado\msado15.dll" -->
<%
Dim company, custID, contact, title, address, city, state, zipcode
company = Request.Form("company")
custID = Request.Form("custID")
contact = Request.Form("contact")
title = Request.Form("title")
address = Request.Form("address")
city = Request.Form("city")
state = Request.Form("state")
zipcode = Request.Form("zipcode")

If company <> "" and custID <> "" then 'Add the customer

    Dim strSQL 'This is the SQL string that inserts the customer

    strSQL = "Insert into customers(CustomerID, CompanyName, ContactName, " _
    & "ContactTitle, Address, City, Region, PostalCode) " _
    & "Values('" & FixIt(custID) & "','" & FixIt(company) & "','" _
    & FixIt(contact) & "','" & FixIt(title) & "','" & FixIt(address) _
    & "','" & FixIt(city) & "','" & FixIt(state) & "','" _
    & FixIt(zipcode) & "');"

    On Error Resume Next
    'Open the connection
```

"What's with the FixIt() function?" you ask. Well, strings are delimited by default by single quotes in SQL. If you want to insert a string that has a single quote in it, like "Mike's" for example, then you need to replace the single quote with two single quotes, like this: "Mike''s." The FixIt() function is a function I wrote that looks for single quotes in a string and replaces them with two single quotes. If you use the Command Object with parameters, you don't have to worry about this because it takes care of replacing the single quotes for you.

```
newCustomer.asp                                                    _ 8 x
        Response.Write(myConn.Errors(0).Description & "<br>")
        myConn.Errors.Clear
    Else
        Response.Write("<h2>Customer successfully added!</h2>")
    End If

    myConn.Close
    Set myConn = Nothing 'Free the memory
End If

'------------FixIt Function--------------------
Function FixIt(str)
    FixIt = Replace(str,"'","''")
End Function
%>
<html>
<head>
<title>Add a Customer</title>
<link rel = "stylesheet" type = "text/css" href = "myStyle.css">
</head>
<body bgcolor = white onload="document.forms[0].elements[0].focus();">
<h1>Northwind Traders</h1>
<blockquote>
    <h2>New Customer Form</h2>
    <form method = "post" action = "newCustomer.asp">
        Company:<input type = "text" name = "company"><br>
        CustomerID:<input type = "text" name = "custID" maxlength = "5">
        <i>5 Characters</i><br>
        Contact Name:<input type = "text" name = "contact"><br>
```

Here is my FixIt() function. It just uses the VBScript Replace function to search for single quotes in the string and replace them with two single quotes.

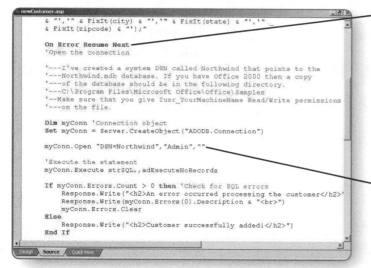

```
                                                                   newCustomer.asp
   & "','" & FixIt(city) & "','" & FixIt(state) & "','" _
   & FixIt(zipcode) & "')";"

   On Error Resume Next
   'Open the connection

   '---I've created a system DSN called Northwind that points to the
   '---Northwind.mdb database. If you have Office 2000 then a copy
   '---of the database should be in the following directory.
   '---C:\Program Files\Microsoft Office\Office\Samples
   '--Make sure that you give Iusr_YourMachineName Read/Write permissions
   '---on the file.

   Dim myConn 'Connection object
   Set myConn = Server.CreateObject("ADODB.Connection")

   myConn.Open "DSN=Northwind","Admin",""

   'Execute the statement
   myConn.Execute strSQL,,adExecuteNoRecords

   If myConn.Errors.Count > 0 then 'Check for SQL errors
       Response.Write("<h2>An error occurred processing the customer</h2>'
       Response.Write(myConn.Errors(0).Description & "<br>")
       myConn.Errors.Clear
   Else
       Response.Write("<h2>Customer successfully added!</h2>")
   End If
```

Design | **Source** | Quick View

I turn on custom error handling because several errors could occur. For one thing, an error will occur if someone tries to use an existing CustomerID. Since the CustomerID is the primary key for the table, it must be unique.

Notice that I've created a DSN called Northwind to connect to the Northwind database. You need to create a similar DSN if you want this example to work on your machine.

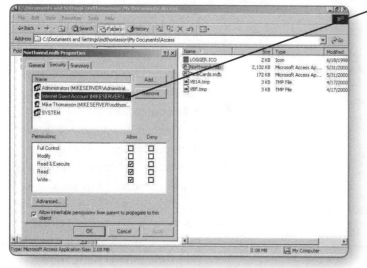

If you're using Windows NT or 2000 with an NTFS-formatted drive, you need to set the permissions on the file so that "Everyone" or "IUSR_machinename" (where machinename is the name of your Web server) has Read/Write permissions on the database. Otherwise, make sure that the permissions of the folder containing the database are set appropriately.

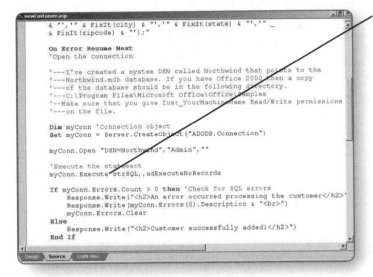

Next I create and open my Connection object. The `Execute` sends the SQL string to the database for processing. I use the `adExecuteNoRecords` option (I'll talk more about this in the Command Object chapter) to increase performance because I'm not expecting any return values or recordsets to be returned from this SQL statement.

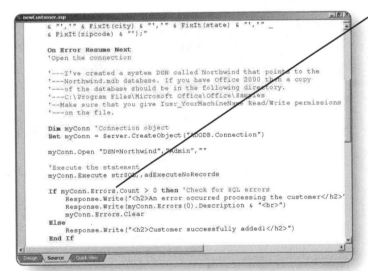

Notice that I'm not checking the VBScript `Err` object for errors, but rather the Connection object's `Errors` collection. The `Errors` collection contains any errors that are thrown by the data source you're connecting to. You can use a loop to iterate through the `Errors` collection and handle each error if there is more than one. I just show the description of the first error and then `Clear` the errors. I display a message to the users letting them know what happened.

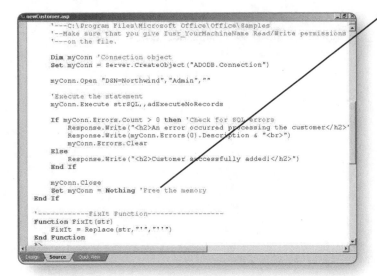

```
newCustomer.asp
      '---C:\Program Files\Microsoft Office\Office\Samples
      '--Make sure that you give Iusr_YourMachineName Read/Write permissions
      '---on the file.

      Dim myConn 'Connection object
      Set myConn = Server.CreateObject("ADODB.Connection")

      myConn.Open "DSN=Northwind","Admin",""

      'Execute the statement
      myConn.Execute strSQL,,adExecuteNoRecords

      If myConn.Errors.Count > 0 then 'Check for SQL errors
          Response.Write("<h2>An error occurred processing the customer</h2>"
          Response.Write(myConn.Errors(0).Description & "<br>")
          myConn.Errors.Clear
      Else
          Response.Write("<h2>Customer successfully added!</h2>")
      End If

      myConn.Close
      Set myConn = Nothing 'Free the memory
  End If

  '-----------FixIt Function------------------
  Function FixIt(str)
      FixIt = Replace(str,"'","''")
  End Function
```

Finally, I close my Connection object and set it equal to `Nothing` to free the memory it was using.

Now let's see if it works. I'll add Prima Publishing to the list of customers.

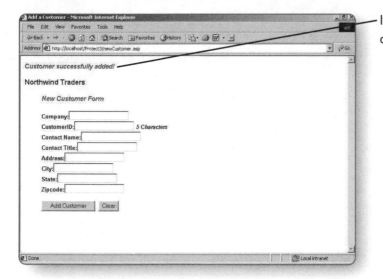

It says it worked. Now let's check the database.

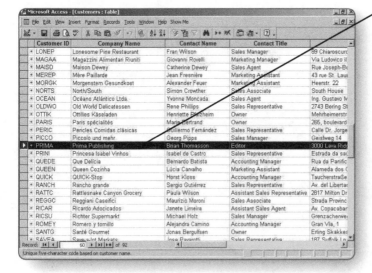

There it is ... the new record.

That's it for the Connection Object. You can also use the Connection Object to run SQL Select statements that return an ADO Recordset Object. However, I rarely use the Connection Object by itself to run SQL statements. It's better to use it in conjunction with ADO Recordset or Command Objects. You'll learn how to do that in the next two chapters.

9

The ADO Recordset Object

The ADO Recordset object is most often used to retrieve and or modify the records returned from an SQL Select statement. Becoming familiar with this object is essential to your success with ASP since it is the primary object used to retrieve data from a database to be presented to the user. In this chapter, you'll learn how to:

- Write an SQL Select statement
- Create and open an ADO Recordset object
- Display information from a recordset
- Modify information in a recordset
- Use some of the other methods of the Recordset

The SQL Select Statement

Before we can get into the ADO Recordset object we'll need to discuss the SQL Select statement since this is usually the source of the data used in a recordset object. The most complex SQL data manipulation statement is the `select` statement. The `select` statement retrieves information from tables in a database. While the `insert`, `update`, and `delete` statements deal only with one table at a time, a single `select` statement can pull data from multiple tables. I can't go into great detail about the `select` statement—chapters could be devoted to such discourse— but I will show you the general syntax of the SQL select statement.

```
Select [columns to retrieve] From [list of tables]
Where [SQL Expression]
[Group by [column list]]
[Having [SQL Expression]]
[Order By [column list]]
```

The list of columns to retrieve is a comma-separated list of table names and column names. Because information can come from more than one table, you need to specify which table and column you want to select using the following syntax:

```
Select authors.au_fname, authors.au_lname From authors
```

In this case, I didn't need to specify the table because we're retrieving information from only one table (`authors`). I specified it for demonstration purposes. Notice that the table name/column name combination is specified using a period between the two. If I want to get all the information from the `authors` table I can use the following syntax:

```
Select * from authors
```

If I want to retrieve the information in a particular order, I can use the `Order by` statement to specify by which columns I want to order the rows. Consider the following:

```
Select au_lname, au_fname from authors order by au_lname
```

If I run this query in the Query Analyzer against the sample Pubs database that ships with Microsoft's SQL Server, I get the following result set:

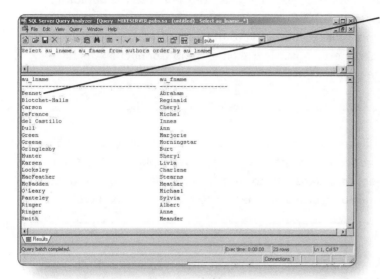

Notice how the rows returned by the query are in alphabetical order by the author last name.

The result set of a query using a select statement is known as a *cursor*, or in ADO terms, a *recordset*.

Creating and Opening an ADO Recordset

With that brief overview of the SQL select statement behind, you're ready to take a look at the ADO Recordset object. A *recordset* is the information returned from a query (a select statement). The ADO Recordset object can retrieve and display—or even modify—information in a database.

Creating a Recordset Object

Creating a Recordset object is similar to creating a Connection object:

```
<%
Dim myRecordset
Set myRecordset = Server.CreateObject("ADODB.Recordset")
%>
```

Opening a Recordset Object

To get a recordset from a database, you first need to connect to the database. You can use either an existing ADO Connection object, or you can create a connection by passing in a ConnectionString to the Recordset Open method as the ActiveConnection parameter. I usually use an existing Connection object. Here is the syntax of the Open method:

```
Recordset.Open Source, ActiveConnection, CursorType, LockType
```

The Source parameter of the Open method can be an SQL select statement, the name of a SQL stored procedure, the name of a database table, a URL, a Command object, or a Stream object that holds a Recordset. You will learn how to use the Command object to obtain a recordset in Chapter 10, "The Command Object."

NOTE

The ADO Stream object can be used to store recordsets as text or XML. I won't discuss the ADO Stream object or the ADO Record object in this book. They are both new to the ADO object model, introduced with the release of ADO 2.5.

The ActiveConnection parameter can be the name of a currently open connection object or a valid connection string. The CursorType can be one of the following:

ADO Constant	Description
adOpenForwardOnly	You can only move forward through the recordset. This is the default cursor type. It is the fastest cursor type, but provides the least functionality. You cannot use the RecordCount property to determine how many records are in this type of cursor.
adOpenKeyset	A complete copy of the cursor is made. Forward and backward movement is allowed within the cursor. Changes made to data by other users can be seen but additions and deletions of data in the cursor cannot be seen. You can use the RecordCount property to determine how many records are in the recordset with this type of cursor.

ADO Constant	Description
adOpenDynamic	The most flexible cursor. Forward and backward movement is allowed within the cursor. Changes, additions and deletions made by other users are reflected dynamically in the recordset. You can sometimes (depends on the provider) use the RecordCount property to determine how many records are in the recordset with this type of cursor.
AdOpenStatic	A complete copy of the cursor is made. Forward and backward movement within the cursor is allowed. No changes, additions, or deletions made by other users are reflected in the recordset. You can use the RecordCount property to determine how many records are in the recordset with this type of cursor.

The LockType parameter specifies how information in the tables is locked while the cursor is in use. When tables or parts of tables are locked, no one else can manipulate data in the locked sections until it's unlocked. Here are the settings you can use:

Constant	Description
adLockReadOnly	The recordset is read-only. This is the default.
adLockPessimistic	The record is locked while you're editing it to ensure that no one else changes it while you're editing.
AdLockOptimisitic	The records are not locked until you actually update a record using the Update method of the Recordset object.
AdLockBatchOptimistic	This allows multiple records to be updated at once. Locking occurs when the UpdateBatch method is called.

Some data sources don't support all possible cursor types and lock types. If you request a type that your data source doesn't support then ADO will automatically select the closest type that the data source does support. You can also set the parameters as properties of the Recordset prior to opening the recordset. Consider the following example:

```
<%
Dim myConn, myRecordset, strSQL
Set myConn = Server.CreateObject("ADODB.Connection")
myConn.Open "DSN=pubs","fast","easy"
Set myRecordset = Server.CreateObject("ADODB.Recordset")
strSQL = "Select * from authors"
myRecordset.CursorType = adOpenForwardOnly
myRecordset.LockType = adLockReadOnly
myRecordset.Open strSQL
%>
```

> ### NOTE
> You can set the properties for the Connection and Command objects in the same way if you prefer. Otherwise, just pass in the parameters in the method call.

I try to use forward only, read only cursors as much as possible since these provide the best performance. I avoid writing scripts that require moving backwards and forwards through cursors. Unfortunately you can't use the Recordset object's RecordCount property with forward only recordsets. The RecordCount property of a recordset (static, keyset or dynamic) will return the number of rows in the recordset.

There are several other properties of the ADO Recordset Object that can be set. You'll see some of them in the examples later in the chapter.

Displaying Information from a Recordset

So you've finally created a connection, built your `select` statement, and created and opened your Recordset. Now what? Well, now you can do something with your data. Usually, the information that you pull out of your back end database is incorporated somehow into the content of your front end Web page. In this section you learn how to handle the data in a Recordset object.

Moving Around in a Recordset

Remember that a recordset is just collection of rows and columns of information. Each row in the recordset is considered a "record." You usually process a recordset one row at a time. If your recordset is a forward only recordset, you start with the first row and step through row by row until you reach the end.

BOF and EOF

There are two Recordset properties that come in handy when you're moving through the records in a recordset. They are the `Recordset.BOF` property and the `Recordset.EOF` property. If the `BOF` (*beginning of file*) property is `true`, the current record pointer is *before* the first record in the recordset. Likewise, if the `EOF` (*end of file*) property is `true` then the current record pointer is *after* the last record of the recordset. When you open a recordset the pointer will automatically be set on the first record. If the recordset is empty, both the `BOF` and `EOF` properties will be `true`.

Move Statements

There are several methods of the Recordset object that have to do with moving from one record to another. To move to the first record in a recordset, use the `Recordset.MoveFirst` method. Likewise, move to the last record using the `Recordset.MoveLast` method. `Recordset.MoveNext` moves to the next record in the Recordset while `Recordset.MovePrevious` moves to the previous record. Finally, the `Recordset.Move` method can be used to move a specified number of records forward or backwards. The syntax of the `Move` method is as follows.

```
Recordset.Move [NumRecords],[Start]
```

The NumRecords parameter specifies how many records forward or backward the record pointer should move. To move forward, use a positive number; to move backward, use a negative number. Be careful though, if you try to move to a record before the BOF marker or after the EOF marker you will get an error. Specify on which record to start the record pointer by supplying the Start parameter. If you omit this parameter, the file pointer will start from the current record.

The Fields Collection

The default collection of the Recordset object is the Fields collection. Remember that each row in a recordset is considered a record. Each column in a record is considered a field. You can refer to a Field by name or by number. Here is the syntax:

```
Recordset.Fields([number of the field in the record])
```

Or

```
Recordset.Fields(["name of the field in the record"])
```

Since the Fields collection is the default collection of the Recordset object, you can omit the word Fields like this.

```
Recordset([name or number of the field in the record])
```

I usually keep the word Fields for clarity.

Using Recordsets

The examples in this chapter all use the Access 2000 Northwind database. This first example, northwind1.asp, pulls information from the database and stores it in a table format.

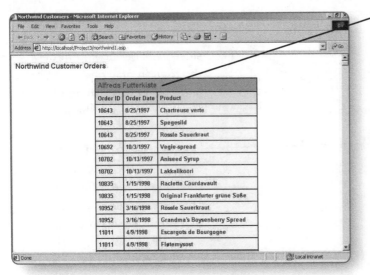

This table shows the name of a customer followed by the products that the customer has ordered. It does this for every customer in the Northwind database, so the page is quite long.

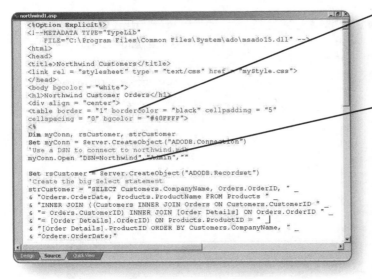

The first thing on the agenda is to start the HTML page. I simply write out the header and the opening `<table>` tag.

After creating a connection to the database, I patch together a `select` statement. I actually cheated and used the query builder in Access to build this `select` statement. It was easiest to do it this way because Access has its own way of joining tables. Notice that there are four tables joined together in this statement; `Customers`, `Orders`, `Order Details`, and `Products`. This query will return a recordset with four columns: "`CompanyName`", "`OrderID`", "`OrderDate`", and "`ProductName`". The rows in the recordset will be ordered first by "`CompanyName`" and then by "`OrderDate`".

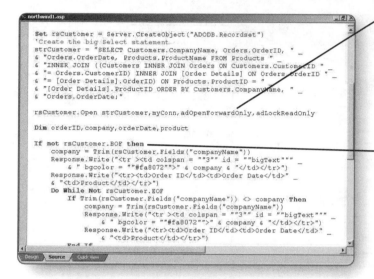

```
Set rsCustomer = Server.CreateObject("ADODB.Recordset")
'Create the big Select statement
strCustomer = "SELECT Customers.CompanyName, Orders.OrderID, " _
& "Orders.OrderDate, Products.ProductName FROM Products " _
& "INNER JOIN ((Customers INNER JOIN Orders ON Customers.CustomerID " _
& "= Orders.CustomerID) INNER JOIN [Order Details] ON Orders.OrderID " _
& "= [Order Details].OrderID) ON Products.ProductID = " _
& "[Order Details].ProductID ORDER BY Customers.CompanyName, " _
& "Orders.OrderDate;"

rsCustomer.Open strCustomer,myConn,adOpenForwardOnly,adLockReadOnly

Dim orderID, company, orderDate, product

If not rsCustomer.BOF then
    company = Trim(rsCustomer.Fields("companyName"))
    Response.Write("<tr ><td colspan = ""3"" id = ""bigText"""
        & " bgcolor = ""#fa8072"">" & company & "</td></tr>")
    Response.Write("<tr><td>Order ID</td><td>Order Date</td>" _
    & "<td>Product</td></tr>")
    Do While Not rsCustomer.EOF
        If Trim(rsCustomer.Fields("companyName")) <> company Then
            company = Trim(rsCustomer.Fields("companyName"))
            Response.Write("<tr ><td colspan = ""3"" id = ""bigText"""
                & " bgcolor = ""#fa8072"">" & company & "</td></tr>")
            Response.Write("<tr><td>Order ID</td><td>Order Date</td>" _
                & "<td>Product</td></tr>")
        End If
```

I've opened this recordset with a forward only, read only cursor since I will be moving through the rows in only one direction and I won't be changing any of the information in the rows.

I next check to see if there is anything in the recordset by checking to see if the BOF property is true. Remember that if there is no information in a recordset, both the BOF and EOF properties will be true. If there is information, the record pointer will be pointing to the first record.

```
Set rsCustomer = Server.CreateObject("ADODB.Recordset")
'Create the big Select statement
strCustomer = "SELECT Customers.CompanyName, Orders.OrderID, " _
& "Orders.OrderDate, Products.ProductName FROM Products " _
& "INNER JOIN ((Customers INNER JOIN Orders ON Customers.CustomerID " _
& "= Orders.CustomerID) INNER JOIN [Order Details] ON Orders.OrderID " _
& "= [Order Details].OrderID) ON Products.ProductID = " _
& "[Order Details].ProductID ORDER BY Customers.CompanyName, " _
& "Orders.OrderDate;"

rsCustomer.Open strCustomer,myConn,adOpenForwardOnly,adLockReadOnly

Dim orderID, company, orderDate, product

If not rsCustomer.BOF then
    company = Trim(rsCustomer.Fields("companyName"))
    Response.Write("<tr ><td colspan = ""3"" id = ""bigText"""
        & " bgcolor = ""#fa8072"">" & company & "</td></tr>")
    Response.Write("<tr><td>Order ID</td><td>Order Date</td>" _
    & "<td>Product</td></tr>")
    Do While Not rsCustomer.EOF
        If Trim(rsCustomer.Fields("companyName")) <> company Then
            company = Trim(rsCustomer.Fields("companyName"))
            Response.Write("<tr ><td colspan = ""3"" id = ""bigText"""
                & " bgcolor = ""#fa8072"">" & company & "</td></tr>")
            Response.Write("<tr><td>Order ID</td><td>Order Date</td>" _
                & "<td>Product</td></tr>")
        End If
```

If the recordset is not empty, I take the value of the "companyName" field from the first row and assign it to the variable company. Next, I write out the first two rows of the table. The first row shows the name of the first company in the recordset. The second row just shows the column headings for the table.

```
northwind1.asp
If not rsCustomer.BOF then
    company = Trim(rsCustomer.Fields("companyName"))
    Response.Write("<tr ><td colspan = ""3"" id = ""bigText""" _
        & " bgcolor = ""#fa8072"">" & company & "</td></tr>")
    Response.Write("<tr><td>Order ID</td><td>Order Date</td>" _
    & "<td>Product</td></tr>")
    Do While Not rsCustomer.EOF
        If Trim(rsCustomer.Fields("companyName")) <> company Then
            company = Trim(rsCustomer.Fields("companyName"))
            Response.Write("<tr ><td colspan = ""3"" id = ""bigText""" _
                & " bgcolor = ""#fa8072"">" & company & "</td></tr>")
            Response.Write("<tr><td>Order ID</td><td>Order Date</td>" _
                & "<td>Product</td></tr>")
        End If

        orderID = rsCustomer.Fields("orderID")
        orderDate = rsCustomer.Fields("orderDate")
        product = rsCustomer.Fields("productName")

        Response.Write("<tr bgcolor=""#FFFF80""><td>" & orderID & "</td>" _
            & "<td>" & orderDate & "</td>" & "<td>" & product _
            & "</td></tr>")
        rsCustomer.MoveNext
    Loop
Else
    Response.Write("<tr><td colspan = ""3"">There were no orders</td></tr>"
End If
```

Now the real work gets done. I use a loop to go through each record in the recordset and write out a row in my table. Remember that the EOF property will be true when the record pointer is pointing to the location *after* the last record in the recordset. This loop continues to get rows from the recordset until the EOF property becomes true.

```
northwind1.asp
If not rsCustomer.BOF then
    company = Trim(rsCustomer.Fields("companyName"))
    Response.Write("<tr ><td colspan = ""3"" id = ""bigText""" _
        & " bgcolor = ""#fa8072"">" & company & "</td></tr>")
    Response.Write("<tr><td>Order ID</td><td>Order Date</td>" _
    & "<td>Product</td></tr>")
    Do While Not rsCustomer.EOF
        If Trim(rsCustomer.Fields("companyName")) <> company Then
            company = Trim(rsCustomer.Fields("companyName"))
            Response.Write("<tr ><td colspan = ""3"" id = ""bigText""" _
                & " bgcolor = ""#fa8072"">" & company & "</td></tr>")
            Response.Write("<tr><td>Order ID</td><td>Order Date</td>" _
                & "<td>Product</td></tr>")
        End If

        orderID = rsCustomer.Fields("orderID")
        orderDate = rsCustomer.Fields("orderDate")
        product = rsCustomer.Fields("productName")

        Response.Write("<tr bgcolor=""#FFFF80""><td>" & orderID & "</td>" _
            & "<td>" & orderDate & "</td>" & "<td>" & product _
            & "</td></tr>")
        rsCustomer.MoveNext
    Loop
Else
    Response.Write("<tr><td colspan = ""3"">There were no orders</td></tr>"
End If
```

The If...End If statement that comes next checks to see whether the "companyName" field of the current record is the same as the value of the company variable. If it is different, I've come to the next company in the recordset. I then set the company variable equal to the new "companyName." The Trim() function removes any extra spaces on the end of the "companyName" field. I also need to write out a row with the name of the company followed by a row with the column headings.

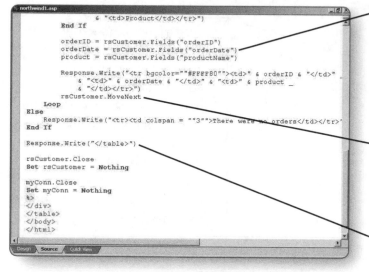

Next I extract the values of the "OrderID", "OrderDate", and "ProductName" fields and put them into variables. These variables are then used to write out another row in the table.

The `rsCustomer.MoveNext` statement moves the record pointer to the next record. The loop continues until `EOF` is `true`.

I clean up by closing the table with the `</table>` tag, closing the recordset and connection objects, and finishing off the HTML page.

Modifying Data with a Recordset

Although you can modify data with the Recordset object, I prefer to use a command object with stored procedures or SQL strings to perform inserts, updates, and deletes. Nevertheless, I'll go over the essential methods used to modify data with the Recordset object. You'll need to make sure that the LockType property of your recordset is something other than adLockReadOnly.

AddNew

The AddNew method of the Recordset object is similar in functionality to the SQL insert statement. There are two ways to use the AddNew method. Here is an example of the first way that uses the AddNew method in conjunction with the Update method to insert a row into a recordset. Here is the syntax for the first method:

```
Recordset.AddNew
Recordset.Fields([name or number of field]) = [some value]
Recordset.Fields([name or number of field]) = [some value]
Recordset.Fields([name or number of field]) = [some value]
...
Recordset.Update
```

Using this method, the AddNew method is called first. Then the values of the individual fields in the new record are set. The Update method is then called to *commit*, or save, the new record to the database.

The second method uses the AddNew method with two arrays as input parameters. The first array contains the names or numbers of the fields to be added, the second array contains the corresponding values to be added to the fields in the new row. Here is the syntax.

```
Recordset.AddNew Array([comma-separated names or numbers of fields]),
Array([comma-separated values corresponding to the fields in the first array])
```

Note that this method does not require that the Update method be used to commit the new row.

Update

The Update method of the Recordset object accomplishes the same task as the SQL update statement. The syntax for this method is similar to the AddNew method.

```
Recordset.Fields([name or number of field]) = [some value]
Recordset.Fields([name or number of field]) = [some value]
Recordset.Fields([name or number of field]) = [some value]
...
Recordset.Update
```

Notice that the only difference between the AddNew method and the Update method is that the AddNew method doesn't need to be called because I am only changing an existing row in the table rather than adding a new row. The changes made are applied to the current record in the recordset.

Delete

The Delete method of the Recordset object accomplishes the same thing as the SQL delete statement. To delete the current record, use this syntax:

```
Recordset.Delete
```

Other Useful Recordset Methods and Properties

Many other methods and properties of the Recordset object become useful from time to time. Here are a few that I've found very helpful.

GetString

The Recordset object's GetString method can be used to return the recordset fields as a string with row and column delimiters that you specify. I've found this to be a useful method for doing things like filling up the options in an HTML <select> tag. Here's the syntax:

```
Dim myString
myString = Recordset.GetString(StringFormat, NumRows, ColumnDelimiter,
RowDelimiter, NullExpr)
```

Because the GetString method is a function that returns a string, you should declare a string to hold the return value of the function. You can then use the string in the appropriate places in your page. For the StringFormat parameter use adClipString. The rest of the parameters are optional. The NumRows parameter is the number of rows of the recordset that you want the string to contain. If you leave this parameter blank then all of the rows will be used. The ColumnDelimiter parameter is the string that you want to use to delimit the columns of the recordset. This string will be inserted when there is a new column. Likewise, the RowDelimiter string will be inserted when there is a new row. The NullExpr parameter is a string that will be inserted when a field in a record is null.

Using the GetString Method

The next example, newCustomer2.asp, is similar to the example you saw in Chapter 8, "The Connection Object." It has a form that can be used to add customers, delete customers, or update customer records. It also makes use of the GetString method.

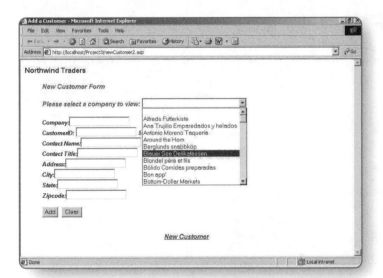

All of the company names are in the drop down list box.

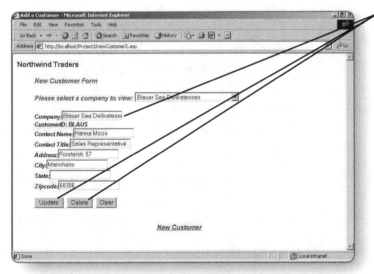

Upon selecting a company, the form is filled with the company information. The information can be changed. Then the user can click on the Update button to save the changes to the record or the Delete button to delete the customers. Clicking on the New Customer link clears the form and shows the Add button.

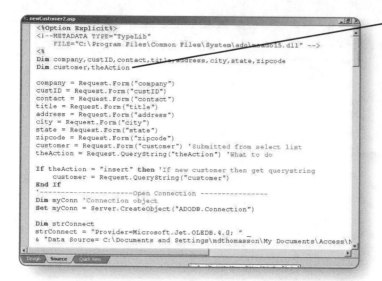

```
newCustomer2.asp
<%Option Explicit%>
<!--METADATA TYPE="TypeLib"
    FILE="C:\Program Files\Common Files\System\ado\msado15.dll" -->
<%
Dim company,custID,contact,title,address,city,state,zipcode
Dim customer,theAction

company = Request.Form("company")
custID = Request.Form("custID")
contact = Request.Form("contact")
title = Request.Form("title")
address = Request.Form("address")
city = Request.Form("city")
state = Request.Form("state")
zipcode = Request.Form("zipcode")
customer = Request.Form("customer") 'Submitted from select list
theAction = Request.QueryString("theAction") 'What to do

If theAction = "insert" then 'If new customer then get querystring
    customer = Request.QueryString("customer")
End If
'----------------------Open Connection ----------------
Dim myConn 'Connection object
Set myConn = Server.CreateObject("ADODB.Connection")

Dim strConnect
strConnect = "Provider=Microsoft.Jet.OLEDB.4.0; " _
& "Data Source= C:\Documents and Settings\mdthomasson\My Documents\Access\N
```

The page starts by retrieving the values from a form into some variables. Notice that there is also one query string value called theAction. You'll look at the form next to see what's going on.

```
newCustomer2.asp
End Function
%>
<html>
<head>
<title>Add a Customer</title>
<link rel = "stylesheet" type = "text/css" href = "myStyle.css">
</head>
<body bgcolor = white onload="document.forms[0].elements[0].focus();">
<h1>Northwind Traders</h1>
<blockquote>
    <h2>New Customer Form</h2>
    <form method = "post" name = "form1" action = "newCustomer2.asp">
        <h2>Please select a company to view:
        <select name = "customer" onchange = "document.form1.submit()">
        <option><%=customer%>
        <%=strCompanies%>
        </select>
    </form>
    <form method = "post" name = "form2" action = "newCustomer2.asp">
        Company:<input type = "text" name = "company" value = "<%=company%>
        CustomerID:
        <% If customer = "" then '-----Get customerID if new cust----%>
        <input type = "text" name = "custID" maxlength = "5">
        <i>5 Characters</i><br>
        <% Else
        Response.Write(custID & "<br>")'---Can't change primary key
        End If
        %>
        Contact Name:<input type = "text" name = "contact"
```

Here is the code at the bottom of the page. Notice that there are two forms. The first form, "form1", simply shows the drop down list with the company names in it. The onchange event of the <select> statement has the following JavaScript: "document.form1.submit()". All this code does is submit "form1" when a new company name is selected from the drop down list.

```
newCustomer2.asp
     End Function
     %>
<html>
<head>
<title>Add a Customer</title>
<link rel = "stylesheet" type = "text/css" href = "myStyle.css">
</head>
<body bgcolor = white onload="document.forms[0].elements[0].focus();">
<h1>Northwind Traders</h1>
<blockquote>
     <h2>New Customer Form</h2>
     <form method = "post" name = "form1" action = "newCustomer.asp">
          <h2>Please select a company to view:
          <select name = "customer" onchange = "document.form1.submit()">
          <option><%=customer%>
          <%=strCompanies%>
          </select>
     </form>
     <form method = "post" name = "form2" action = "newCustomer2.asp">
          Company:<input type = "text" name = "company" value = "<%=company%>
          CustomerID:
          <% If customer = "" then '-----Get customerID if new cust----%>
          <input type = "text" name = "custID" maxlength = "5">
          <i>5 Characters</i><br>
          <% Else
          Response.Write(custID & "<br>")'---Can't change primary key
          End If
          %>
          Contact Name:<input type = "text" name = "contact"
```

If "form1" has been submitted then the customer variable will have the name of the customer that was selected. In that case, I write out that customer as the first <option> in the <select> statement. After that, the rest of the customer names are written in. Believe it or not, all the rest of the <option> statements are in the strCompanies variable. You'll see how they got there momentarily.

```
newCustomer2.asp
          <%=strCompanies%>
          </select>
     </form>
     <form method = "post" name = "form2" action = "newCustomer2.asp">
          Company:<input type = "text" name = "company" value = "<%=company%>
          CustomerID:
          <% If customer = "" then '-----Get customerID if new cust----%>
          <input type = "text" name = "custID" maxlength = "5">
          <i>5 Characters</i><br>
          <% Else
          Response.Write(custID & "<br>")'---Can't change primary key
          End If
          %>
          Contact Name:<input type = "text" name = "contact"
               value ="<%=contact%>"><br>
          Contact Title:<input type = "text" name = "title"
               value = "<%=title%>"><br>
          Address:<input type = "text" name = "address"
               value = "<%=address%>"><br>
          City:<input type = "text" name = "city"
               value = "<%=city%>"><br>
          State:<input type = "text" name = "state"
               value = "<%=state%>"><br>
          Zipcode:<input type = "text" name = "zipcode"
               maxlength = "10" value="<%=zipcode%>"><br>

          <input type = "hidden" name = "customer" value = "<%=customer%>">
          <br>
          <% If customer = "" then %>
```

The second form is the data entry form. Notice that each of the text box elements has a variable in the "value" attribute. If "form1" has been submitted, a query will have filled those variables with the information corresponding to whichever customer was selected.

```
newCustomer2.asp                                          _ 8 X
            <%=strCompanies%>
            </select>
    </form>
    <form method = "post" name = "form2" action = "newCustomer2.asp">
        Company:<input type = "text" name = "company" value = "<%=company%>
        CustomerID:
        <% If customer = "" then '-----Get customerID if new cust----%>
        <input type = "text" name = "custID" maxlength = "5">
        <i>5 Characters</i><br>
        <% Else
        Response.Write(custID & "<br>")'---Can't change primary key
        End If
        %>
        Contact Name:<input type = "text" name = "contact"
            value ="<%=contact%>"><br>
        Contact Title:<input type = "text" name = "title"
            value = "<%=title%>"><br>
        Address:<input type = "text" name = "address"
            value = "<%=address%>"><br>
        City:<input type = "text" name = "city"
            value = "<%=city%>"><br>
        State:<input type = "text" name = "state"
            value = "<%=state%>"><br>
        Zipcode:<input type = "text" name = "zipcode"
            maxlength = "10" value="<%=zipcode%>"><br>

        <input type = "hidden" name = "customer" value = "<%=customer%>">
        <br>
        <% If customer = "" then %>
Design  Source   Quick View
```

If the customer is new, I have the user choose a "custID." Otherwise the "custID" is read-only because you can't change the value of "CustomerID" on an existing record— it is the primary key for the customers table.

Notice we also pass along the customer variable's value as a "hidden" form element.

```
newCustomer2.asp                                          _ 8 X
        City:<input type = "text" name = "city"
            value = "<%=city%>"><br>
        State:<input type = "text" name = "state"
            value = "<%=state%>"><br>
        Zipcode:<input type = "text" name = "zipcode"
            maxlength = "10" value="<%=zipcode%>"><br>

        <input type = "hidden" name = "customer" value = "<%=customer%>">
        <br>
        <% If customer = "" then %>
        <input type = "submit" value = "Add" onclick =
        "document.form2.action='newCustomer2.asp?theAction=insert&customer=new'">
        <% Else %>
        <input type = "submit" value = "Update"
        onclick = "document.form2.action='newCustomer2.asp?theAction=update'">&nbs
        <input type = "submit" value = "Delete"
        onclick = "document.form2.action='newCustomer2.asp?theAction=delete'">&nbs
        <% End If %>
        <input type = "reset" value = "Clear">
    </form>
    quote><br>
    ><a href = "newCustomer2.asp">New Customer</a></center>
Design  Source   Quick View
```

At the bottom of the form I add the applicable buttons. If the customer variable is blank, the customer is new and must be added to the database. In that case, the "Add" button must be shown. Notice that I use the onclick event of the "submit" button to change the action attribute of form2 via JavaScript. I simply append a query string to the URL that contains an element called theAction that is set equal to insert and one called customer that is set equal to new.

If the customer variable was not blank, the customer is not new and can only be updated or deleted. I show only the "Update" and "Delete" buttons and append the appropriate query string to the URL. Now I'll go back to the top of the page.

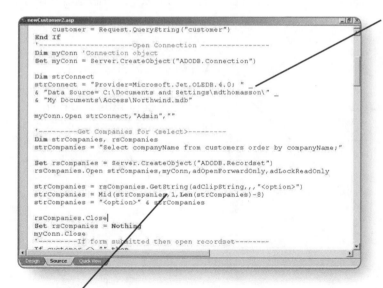

```
newCustomer2.asp                                            _ 8 x
<%Option Explicit%>
<!--METADATA TYPE="TypeLib"
    FILE="C:\Program Files\Common Files\System\ado\msado15.dll" -->
<%
Dim company,custID,contact,title,address,city,state,zipcode
Dim customer,theAction

company = Request.Form("company")
custID = Request.Form("custID")
contact = Request.Form("contact")
title = Request.Form("title")
address = Request.Form("address")
city = Request.Form("city")
state = Request.Form("state")
zipcode = Request.Form("zipcode")
customer = Request.Form("customer") 'Submitted from select list
theAction = Request.QueryString("theAction") 'what to do

If theAction = "insert" then 'If new customer then get querystring
    customer = Request.QueryString("customer")
End If
'-------------------Open Connection ----------------
Dim myConn 'Connection object
Set myConn = Server.CreateObject("ADODB.Connection")

Dim strConnect
strConnect = "Provider=Microsoft.Jet.OLEDB.4.0; " _
& "Data Source= C:\Documents and Settings\mdthomasson\My Documents\Access\N
Design  Source  Quick View
```

Now you can see what the theAction variable is all about. It tells the active server script whether the customer is to be inserted, updated, or deleted.

Remember that if the customer was new we appended the customer element onto the query string with a value of new. If theAction is equal to "insert" then the customer is new and the value of the customer element must be taken from the QueryString collection rather than the Form collection.

```
newCustomer2.asp                                            _ 8 x
    customer = Request.QueryString("customer")
End If
'-------------------Open Connection ----------------
Dim myConn 'Connection object
Set myConn = Server.CreateObject("ADODB.Connection")

Dim strConnect
strConnect = "Provider=Microsoft.Jet.OLEDB.4.0; " _
& "Data Source= C:\Documents and Settings\mdthomasson\" _
& "My Documents\Access\Northwind.mdb"

myConn.Open strConnect,"Admin",""

'---------Get Companies for <select>---------
Dim strCompanies, rsCompanies
strCompanies = "Select companyName from customers order by companyName;"

Set rsCompanies = Server.CreateObject("ADODB.Recordset")
rsCompanies.Open strCompanies,myConn,adOpenForwardOnly,adLockReadOnly

strCompanies = rsCompanies.GetString(adClipString,,,"<option>")
strCompanies = Mid(strCompanies,1,Len(strCompanies)-8)
strCompanies = "<option>" & strCompanies

rsCompanies.Close
Set rsCompanies = Nothing
myConn.Close
'---------If form submitted then open recordset--------
If customer <> "" then
Design  Source  Quick View
```

Moving on, I create a Connection object and open it. Note that this time I'm connecting to the Northwind database with an OLE DB native driver rather than with a DSN. I made a copy of the Northwind database and put it in my My Documents folder.

Next I create and open the recordset that fills up the <select> element named customers in the first form, form1. I used the GetString method to get the information from the recordset and put it into the strCompanies variable. Notice that I used <option> as the RowDelimeter value. That way every new row would have the <option> tag appended to the end of it.

I have to do a little clean up to our strCompanies variable. First I need to get rid of the extra <option> tag that was added to the end of the last row. I do that by using the VBScript Mid() function and Len() function. The Mid() function extracts a specified part of a string. It takes three parameters. The first one is the string (in this case strCompanies). The next is the starting location (in this case 1 since I want to start at the beginning). And finally, the last

parameter is the length of the string I want to extract (in this case I want everything but the last eight characters – <option>). The Len() function returns the length of a string as an integer.

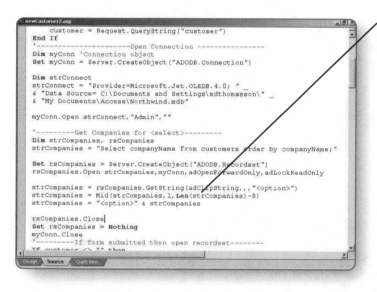

After I get rid of the extra <option> tag we need to add an <option> tag to the beginning of the string. After I've gotten the information in our string, I can close the recordset.

```
newCustomer2.asp                                                    _|8|X
   rsCompanies.Close
   Set rsCompanies = Nothing
   myConn.Close
   '---------If form submitted then open recordset--------
   If customer <> "" then
       myConn.Open
       Dim rsCustomer, strCustomer
       If customer <> "new" then
           strCustomer = "select * from customers where companyName " _
           & "= '" & FixIt(customer) & "';"
       Else
           strCustomer = "customers"
       End If

       Set rsCustomer = Server.CreateObject("ADODB.Recordset")
       rsCustomer.Open strCustomer,myConn,adOpenDynamic,adLockOptimistic

   '---------See if the user wants to insert,update or delete------
       Select Case theAction
           Case "update"
               With rsCustomer
                   .Fields("companyName") = company
                   .Fields("contactName") = contact
                   .Fields("contactTitle") = title
                   .Fields("address") = address
                   .Fields("city") = city
                   If state <> "" then
                   .Fields("region") = state
                   End If
 Design   Source   Quick View
```

If the customer variable is not blank, one of the two forms has been submitted. If that is the case, I reopen my Connection object and proceed to build a recordset.

If the customer is new, I will just open the customers table so I can append to it. Otherwise I just get the information pertaining to the selected customer. Notice that I have to use my handy FixIt() function (from Chapter 8) to replace any single quote marks with two single quote marks.

```
newCustomer2.asp                                                    _|8|X
   rsCompanies.Close
   Set rsCompanies = Nothing
   myConn.Close
   '---------If form submitted then open recordset--------
   If customer <> "" then
       myConn.Open
       Dim rsCustomer, strCustomer
       If customer <> "new" then
           strCustomer = "select * from customers where companyName " _
           & "= '" & FixIt(customer) & "';"
       Else
           strCustomer = "customers"
       End If

       Set rsCustomer = Server.CreateObject("ADODB.Recordset")
       rsCustomer.Open strCustomer,myConn,adOpenDynamic,adLockOptimistic

   '---------See if the user wants to insert,update or delete------
       Select Case theAction
           Case "update"
               With rsCustomer
                   .Fields("companyName") = company
                   .Fields("contactName") = contact
                   .Fields("contactTitle") = title
                   .Fields("address") = address
                   .Fields("city") = city
                   If state <> "" then
                   .Fields("region") = state
                   End If
 Design   Source   Quick View
```

After setting up my SQL string I create and open the recordset. Notice that I am not using a read-only recordset because I might be adding, updating, or deleting records.

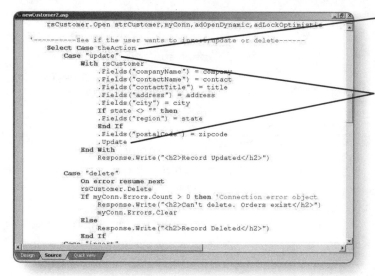

```
newCustomer2.asp
    rsCustomer.Open strCustomer,myConn, adOpenDynamic,adLockOptimistic

    '---------See if the user wants to insert,update or delete------
    Select Case theAction
        Case "update"
            With rsCustomer
                .Fields("companyName") = company
                .Fields("contactName") = contact
                .Fields("contactTitle") = title
                .Fields("address") = address
                .Fields("city") = city
                If state <> "" then
                .Fields("region") = state
                End If
                .Fields("postalCode") = zipcode
                .Update
            End With
                Response.Write("<h2>Record Updated</h2>")

        Case "delete"
            On error resume next
            rsCustomer.Delete
            If myConn.Errors.Count > 0 then 'Connection error object
                Response.Write("<h2>Can't delete. Orders exist</h2>")
                myConn.Errors.Clear
            Else
                Response.Write("<h2>Record Deleted</h2>")
            End If
        Case "insert"

Design  Source  Quick View
```

Next I check the theAction variable to see if I need to insert, update, or delete anything.

If theAction equals "update", I set the value of the recordset fields equal to the values of the variables passed in from form. Not all the records had a "region", so I had to put the If…End If to check whether the state variable was blank (my state variable is the same as their "region"). The customers table is set up so that the columns can not have zero length strings. Finally, I call the Update method to save the changes.

NOTE

Starting with VBScript 5.0, you can use the With…End With notation when dealing with objects. Just put the name of the object after the With statement. After that you can just use a period followed by any method or property of the object that you want to reference. When you're done with the object, use End With. This technique saves typing.

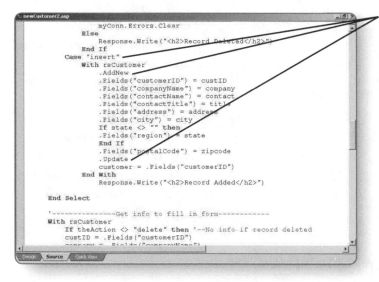

```
newCustomer2.asp
        rsCustomer.Open strCustomer,myConn, adOpenDynamic, adLockOptimistic

'----------See if the user wants to insert,update or delete------
    Select Case theAction
        Case "update"
            With rsCustomer
                .Fields("companyName") = company
                .Fields("contactName") = contact
                .Fields("contactTitle") = title
                .Fields("address") = address
                .Fields("city") = city
                If state <> "" then
                .Fields("region") = state
                End If
                .Fields("postalCode") = zipcode
                .Update
            End With
                Response.Write("<h2>Record Updated</h2>")

        Case "delete"
            On error resume next
            rsCustomer.Delete
            If myConn.Errors.Count > 0 then 'Connection error object
                Response.Write("<h2>Can't delete. Orders exist</h2>")
                myConn.Errors.Clear
            Else
                Response.Write("<h2>Record Deleted</h2>")
            End If
        Case "insert"
```

If `theAction` equals "delete", I call the recordset's `Delete` method to delete the record. If the customer has placed orders, an error will be thrown due to the integrity constraints imposed by the primary/foreign key constraints. If this occurs, the record will not be deleted and I can catch the error by checking the Connection object's `Errors` collection. I then let the user know what happened.

```
newCustomer2.asp
                myConn.Errors.Clear
            Else
                Response.Write("<h2>Record Deleted</h2>")
            End If
        Case "insert"
            With rsCustomer
                .AddNew
                .Fields("customerID") = custID
                .Fields("companyName") = company
                .Fields("contactName") = contact
                .Fields("contactTitle") = title
                .Fields("address") = address
                .Fields("city") = city
                If state <> "" then
                .Fields("region") = state
                End If
                .Fields("postalCode") = zipcode
                .Update
                customer = .Fields("customerID")
            End With
                Response.Write("<h2>Record Added</h2>")

    End Select

'----------------Get info to fill in form------------
With rsCustomer
    If theAction <> "delete" then '--No info if record deleted
    custID = .Fields("customerID")
    company = .Fields("companyName")
```

If `theAction` equals "insert", I call the `AddNew` method, then proceed to set the fields equal to the appropriate variable values. Finally, I call the `Update` method to seal the deal.

Finally, I need to put the correct information into the form variables. If the record was deleted then I skip this step since there won't be any information to put into the variables. Notice that if the recordset was changed then the new values of the fields will be put into the variables. Otherwise, the `Select…End Select` statement would have been skipped and the original values of the recordset fields would be put into the variables.

Remember that these variables will now be used as the values of the text box elements in `form2`.

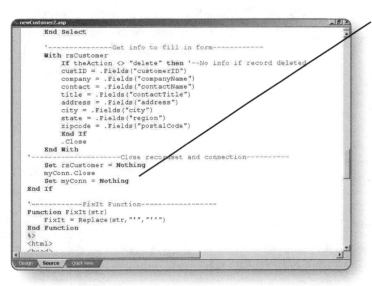

At last, I close the recordset and the connection. Yet another script is finished…. If you want to see another example of using recordsets with the `GetString` method, check out northwind2.asp. It allows the user to select a company from the drop down list. The selected customer's orders are then listed in table format.

Recordset Paging Using the PageSize, PageCount, CacheSize and AbsolutePage Properties

We've all seen Web site search pages that return only a certain number of results at a time. For example, if you do a search that returns 10,000 results, you will usually "page" through the results by smaller increments of, say, ten or twenty-five results per page. One way to accomplish such paging is using the `PageSize`, `PageCount`, `CacheSize`, and `AbsolutePage` properties of the Recordset object. The `PageSize` property of a Recordset object is the number of records in a page. The default `PageSize` is ten. The `CacheSize` property determines how many records ADO will grab from the database and put into local memory at one time. The default `CacheSize` is 1. Increasing the `CacheSize` property will increase performance since fewer trips have to be made between the provider and ADO. The `PageCount` property returns the total number of pages in the recordset. Finally, the `AbsolutePage` property returns the page number that the record pointer is currently on. Using these properties you can set up recordset paging.

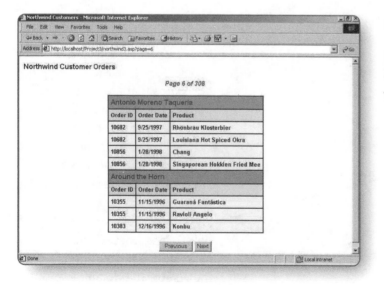

Using Paging

Here it is, northwind3.asp. You can page to your heart's content with this one!

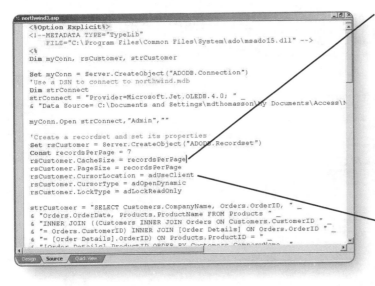

```
northwind3.asp
<%Option Explicit%>
<!--METADATA TYPE="TypeLib"
    FILE="C:\Program Files\Common Files\System\ado\msado15.dll" -->
<%
Dim myConn, rsCustomer, strCustomer

Set myConn = Server.CreateObject("ADODB.Connection")
'Use a DSN to connect to northwind.mdb
Dim strConnect
strConnect = "Provider=Microsoft.Jet.OLEDB.4.0; " _
& "Data Source=C:\Documents and Settings\mdthomasson\My Documents\Access\N

myConn.Open strConnect,"Admin",""

'Create a recordset and set its properties
Set rsCustomer = Server.CreateObject("ADODB.Recordset")
Const recordsPerPage = 7
rsCustomer.CacheSize = recordsPerPage
rsCustomer.PageSize = recordsPerPage
rsCustomer.CursorLocation = adUseClient
rsCustomer.CursorType = adOpenDynamic
rsCustomer.LockType = adLockReadOnly

strCustomer = "SELECT Customers.CompanyName, Orders.OrderID, " _
& "Orders.OrderDate, Products.ProductName FROM Products "
& "INNER JOIN ((Customers INNER JOIN Orders ON Customers.CustomerID "
& "= Orders.CustomerID) INNER JOIN [Order Details] ON Orders.OrderID "
& "= Products].OrderID) ON Products.ProductID = "
```

This page is similar to northwind1.asp, so I'll focus on only the differences. After creating the recordset object, the differences start to appear. First, I declare a Const called recordsPerPage and set it equal to 7. This is obviously the number of records I show per page. I used a Const so that if I want to change the records per page to something else, I only have to do it in one place.

```
northwind3.asp
<%Option Explicit%>
<!--METADATA TYPE="TypeLib"
    FILE="C:\Program Files\Common Files\System\ado\msado15.dll" -->
<%
Dim myConn, rsCustomer, strCustomer

Set myConn = Server.CreateObject("ADODB.Connection")
'Use a DSN to connect to northwind.mdb
Dim strConnect
strConnect = "Provider=Microsoft.Jet.OLEDB.4.0; " _
& "Data Source=C:\Documents and Settings\mdthomasson\My Documents\Access\N

myConn.Open strConnect,"Admin",""

'Create a recordset and set its properties
Set rsCustomer = Server.CreateObject("ADODB.Recordset")
Const recordsPerPage = 7
rsCustomer.CacheSize = recordsPerPage
rsCustomer.PageSize = recordsPerPage
rsCustomer.CursorLocation = adUseClient
rsCustomer.CursorType = adOpenDynamic
rsCustomer.LockType = adLockReadOnly

strCustomer = "SELECT Customers.CompanyName, Orders.OrderID, " _
& "Orders.OrderDate, Products.ProductName FROM Products "
& "INNER JOIN ((Customers INNER JOIN Orders ON Customers.CustomerID "
& "= Orders.CustomerID) INNER JOIN [Order Details] ON Orders.OrderID "
& "= [Order Details].OrderID) ON Products.ProductID = "
```

Notice that I set both the PageSize and CacheSize equal to the recordsPerPage constant. To review, PageSize is the number of records that are considered a page in the recordset. CacheSize is the number of records that ADO will grab from the database and cache locally in one hit to the database.

The CursorLocation property determines what will be handling the processing of the cursor. The default is adUseServer which means that the database will handle the cursor. In this case I used adUseClient, which means that ADO will handle the cursor processing. A forward only, read only recordset works fine here. The SQL select statement is the same as in northwind1.asp.

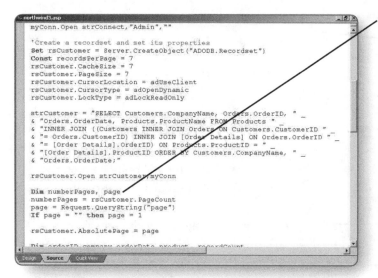

```
- northwind3.asp
myConn.Open strConnect, "Admin", ""

'Create a recordset and set its properties
Set rsCustomer = Server.CreateObject ("ADODB.Recordset")
Const recordsPerPage = 7
rsCustomer.CacheSize = 7
rsCustomer.PageSize = 7
rsCustomer.CursorLocation = adUseClient
rsCustomer.CursorType = adOpenDynamic
rsCustomer.LockType = adLockReadOnly

strCustomer = "SELECT Customers.CompanyName, Orders.OrderID, " _
& "Orders.OrderDate, Products.ProductName FROM Products " _
& "INNER JOIN ((Customers INNER JOIN Orders ON Customers.CustomerID " _
& "= Orders.CustomerID) INNER JOIN [Order Details] ON Orders.OrderID " _
& "= [Order Details].OrderID) ON Products.ProductID = " _
& "[Order Details].ProductID ORDER BY Customers.CompanyName, " _
& "Orders.OrderDate;"

rsCustomer.Open strCustomer, myConn

Dim numberPages, page
numberPages = rsCustomer.PageCount
page = Request.QueryString("page")
If page = "" then page = 1

rsCustomer.AbsolutePage = page

Dim orderID company orderDate product   recordCount

Design  Source  Quick View
```

After opening the recordset, I declare two new variables. The numberPages variable holds the number of pages in the recordset as determined by the PageCount property. Obviously, the PageSize property needs to be set before the PageCount can be determined (although PageSize defaults to 10). The "page" variable will contain the page number passed in from a query string. If the "page" variable is blank, we must be on the first page, so I set "page = 1".

NOTE

Yes, I know that I didn't use an End If on the line that checks to see if the page is blank. If you are only doing one thing in the Then part of your If statement, you don't need to use an End If.

```
- northwind3.asp
& "[Order Details].ProductID ORDER BY Customers.CompanyName, " _
& "Orders.OrderDate;"

rsCustomer.Open strCustomer, myConn

Dim numberPages, page
numberPages = rsCustomer.PageCount
page = Request.QueryString("page")
If page = "" then page = 1
%>
<html>
<head>
<title>Northwind Customers</title>
<link rel = "stylesheet" type = "text/css" href = "myStyle.css">
</head>
<body bgcolor = "white">
<h1>Northwind Customer Orders</h1>
<h2 align = "center">Page <%=page%> of <%=numberPages%></h2>
<div align = "center">
<table border = "1" bordercolor = "black" cellpadding = "5"
cellspacing = "0" bgcolor = "#40FFFF">
<%
rsCustomer.AbsolutePage = page

Dim orderID, company, orderDate, product, recordCount

If not rsCustomer.BOF then
    company = Trim(rsCustomer.Fields("companyName"))
    recordCount = 0

Design  Source  Quick View
```

I had to move the top of the HTML page code down below the recordset Open method so that I could write out the line that says "Page # of #".

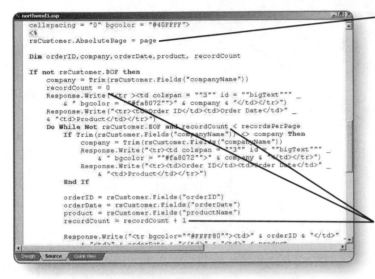

```
cellspacing = "0" bgcolor = "#40FFFF">
<%
rsCustomer.AbsolutePage = page

Dim orderID,company,orderDate,product, recordCount

If not rsCustomer.BOF then
     company = Trim(rsCustomer.Fields("companyName"))
     recordCount = 0
     Response.Write("<tr ><td colspan = ""3"" id = ""bigText"""
          & " bgcolor = ""#fa8072"">" & company & "</td></tr>")
     Response.Write("<tr><td>Order ID</td><td>Order Date</td>"
          & "<td>Product</td></tr>")
     Do While Not rsCustomer.EOF and recordCount < recordsPerPage
          If Trim(rsCustomer.Fields("companyName")) <> company Then
               company = Trim(rsCustomer.Fields("companyName"))
               Response.Write("<tr><td colspan = ""3"" id = ""bigText"""
                    & " bgcolor = ""#fa8072"">" & company & "</td></tr>")
               Response.Write("<tr><td>Order ID</td><td>Order Date</td>"
                    & "<td>Product</td></tr>")
          End If

          orderID = rsCustomer.Fields("orderID")
          orderDate = rsCustomer.Fields("orderDate")
          product = rsCustomer.Fields("productName")
          recordCount = recordCount + 1

          Response.Write("<tr bgcolor=""#FFFF80""><td>" & orderID & "</td>"
```

The next thing to do is to set the AbsolutePage property to whatever page we're on. Remember that the AbsolutePage property sets which page in the recordset the record pointer is to be placed on. When set, the record pointer will be placed on the first record in that page.

Only a few changes were made to this looping section of code. Notice that I added a variable named recordCount. Before the loop begins, I set the variable equal to zero. With each iteration of the loop, the recordCount is incremented by one. The loop will continue writing out table rows as long as the EOF property of the recordset is false and the recordCount variable is less than the recordsPerPage constant (which is 7 in this case).

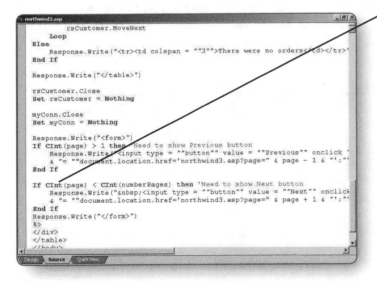

```
          rsCustomer.MoveNext
     Loop
Else
     Response.Write("<tr><td colspan = ""3"">There were no orders</td></tr>")
End If

Response.Write("</table>")

rsCustomer.Close
Set rsCustomer = Nothing

myConn.Close
Set myConn = Nothing

Response.Write("<form>")
If CInt(page) > 1 then 'Need to show Previous button
     Response.Write("<input type = ""button"" value = ""Previous"" onclick '
          & "= ""document.location.href='northwind3.asp?page=" & page - 1 & "';""
End If

If CInt(page) < CInt(numberPages) then 'Need to show Next button
     Response.Write(" <input type = ""button"" value = ""Next"" onclick
          & "= ""document.location.href='northwind3.asp?page=" & page + 1 & "';""
End If
Response.Write("</form>")
%>
</div>
</table>
</body>
```

The next real difference in the code comes at the bottom of the page. I've added the "Previous" and "Next" buttons to the page. First of all, the CInt() function converts the value passed to it into an integer. If the integer value of page is greater than one, I am past the first page and need to show the "Previous" button so that the user can go back. Likewise, if the page number is less than the total number of pages, I need to show the "Next" button so that the user can move to the next page.

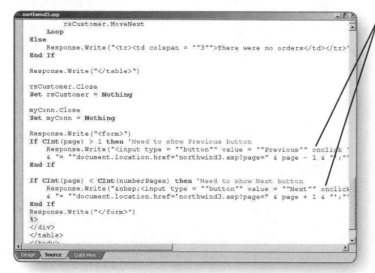

In the buttons' `onclick` events, I use the JavaScript statement "`document.location.href`" to set the URL that the page should navigate to. If it is the "Previous" button, one is subtracted from the `page` variable and set equal to the `page` query string element. Similarly, if the "Next" button is clicked on, one is added to the current page number.

NOTE

If you don't put these buttons between `<form></form>` tags, they won't show up in Netscape.

This is just one way to do recordset paging. It is not necessarily the best way. With this method the entire recordset still needs to be passed from the database to ADO. Then just part of the recordset is displayed to the user. You might want to look into using a stored procedure that passes a recordset back to ADO that contains only one page's information.

10

The ADO Command Object

The ADO Command object enables you to take advantage of the power of database stored procedures. A *stored procedure* is basically a predefined package of one or more SQL statements. Stored procedures can be set up to accept parameters that can be plugged into SQL statements. Stored procedures can also send values back to the code that called the stored procedure. Queries in stored procedures also provide much greater performance because the database already knows how to execute the query in an optimal way. Often, frequently used stored procedures will also remain in the database server's memory, providing additional performance increases. For these reasons alone it pays to use stored procedures whenever possible. In this chapter, you'll learn how to:

- Use the ADO Command object to modify data
- Use the ADO Command object to pass parameters to a stored procedure
- Retrieve return values and output parameters from a stored procedure
- Retrieve recordsets from a stored procedure

Using the Command Object to Modify Data

The ADO Command object can be used to send information to database stored procedures that can modify information in the database. If you're going to modify information in a database then using a stored procedure is the best way to do it.

NOTE

Not all databases support stored procedures. High-end databases like Oracle, DB2, and Microsoft's SQL server support stored procedures whereas "desktop" type databases like Access and FileMaker Pro don't. Some of the desktop databases like Access support *parameterized* queries, but they don't provide the same performance as stored procedures.

Creating a Command Object

ADO Command objects are created in much the same fashion as the other ADO objects. Here is the syntax:

```
Set command = Server.CreateObject("ADODB.Command")
```

The primary method of the command object is the Execute method. Before executing a command, however, there are a few properties that need to be set. Consider the following example:

```
<%
Dim myConn, myCommand
Set myConn = Server.CreateObject("ADODB.Connection")
myConn.Open "DSN=pubs","fast","easy"
myCommand.ActiveConnection = myConn
myCommand.CommandText = "usp_myStoredProc"
myCommand.CommandType = adCmdStoredProc
myCommand.CommandTimeout = 60

myCommand.Execute
%>
```

The `ActiveConnection` property establishes the database connection that the command object uses. The `CommandText` property is a string that represents the command to be run. This string can be the name of a stored procedure, a SQL string, a table name, and so on. The `CommandType` property specifies what type of command the Command object is going to run. There are several different ADO constants you can use, but the two most commonly used are `adCmdText` and `adCmdStoredProc`. The `adCmdText` constant should be used if you are just passing in a SQL string as the `CommandText`. Use the `adCmdStoredProc` setting if you are passing in the name of a stored procedure as the `CommandText`. If you want to specify how long the command should be allowed to run before timing out, you can set the `CommandTimeout` property. This property sets the number of seconds allowed to elapse before a timeout error occurs. The default `CommandTimeout` setting is 30 seconds. After you've set all of the properties you can execute the Command object using the `Execute` method. I'll now consider the `Execute` method in a little more detail.

Executing Commands with the Command Object

In the preceding example I executed the Command object named `myCommand` without any additional parameters. There are some parameters that you can pass to the `Execute` method if you choose to. Here is the complete syntax for the `Execute` method.

```
Command.Execute [Records Affected],[Parameters],[Options]
```

If you want to know how many rows in a table were affected by an `insert`, `update`, or `delete` statement, you can pass in a variable as the `Records Affected` parameter. After the command has been executed, the variable you passed in will contain the number of records affected. The second parameter, `Parameters`, is an array of parameter values. Some stored procedures can accept parameters (you'll see examples later). You can pass in the values of the parameters as an array in the `Execute` method. I'll go over a different way of passing in parameters that yields better performance. Finally, the `Options` parameter allows you to pass in the `CommandType` or other options. One option that you can use if the command will not be returning a recordset is the `adExecuteNoRecords`. Passing in this constant to the `Options` parameter will increase performance on commands that don't need to return anything.

Using a Stored Procedure

Before we move on to a discussion of parameters we'll consider an example of a simple stored procedure that modifies data in the database.

First, I modified all of the examples from Chapter 9, "The ADO Recordset Object," to use the SQL Server Northwind database instead of the Access 2000 Northwind database. The names of the active server pages are the same except that I put "SQL"

in front of the name. The only changes I had to make to the code were the connection strings and any Select statements with Joins in them. For example, here is northwind1.asp from the last chapter.

```
<%Option Explicit%>
<!--METADATA TYPE="TypeLib"
    FILE="C:\Program Files\Common Files\System\ado\msado15.dll" -->
<html>
<head>
<title>Northwind Customers</title>
<link rel = "stylesheet" type = "text/css" href = "myStyle.css">
</head>
<body bgcolor = "white">
<h1>Northwind Customer Orders</h1>
<div align = "center">
<table border = "1" bordercolor = "black" cellpadding = "5"
cellspacing = "0" bgcolor = "#40FFFF">
<%
Dim myConn, rsCustomer, strCustomer
Set myConn = Server.CreateObject("ADODB.Connection")
'Use a DSN to connect to northwind.mdb
myConn.Open "DSN=Northwind", "Admin", ""

Set rsCustomer = Server.CreateObject("ADODB.Recordset")
'Create the big Select statement
strCustomer = "SELECT Customers.CompanyName, Orders.OrderID, " _
& "Orders.OrderDate, Products.ProductName FROM Products " _
& "INNER JOIN ((Customers INNER JOIN Orders ON Customers.CustomerID " _
& "= Orders.CustomerID) INNER JOIN [Order Details] ON Orders.OrderID " _
& "= [Order Details].OrderID) ON Products.ProductID = " _
& "[Order Details].ProductID ORDER BY Customers.CompanyName, " _
& "Orders.OrderDate;"
```

Here is SQLNorthwind1.asp.

Notice that I used an OLE DB connection to connect to the Northwind SQL Server database. You can see that the Select statement is a lot simpler in this example as well. SQL Server uses ANSI SQL join syntax whereas Access doesn't.

```
<h1>Northwind Customer Orders</h1>
<div align = "center">
<table border = "1" bordercolor = "black" cellpadding = "5"
cellspacing = "0" bgcolor = "#40FFFF">
<%

'Record Hits

Server.Execute("northwindHits.asp")

Dim myConn, rsCustomer, strCustomer, strConnection

'Connect to SQL Server Northwind
strConnection = "PROVIDER=SQLOLEDB; DATA SOURCE=MIKESERVER;" _
    & "INITIAL CATALOG=Northwind; USER ID=fast; PASSWORD=easy"

Set myConn = Server.CreateObject("ADODB.Connection")
myConn.Open strConnection

Set rsCustomer = Server.CreateObject("ADODB.Recordset")
'Create the big Select statement

strCustomer = "Select CompanyName, o.OrderID, OrderDate, ProductName " _
& "From Customers c inner join Orders o on c.CustomerID = o.CustomerID " _
& "inner join [Order Details] d on o.OrderID = d.OrderID inner join " _
& "Products p on d.ProductID = p.ProductID " _
& "Order by CompanyName, OrderDate;"

rsCustomer.Open strCustomer, myConn, adOpenForwardOnly, adLockReadOnly
```

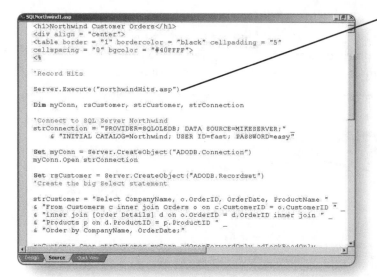

```
<h1>Northwind Customer Orders</h1>
<div align = "center">
<table border = "1" bordercolor = "black" cellpadding = "5"
cellspacing = "0" bgcolor = "#40FFFF">
<%

'Record Hits

Server.Execute("northwindHits.asp")

Dim myConn, rsCustomer, strCustomer, strConnection

'Connect to SQL Server Northwind
strConnection = "PROVIDER=SQLOLEDB; DATA SOURCE=MIKESERVER;" _
      & "INITIAL CATALOG=Northwind; USER ID=fast; PASSWORD=easy"

Set myConn = Server.CreateObject("ADODB.Connection")
myConn.Open strConnection

Set rsCustomer = Server.CreateObject("ADODB.Recordset")
'Create the big Select statement
strCustomer = "Select CompanyName, o.OrderID, OrderDate, ProductName "
& "From Customers c inner join Orders o on c.CustomerID = o.CustomerID "
& "inner join [Order Details] d on o.OrderID = d.OrderID inner join "
& "Products p on d.ProductID = p.ProductID "
& "Order by CompanyName, OrderDate;"
```

These pages have one more change as well. I added a hit counter to all of them. Not just any hit counter—a SQL hit counter! Here's the code that calls the hit counter on SQLNorthwind1.asp. You'll find it on SQLNorthwind2.asp, SQLNorthwind3.asp, and SQLnewCustomer2.asp as well. That's it, a simple `Server.Execute` statement that runs the NorthwindHits.asp page. Remember that the `Server.Execute` method

transfers control to another active server page, executes that page, and then returns to the original active server page. The NorthwindHits.asp page is run in the context of the SQLNorthwind1.asp page, so it has access to all of the Collections that SQLNorthwind1.asp has. You'll see why that's important in a while.

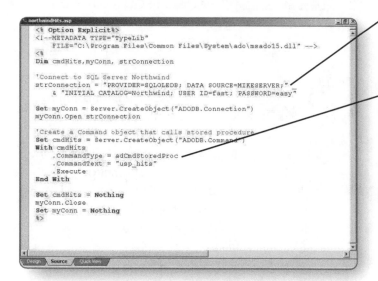

```
<% Option Explicit%>
<!--METADATA TYPE="TypeLib"
    FILE="C:\Program Files\Common Files\System\ado\msado15.dll" -->
<%
Dim cmdHits, myConn, strConnection

'Connect to SQL Server Northwind
strConnection = "PROVIDER=SQLOLEDB; DATA SOURCE=MIKESERVER;"
      & "INITIAL CATALOG=Northwind; USER ID=fast; PASSWORD=easy"

Set myConn = Server.CreateObject("ADODB.Connection")
myConn.Open strConnection

'Create a Command object that calls stored procedure
Set cmdHits = Server.CreateObject("ADODB.Command")
With cmdHits
    .CommandType = adCmdStoredProc
    .CommandText = "usp_hits"
    .Execute
End With

Set cmdHits = Nothing
myConn.Close
Set myConn = Nothing
%>
```

Here's the NorthwindHits.asp page. This page first connects to the SQL Northwind database.

Next I create my first Command object. Note that the `CommandType` property has been set to `adCmdStoredProc` because I'm going to use the Command object to execute a stored procedure. After that I set the `CommandText` property to "usp_hits". Finally, I call the `Execute` method and let 'er rip. When I'm all done I get rid of the Connection and Command objects explicitly.

NOTE

I start all of my stored procedures with "usp_" (*user stored procedure*) so that I can tell them apart from "system" stored procedures.

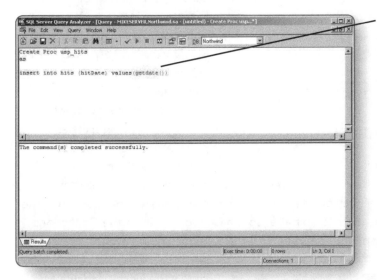

Here's the "usp_hits" stored procedure. At least this is the way it started out. It "morphs" as the chapter moves on. I usually create my stored procedures in the Query Analyzer that ships with SQL Server. As you can see, all that this stored procedure does is insert a date/time into the "hitDate" column of the hits table. The getdate() function is a TSQL (Transact SQL – aka. Microsoft SQL) function that returns the current system date and time.

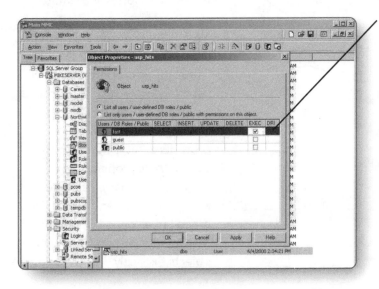

I had to make sure to give the "fast" user the permission to Execute this stored procedure. Remember that I'm connecting to the database with the login "fast." I must grant permission to this login to execute all of the stored procedures that these Web pages use.

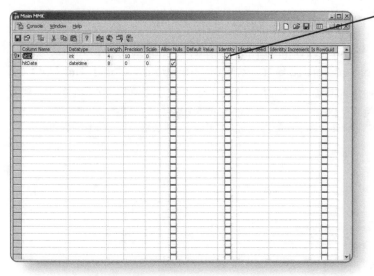

Here is the hits table that I created. It too will change as we add more functionality to our hit counter. It starts out with two columns: hitID and hitDate". Notice that hitID is an Identity column. This is essentially the same thing as an Access Autonumber column. It simply increments by whatever increment value you specify (defaults to 1). SQL Server takes care of inserting into the column for you whenever you insert a row. Recall that in my stored procedure I only inserted into the hitDate column. You will get an error if you try to insert something directly into the hitID column.

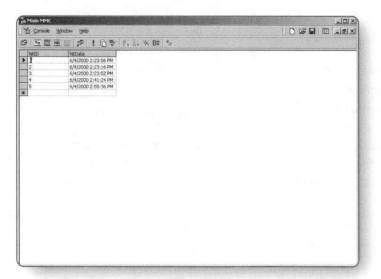

Here are the first few hits recorded in the hits table.

Using Stored Procedures with Parameters

Not only can we create stored procedures that simply execute SQL statements, but we can also pass in parameters to be used in the stored procedures. The ADO Command Object has a collection called the Parameters collection that can be used to accomplish this. There are two ways to pass in parameters to a stored procedure with an ADO Command. There's the hard way and the easy way. Here's the easy way:

```
<%
Dim myCommand
Set myCommand = Server.CreateObject("ADODB.Command")
With myCommand
        .ActiveConnection = myConn
        .CommandType = adCmdStoredProc
        .CommandText = "usp_myProc"
        .Parameters("@parameter1") = "something"
        .Parameters("@paremeter2") = "something else"
        ...

End With
myCommand.Execute
Set myCommand = Nothing
%>
```

In this scenario we simply reference the name of the parameter and set the parameter equal to some value that we want to pass to the stored procedure. While this technique is great for testing, it is not as efficient as the hard method because it has to make extra trips to the database to find the attributes of the parameters. Here's how to do it the hard way:

> **NOTE**
>
> Parameters in SQL Server stored procedures start with the @ symbol.

```
<%
Dim myCommand
Set myCommand = Server.CreateObject("ADODB.Command")
With myCommand
        .ActiveConnection = myConn
        .CommandType = adCmdStoredProc
        .CommandText = "usp_myProc"
        .Parameters.Append .CreateParameter("@parameter1",adVarchar, _
        adParamInput,20,"something")
        .Parameters.Append .CreateParameter("@parameter2",adInteger, _
        adParamInput,,7)
```

```
    ...
End With
myCommand.Execute
Set myCommand = Nothing
%>
```

In this method we Append a parameter to the Parameters collection. The Command Object has a CreateParameter method that can be used to specify all the details of a parameter that is to be passed to a stored procedure. You can declare a variable to hold the parameter and then Append the variable to the Parameters collection if you like. Here is the syntax of the Command.CreateParameter method.

```
Command.CreateParameter([Name],[Type],[Direction],[Size],[Value])
```

The Name is the name of the parameter. Although you can make up whatever name you want for your parameters, I usually name them after the corresponding parameter in the stored procedure. Type is the data type of the parameter, direction specifies whether this is an input parameter, output parameter, or the like. Size is used to specify the size of a variable length data type. Value is the value to be passed to the stored procedure.

Using Parameters

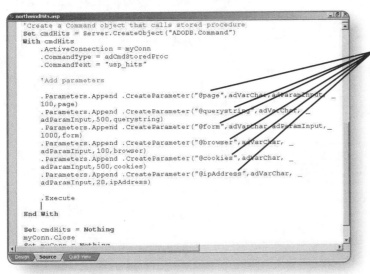

Time to see parameters in action.

As you can see, I've added quite a few parameters to our hit counter. The "@page" parameter sends in the URL of the page. The "@querystring" parameter sends in any query string data, while "@form" sends any form data. "@browser" passes in the "HTTP_USER_AGENT" header that contains browser specifics. Lastly, I pass in any cookies and the client server's IP address using the "@cookies" and "@ipAddress" parameters respectively.

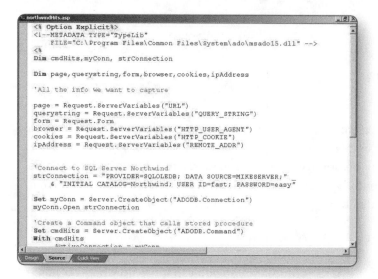

Here is the top of the northwindHits.asp page where I collect all of this data. Remember that the Server.Execute method executes one page in the context of another. So all of the information I'm gathering to send to "usp_hits" will be information from the calling page (the page with the Server.Execute statement in it), not the northwindHits.asp page.

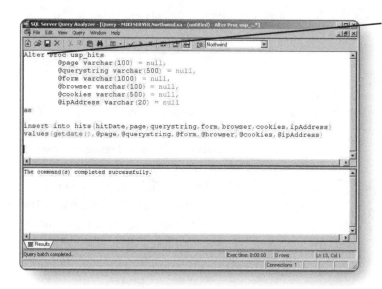

Here is the updated "usp_hits" stored procedure. Notice that I changed the word Create to Alter since I am now altering an existing stored procedure. I also added all of the additional columns to my hits table.

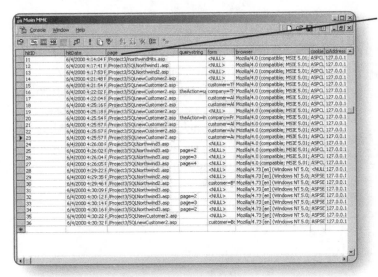

Here are the values in my `hits` table after "hitting" a few pages. Notice that the values of the `page` column indeed reflect the calling page, not the northwindHits.asp page. Such a page hit active server page can be useful for doing analysis of your Web site.

Return Values, Output Parameters, and the Command Object

Not only can Command objects be used to pass parameters into stored procedures, but they can be used to retrieve parameter values as well. There are two types of parameters that can be passed back from a stored procedure: return values and output parameters. If the stored procedure will be sending back a return value, it should be the first parameter in the Parameters collection. Here's the syntax for a return value:

```
MyCommand.CreateParameter("Return Value",adInteger, adParamReturnValue)
```

Output parameters are similar to return values except that they do not have to be the first parameter in the parameters collection. The only difference between an output parameter and a regular input parameter is the direction. For output parameters you use a direction of `adParamOutput`. You can have both a return value and an output parameter in the same Command object. After the Command object has been executed, the output parameters and return values can be referenced through their names to obtain their values.

Using the Command Object

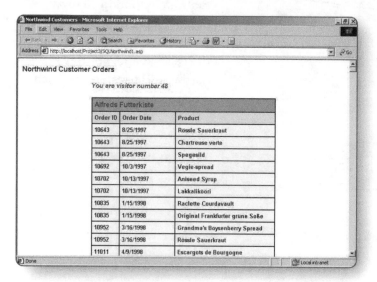

Here is the final version of our hit counter. The only new feature I've added is a return value parameter that passes back the total number of hits. This number is then displayed to the user.

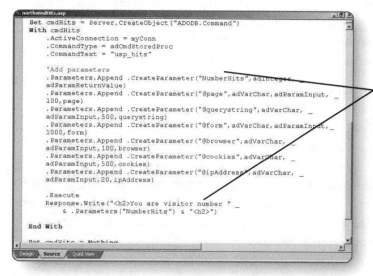

The following code has been added to northwindHits.asp to implement the return value.

It doesn't matter what name you give your return value. I named this one "NumberHits". After the command has been executed, I grab the value from the "NumberHits" parameter and show the user the current number of hits.

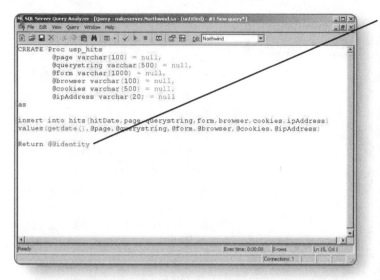

Notice that I don't have to add the return value to the list of parameters accepted by the stored procedure. The only line I added to the stored procedure is the last line that returns the value of the last "hit." Recall that the `hitID` column is an `Identity` column that automatically increments by one every time a row is inserted into the hits table. Well, the last value inserted into an `Identity` column can be referenced through the SQL Server variable named `@@identity`. In this example, I just send that value back as a return value. I could have done the same thing with an output parameter, but you'll see another example that uses output parameters.

Returning Recordsets with the Command Object

As you can see, the Command object is just chock full of features. Not only can it be used to run stored procedures and return values back from stored procedures, but it can return entire recordsets from stored procedures as well. In fact, it can send back more than one recordset! If a command object will be returning a recordset then you need to create a Recordset object to hold it. You'll see this in the following example.

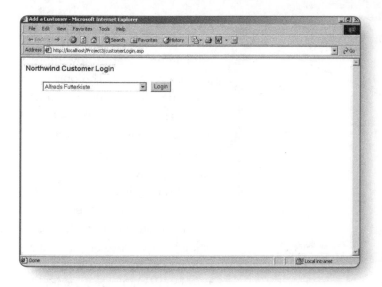

I've created an online storefront for the Northwind Trading Company. Now, mind you, this is not a finished storefront, but it does use all the features of the Command object. This first page, called customerLogin.asp, simply has a drop down list box with all of the customer names in it. To login, a customer selects the name of his or her company and clicks on Login. All this page does is set cookies on the client machine. Normally, this page would be some kind of a "Create Account" page where a user fills in a form. In this case, however, the customers are already in the database. The page posts its information to NorthwindStore.asp where the value of the customer name is retrieved and saved as a cookie.

Here is the Northwind Traders Online Storefront. You'll look at the code behind the pages momentarily. For now you'll just experience the page.

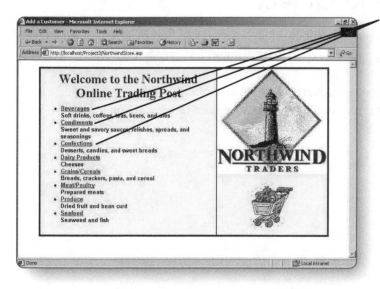

Notice that the page lists the various categories of goods sold at the online trading post. A user can view the products in a category by clicking on the hyperlink.

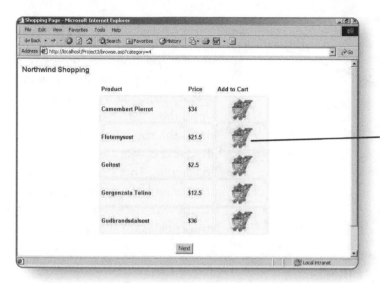

The user can then browse for products in that category on the browse.asp page. Notice that the shopping cart is available for our online shopper.

By clicking on the cart, the specified item is added to the cart.

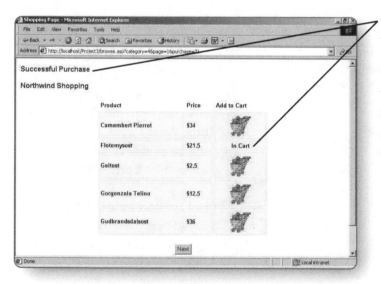

Notice that the shopping cart turns to "In Cart" when the user purchases a product.

That's pretty much it. I didn't build an online checkout stand, so all our shoppers can do is add things to their cart.

Here's the code for NorthwindStore.asp. I won't look at the customerLogin.asp script since you've already seen `GetString` code. Note that I grab the `"customerID"` cookie from the customer using the Request object's cookies collection. That's great if the customer has already logged in. Otherwise we will need to set the cookies for the customer.

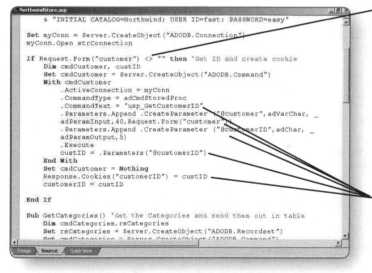

If the customer just logged in, the `Request.Form("customer")` statement will have the `"CompanyName"` of the customer in it because that is what was selected from the drop down list box. What I want, however, is the `"CustomerID"`. To get it, I'll use a stored procedure.

I've created a stored procedure called `"usp_GetCustomerID"` that expects an input parameter called `"@customer"` and an output parameter called `"@customerID."` Notice that I didn't send a value into the `"@customerID"` parameter because it is an output parameter and will be sending back a value. After the command is executed, I get the value from the `"@customerID"` and put it into the variable `"custID."` This variable is then used to send a `"customerID"` cookie back to the client. I also set the variable `"customerID"` equal to `"custID"` because I need to know the `"customerID"` in other parts of the page.

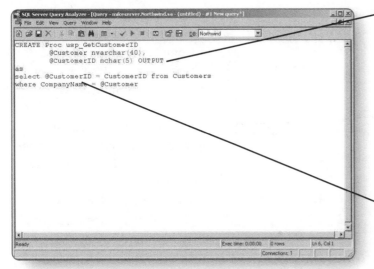

Here is the usp_GetCustomerID stored procedure. Notice that the output parameter does have to be declared in the parameter list (as opposed to return values, which don't have to be declared). The keyword OUTPUT is used to declare that @customerID is an output parameter.

In TSQL you can use this syntax to select a value from a query into a variable. In this case, I'm selecting the customerID into the @customerID output parameter.

Here's the bottom of the NorthwindStore.asp page. You can see that it's all HTML except for the <%GetCategories%> statement. This statement is actually a subroutine that displays all of the categories in the table. Notice that I used <% instead of <%=. The <%= can be used only to output the value of a variable. In this case I'm running a subroutine.

NOTE

I could have made GetCategories() a function that returned an HTML string. In that case I would have just output the string using the <%= ...%> syntax.

```
NorthwindStore.asp
        Set cmdCustomer = Nothing
        Response.Cookies("customerID") = custID
        customerID = custID

    End If

    Sub GetCategories() 'Get the Categories and send them out in table
        Dim cmdCategories, rsCategories
        Set rsCategories = Server.CreateObject("ADODB.Recordset")
        Set cmdCategories = Server.CreateObject("ADODB.Command")
        With cmdCategories
            .ActiveConnection = myConn
            .CommandType = adCmdStoredProc
            .CommandText = "usp_GetCategories"
            Set rsCategories = .Execute
        End With
        Set cmdCategories = Nothing

        If not rsCategories.BOF then 'Write out the Categories
            Response.Write("<ul>")
            Dim CategoryID, CategoryName, Description
            Do While Not rsCategories.EOF
                CategoryID = rsCategories.Fields("categoryID")
                CategoryName = rsCategories.Fields("CategoryName")
                Description = rsCategories.Fields("Description")

                Response.Write("<li><a href = ""browse.asp?category=" _
                    & CategoryID & """>" & CategoryName & "</a>")
                Response.Write("<br>" & Description)
```

Design **Source** Quick View

Here's the `GetCategories()` subroutine. I've created both a Command and a Recordset object because this Command object returns a recordset.

This Command object doesn't have any parameters. All it does is run a stored procedure that returns a recordset. I then set the Recordset object that I created equal to the result of the Command object's `execute` method. After I have my recordset, I can get rid of the Command object.

NOTE

You may have noticed that I didn't set the `CursorType` or `LockType` properties of the recordset object. That's because when you retrieve a recordset from a command object you can only get a forward only, read only recordset.

```
NorthwindStore.asp
        End With
        Set cmdCategories = Nothing

        If not rsCategories.BOF then 'Write out the Categories
            Response.Write("<ul>")
            Dim CategoryID, CategoryName, Description
            Do While Not rsCategories.EOF
                CategoryID = rsCategories.Fields("categoryID")
                CategoryName = rsCategories.Fields("CategoryName")
                Description = rsCategories.Fields("Description")

                Response.Write("<li><a href = ""browse.asp?category=" _
                    & CategoryID & """>" & CategoryName & "</a>")
                Response.Write("<br>" & Description)
                rsCategories.MoveNext
            Loop
            Response.Write("</ul>")
            rsCategories.Close
            Set rsCategories = Nothing
            myConn.Close
            Set myConn = Nothing
        End If
    End Sub

%>
<html>
<head>
<title>Add a Customer</title>
<link rel = "stylesheet" type = "text/css" href = "myStyle.css">
```

Design **Source** Quick View

If the Recordset object has information in it (`BOF` is false), I can display the info. All I'm doing here is creating an unordered list that displays the information from the recordset. Notice that each list item contains a hyperlink that sends the "categoryID" to the browse.asp page. When I'm done looping through the recordset I can write the "`</ul>`" tag and close the recordset and the connection.

Here is the usp_GetCategories stored procedure. All it does is run a Select statement that gets the CategoryName, CategoryID, and Description from the Categories table.

I'll start at the bottom of the browse.asp page. This page has mostly HTML at the bottom as well. Notice the call to the ShowProducts() sub. That sub builds the table and navigation buttons for the page. I close the Connection object at the end of the page.

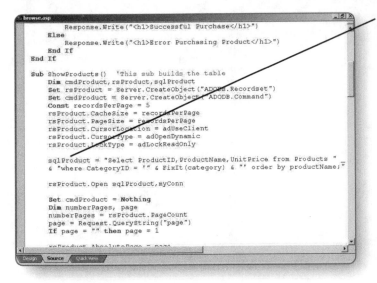

```
        Response.Write("<h1>Successful Purchase</h1>")
    Else
        Response.Write("<h1>Error Purchasing Product</h1>")
    End If
End If

Sub ShowProducts()  'This sub builds the table
    Dim cmdProduct, rsProduct, sqlProduct
    Set rsProduct = Server.CreateObject("ADODB.Recordset")
    Set cmdProduct = Server.CreateObject("ADODB.Command")
    Const recordsPerPage = 5
    rsProduct.CacheSize = recordsPerPage
    rsProduct.PageSize = recordsPerPage
    rsProduct.CursorLocation = adUseClient
    rsProduct.CursorType = adOpenDynamic
    rsProduct.LockType = adLockReadOnly

    sqlProduct = "Select ProductID,ProductName,UnitPrice from Products " _
    & "where CategoryID = '" & FixIt(category) & "' order by productName;"

    rsProduct.Open sqlProduct,myConn

    Set cmdProduct = Nothing
    Dim numberPages, page
    numberPages = rsProduct.PageCount
    page = Request.QueryString("page")
    If page = "" then page = 1

    rsProduct.AbsolutePage = page
```

Next I'll look at the ShowProducts() sub because it builds most of the page. I won't discuss much from this sub because it is essentially just a modification of the recordset paging code you saw in Chapter 9. The sqlProduct statement looks up all the products that have the categoryID passed in from the NorthwindStore.asp page. After opening the recordset and setting up the paging properties of the recordset, I'm ready to write out the table.

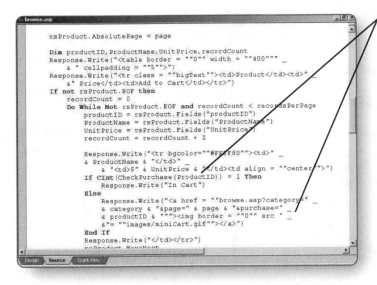

```
    rsProduct.AbsolutePage = page

    Dim productID, ProductName, UnitPrice, recordCount
    Response.Write("<table border = ""0"" width = ""400""" _
    & " cellpadding = ""5"">")
    Response.Write("<tr class = ""bigText""><td>Product</td><td>" _
    & " Price</td><td>Add to Cart</td></tr>")
    If not rsProduct.BOF then
        recordCount = 0
        Do While Not rsProduct.EOF and recordCount < recordsPerPage
            productID = rsProduct.Fields("productID")
            ProductName = rsProduct.Fields("ProductName")
            UnitPrice = rsProduct.Fields("UnitPrice")
            recordCount = recordCount + 1

            Response.Write("<tr bgcolor=""#FEFF80""><td>" _
            & ProductName & "</td>" _
                & "<td>$" & UnitPrice & "</td><td align = ""center"">")
            If CInt(CheckPurchase(ProductID)) = 1 Then
                Response.Write("In Cart")
            Else
                Response.Write("<a href = ""browse.asp?category=" _
                & category & "&page=" & page & "&purchase=" _
                & productID & """><img border = ""0"" src " _
                &"= ""images/miniCart.gif""></a>")
            End If
            Response.Write("</td></tr>")
            rsProduct.MoveNext
```

The code then loops through the recordset printing out table rows. Everything is pretty normal until you get down to the If…End If with the following statement: CInt(CheckPurchase (ProductID)). This statement passes in the productID of the current record to the CheckPurchase() function to find out whether the customer has added this product to their cart already. If they have, the function will return "1" and I write out "In Cart," otherwise I display the shopping cart as a hyperlink. Notice that the hyperlink attached to the shopping cart points to the browse.asp page and passes in the categoryID, productID, and page as query string elements.

```
                         & productID & """><img border = ""0"" src " _
                         &"= ""images/miniCart.gif""></a>")
                 End If
                 Response.Write("</td></tr>")
                 rsProduct.MoveNext
         Loop
     Else
             Response.Write("<tr><td colspan = ""3"">There were no orders" _
                 &"</td></tr>")
     End If

     Response.Write("</table>")

     rsProduct.Close
     Set rsProduct = Nothing


     Response.Write("<form>")
     If CInt(page) > 1 then 'Need to show Previous button
         Response.Write("<input type = ""button"" value " _
             & "= ""Previous"" onclick= ""document.location.href='Browse.asp
     End If

     If CInt(page) < CInt(numberPages) then 'Need to show Next button
         Response.Write(" <input type = ""button"" value = ""Next"" onc
             & "= ""document.location.href='Browse.asp?page=" & page + 1 & "&cat
     End If
     Response.Write("</form>")
```

You've already seen the code that writes out the navigation buttons in Chapter 9 so I won't explain those again.

```
             & "= ""document.location.href='Browse.asp?page=" & page + 1 & "&cat
         End If
         Response.Write("</form>")
 End Sub
 Function FixIt(str)
     FixIt = Replace(str,"'","''")
 End Function
 Function CheckPurchase(theProduct) 'See if customer has purchased product
     Dim cmdCheck, theValue
         Set cmdCheck = Server.CreateObject("ADODB.Command")
         With cmdCheck
             .ActiveConnection = myConn
             .CommandType = adCmdStoredProc
             .CommandText = "usp_CheckPurchase"
             .Parameters.Append .CreateParameter("ReturnValue",adInteger, _
             adParamReturnValue)
             .Parameters.Append .CreateParameter("@customerID",adChar, _
             adParamInput,5,customerID)
             .Parameters.Append .CreateParameter("@productID",adInteger, _
             adParamInput,,theProduct)
             .Execute
             CheckPurchase = .Parameters("ReturnValue")
         End With
         Set cmdCheck = Nothing
 End Function
 Function AddToCart(theProduct)'Customer purchases product
     Dim cmdPurchase
         Set cmdPurchase = Server.CreateObject("ADODB.Command")
         With cmdPurchase
```

Here is the CheckPurchase() function that was referenced from the ShowProducts() subroutine. This procedure has a Command object that plugs parameters into the "usp_CheckPurchase" stored procedure. Notice that it also expects a return value. The stored procedure sends back a "1" if the customer has purchased the product already, or a "0" if not. This value then becomes the return value of the function.

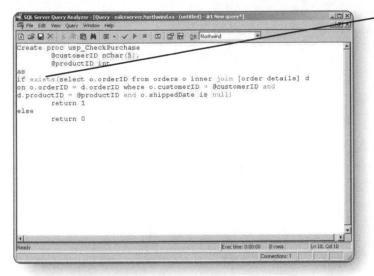

Here is the "usp_CheckPurchase" stored procedure. Notice that it uses the TSQL Exists() function to determine if the Select statement is true. The Exists() function runs the Select statement. If any rows are returned, it will return true; otherwise it returns false. If the customer has purchased the product, I return 1; otherwise I return 0.

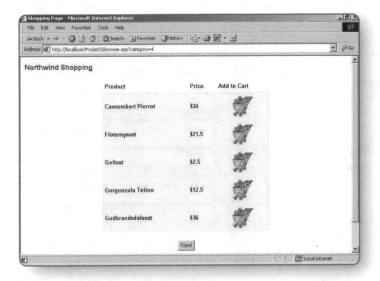

Recall that the customer can purchase a product by clicking on the "shopping cart" next to the product they want to buy.

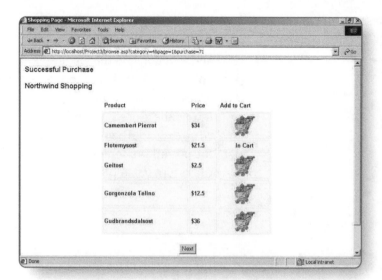

After the product is purchased, the shopping cart turns to the phrase "In Cart." Next you'll see what really goes on when the customer "hits the cart."

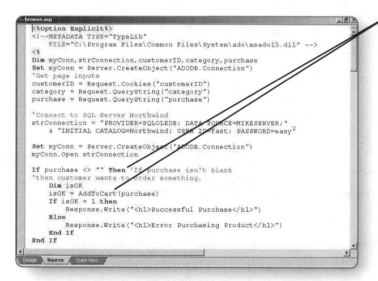

Here is the top of the browse.asp page. Notice the If...End If statement that checks to see whether the purchase variable is blank or not. If it's not blank, the customer "hit the cart." In that case we need to place the order. I do so by calling the AddToCart() which returns a "1" if the purchase was successful or a "0" if it was not. Depending on the outcome, I write out an appropriate response to the customer.

```
browse.asp
          adParamInput,5,customerID)
        .Parameters.Append .CreateParameter("@productID",adInteger, _
        adParamInput,,theProduct)
        .Execute
        CheckPurchase = .Parameters("ReturnValue")
    End With
    Set cmdCheck = Nothing
End Function
Function AddToCart(theProduct)'Customer purchases product
    Dim cmdPurchase
    Set cmdPurchase = Server.CreateObject("ADODB.Command")
    With cmdPurchase
        .ActiveConnection = myConn
        .CommandType = adCmdStoredProc
        .CommandText = "usp_Order"
        .Parameters.Append .CreateParameter("ReturnValue",adInteger, _
        adParamReturnValue)
        .Parameters.Append .CreateParameter("@customerID",adChar, _
        adParamInput,5,customerID)
        .Parameters.Append .CreateParameter("@productID",adInteger, _
        adParamInput,,theProduct)
        .Execute
        AddToCart = .Parameters("ReturnValue")
    End With
    Set cmdPurchase = Nothing
End Function
%>
<html>
<head>

Design    Source    Quick View
```

Finally, the AddToCart() function, the last in a long line of subs and functions on this page. This function is similar to the CheckPurchase() function. It runs the stored procedure "usp_Order". The return value of the stored procedure becomes the return value of the function.

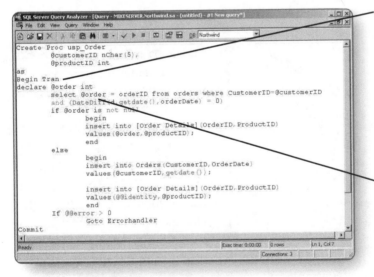

```
SQL Server Query Analyzer - [Query - MIKESERVER.Northwind.sa - (untitled) - #1 New query*]
File Edit View Query Window Help
                                                   DB: Northwind
Create Proc usp_Order
        @customerID nChar(5),
        @productID int
as
Begin Tran
declare @order int
        select @order = orderID from orders where CustomerID=@customerID
        and (DateDiff(d,getdate(),orderDate) = 0)
        if @order is not null
                begin
                insert into [Order Details](OrderID,ProductID)
                values(@order,@productID);
                end
        else
                begin
                insert into Orders(CustomerID,OrderDate)
                values(@customerID,getdate());

                insert into [Order Details](OrderID,ProductID)
                values(@@identity,@productID);
                end
        If @@error > 0
                Goto Errorhandler
Commit

Ready                              Exec time: 0:00:00   0 rows       Ln 1, Col 7
                                                  Connections: 3
```

Here is the "usp_Order" stored procedure. This one is a little fancier than the rest. It uses a transaction to insure that all of the statements succeed or none of them succeed. The Begin Tran statement starts the transaction.

The [Order Details] table is a many to many table that joins the Products table to the Orders table. A customer might purchase several products at once, all of which would have the same "OrderID." I decided that if the customer has an "OrderID" for a particular day then anything else the customer orders on that day will have the same "OrderID." To implement this I declared a variable named "@order." I select into "@order" the "OrderID" from the Orders table that has the same "customerID" that was passed into the stored procedure and was also placed today.

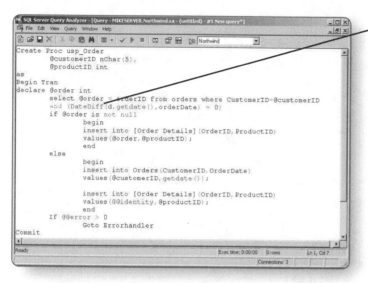

I know this is complicated, but bear with me for a moment. To see if the "OrderID" was for an order placed today I use the TSQL `DateDiff()` function. The first parameter of the function specifies that I want the difference in time to be in days (d). The second parameter is the start date, which would be today, the third parameter is the end date which would be a date in the `Orders` table. If the difference between these two dates is zero then the order must have been placed today.

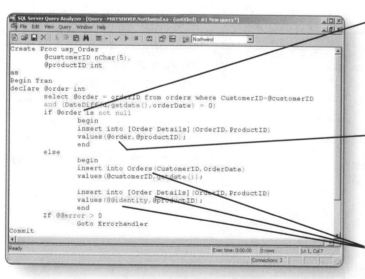

If there is an `OrderID` that fits the query then the `@order` variable will not be `null` but will have the value of today's `OrderID` for the customer.

If that's true then all I have to do is insert a row into the [Order Details] table with the same `OrderID` that is in the `@order` variable.

If there was no `OrderID` returned from the query then this must be the customer's first order of the day. In that case, the new order is inserted into the `Orders` Table. Next the `OrderID` and `ProductID` are inserted into the [Order Details] table. The `@@identity` variable will have the value of the last `orderID` inserted into the `Orders` table.

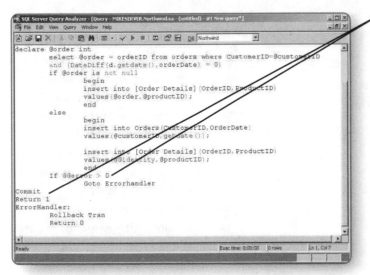

After I'm done with the insert statements, I check the @@Error variable to see whether any errors occurred. The @@Error variable contains the error number of the last error that occurred. If @@Error is greater than zero, then an error occurred and I need to go to the error handler. Otherwise the Commit statement commits the transaction and a "1" is returned to the ADO Command Object.

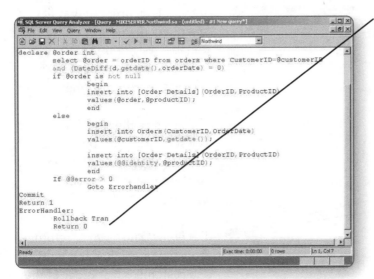

If an error has occurred, the error-handler will rollback the transaction and return "0." When a transaction is rolled back, all the changes that were made by any of the statements in the transaction are discarded. All the tables will remain as they were before the transaction began.

11

Introducing COM/COM+

COM and COM+ are common buzzwords in the world of Web development (especially Microsoft-based Web development). This chapter will give you an introduction to the world of COM (*Component Object Model*). COM+ is an enhanced version of COM that shipped with Windows 2000. I'll use COM/COM+ interchangeably in this chapter. In this chapter, you'll learn how to:

- Create a COM+ Component with Visual Basic
- Create a COM+ Application with Component Services
- Use a COM+ component in an Active Server Page

Creating a COM/COM+ Component

Components are essentially packages of reusable code that are usually written in a programming language other than a scripting language (Windows Scripting Components are an exception to this.) They are based on XML and VBScript. Components can be used to implement what is referred to as a 3-tier or n-tier Web application. A 3-tier application is divided into a *User Services*, or *Presentation* tier, a *Business Services* tier, and a *Data Services* tier. The User Services tier is responsible for the presentation of information to a user. It is the front-end interface to an application. In a Web application the presentation layer is created with Web pages. The User Services tier knows how to hook into the Business Services tier. The Business Services layer is where all of the business logic is supposed to take place. This is where most of the If...Then...Else and Select Case statements are found. This layer knows how to communicate with both the User Services layer and the Data Services layer of the application. The Data Services layer is responsible for managing the information in data sources. These data sources can be a database or other source of information like Exchange or an active directory. Each of these layers can be created using components. Often however, components are used in just one or two of the tiers. In the example in this chapter, the Presentation layer consists of active server pages, the Business Services layer consists of the COM component we'll create, and the Data Services layer consists of several SQL Server stored procedures.

There are several reasons for using components and a three-tier approach to Web applications. One reason is that it breaks up the tasks of creating a Web application. People who are good at presentation can concentrate on getting the web front end the way they want it without worrying about programming the business logic behind the front end. Likewise, programmers writing the business components don't have to know everything about the database or data source that supplies information for the application. Finally, the database experts can work on optimizing the collection and retrieval of data in the data sources. The internal workings of any one of the layers can be changed without breaking the application as long as the interfaces between the layers remain unchanged. A second reason for going with a three-tier model is that it facilitates code reuse. Business components, for example, are often reused in a variety of different applications. You can also have different Presentation layers hook up to the same business components. For example, you might have a Visual Basic form front ends use the same business components as a web front end. Another reason for using components is that they provide greater performance and scalability because they usually consist of precompiled code written with programming languages that are more efficient than scripting languages. The list of reasons for using components and a multi-tier approach to Web applications could go on, but I hope by now you've gotten the idea that it's a good direction to go.

Using Visual Basic to Create a COM+ Component

Now that you have an idea of what a component is we can take a look at how to create one. COM components can be written using a variety of programming languages including Visual Basic, Java, and C++. I'll create one using Visual Basic because it's the easiest language to use. Components created with a lower level programming language like C++ are faster and provide more functionality, but are much more difficult to create. COM Components created with C++ and Visual Basic are compiled into .dll files. Here are the steps to create a DLL with Visual Basic 6.0:

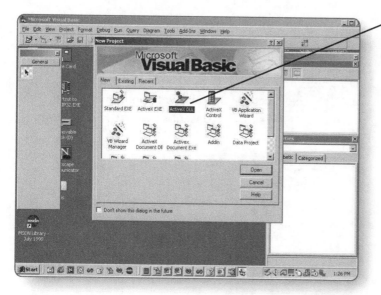

1. Open Visual Basic. You should see a screen that looks like this. Click on the icon that says ActiveX DLL.

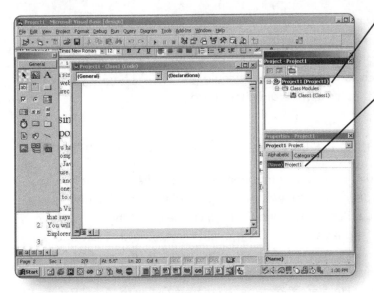

2. You now have a blank project screen. Click on Project1 in the Project Explorer.

3. In the Properties section, change the name of the Project to a one-word name that describes what the project does. I'm using "myProject" as an example.

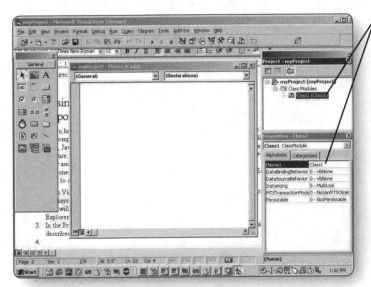

4. Next click on Class1 in the Class Modules folder. Rename the class in the properties window to something that describes what the class does.

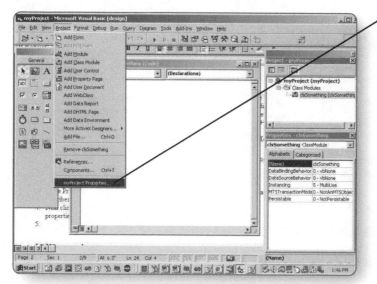

5. Next click on Project on the Menu Bar and click on Properties.

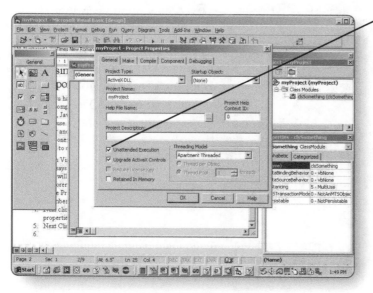

6. I'll use all the default settings except that I'll check the Unattended Execution box. That makes sure that any errors are recorded to the NT Event log rather than putting up a message box on the server. Click on OK.

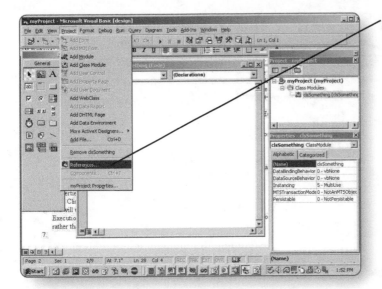

7. Next click on Project, then References.

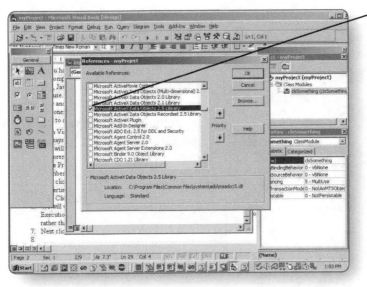

8. A new popup window opens. Scroll down and check the box next to "Microsoft ActiveX Data Objects 2.5 Library." That way you will be able to use ADO in your component. Click on OK.

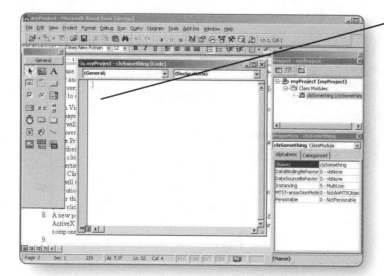

9. At this point you are ready to start coding the class.

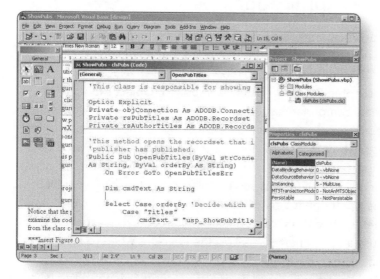

Here is the project that I use as an example in this chapter.

Notice that the project is named "ShowPubs" and the class is named "clsPubs." We'll examine the code later. For now I just want to show you how to create a compiled DLL from the class code.

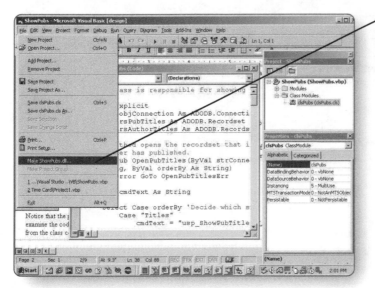

After you've written all your code, click on File on the menu bar, then Make ShowPubs.dll. (The name of your project will show up between Make and .dll.) The machine will then compile your code and make the .dll. You may have to fix a few compilation errors (if you're like most of us) before you get your DLL to compile.

Creating a COM+ Application

When you make your DLL, Visual Basic automatically registers the component on your machine. You could use the component at that point, but it wouldn't really be a COM component. A COM component has to meet the COM specification. As mentioned earlier in the chapter, COM stands for *Component Object Model*. This *model* is a standard for how components should interface with each other and with other programs. We can make our component a COM/COM+ component by making it part of a COM+ application. COM+ applications are managed by Windows 2000 using Microsoft Component Services (this used to be called MTS, Microsoft Transaction Server, in Windows NT 4.0). This service takes care of making your DLL a COM+ component. The Component Services is a component "object broker." As a broker it manages the lifetime of a COM component. It intercepts requests from applications wanting to use a component's services, then decides when to instantiate the requested object and when to destroy it. Component Services can also facilitate the use of components in transactions as well as provide security by controlling who can use the component. Component Services can also pool components created in C++ so an application requesting a particular component can use an instance of the component that is already in memory. When the application is done with the object, the instance goes back into the pool until someone else requests the component. Such pooling increases performance significantly. Unfortunately, components made with Visual Basic don't support object pooling as yet.

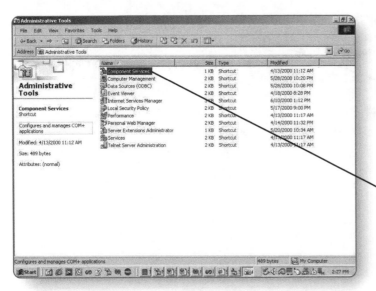

I will demonstrate how to create a COM+ application that uses the DLL that I created in the example. Here are the steps:

1. Click on Start, Settings, Control Panel. Then double-click on Administrative Tools.

2. Double-click on Component Services.

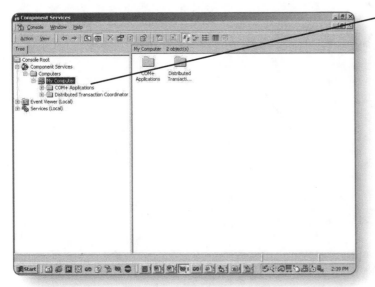

3. Keep expanding the + signs, starting with the one next to Component Services, until you get down to two folders that say COM+ Applications and Distributed Transaction Coordinator. Click on COM+ Applications.

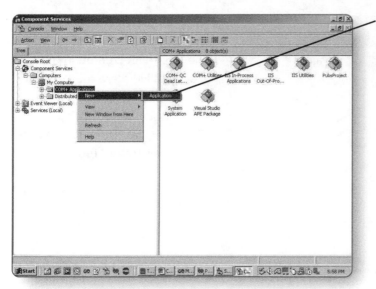

4. Right click on COM+ Applications, put the mouse over New and then click on Application.

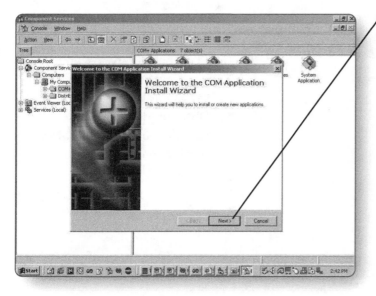

5. This launches a Wizard. Click on Next on the Wizard screen.

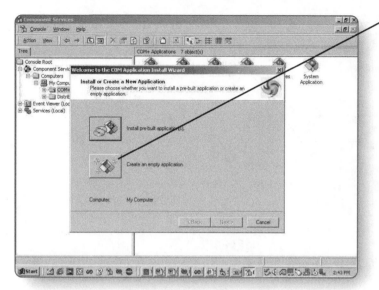

6. Click the button next to "Create an empty application."

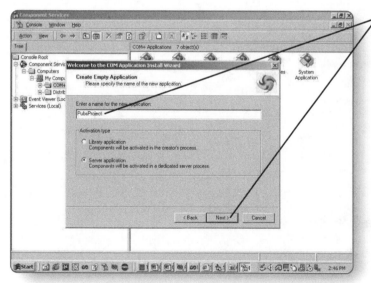

7. Type a name for your application. Leave the activation type at the default setting of Server Application. Click on Next.

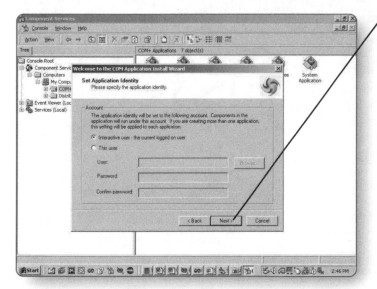

8. Leave the Account setting at Interactive User. Click on Next.

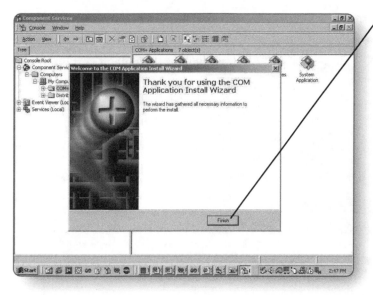

9. Click on Finish.

10. The new application has been created.

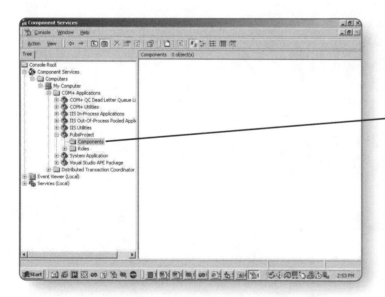

Now that you've created the application, you need to add your component to the application. Follow these steps:

1. Double click on the name of the application. Expand the + sign next to the application name. Mine is named PubsProject. Click on the Components folder.

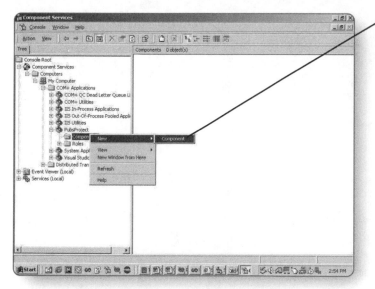

2. Right click on the Components folder. Hold the mouse over New and then click on Component.

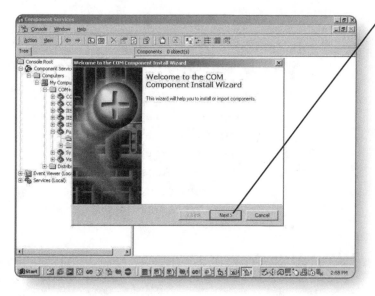

3. This starts yet another Wizard. Click on Next.

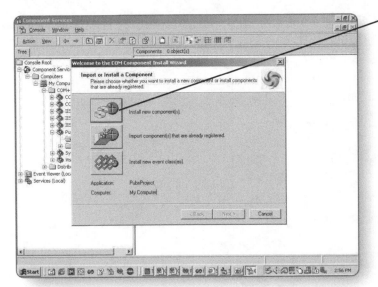

4. Click on the button next to "Install new component(s)."

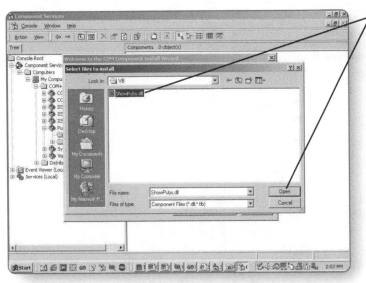

5. Browse for the DLL. It will have the same name as your Visual Basic project and will be in the same directory. Mine is called ShowPubs.dll. Click on Open.

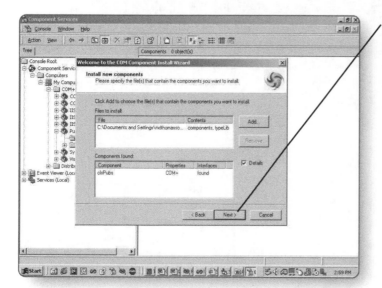

6. Because we're only installing one component for now, click on Next.

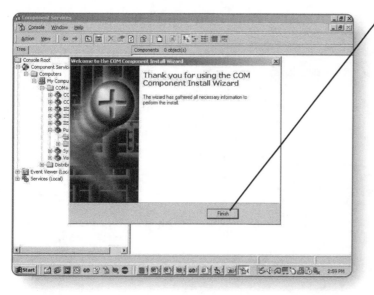

7. Click on Finish.

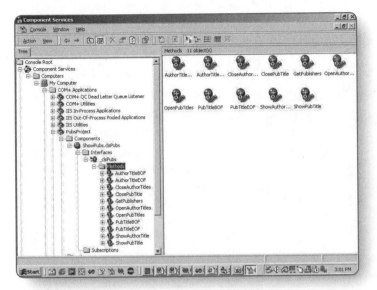

If you expand all of the + signs next to the Components folder you will be able to see the class and all of the methods it supports. You can right click on the component and set all kinds of properties, but we won't do that right now.

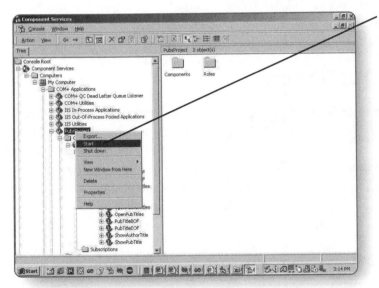

Lastly, we need to start our application. Right-click on the name of the application and click on Start.

At this point the component is ready to use. Your component will now be managed by Component Services.

If you go back and make changes to your Visual Basic project and try to re-make your DLL, you may get an error message that looks something like this:

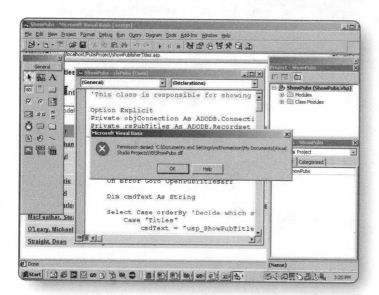

If that happens then you will have to Stop your COM+ application, close Visual InterDev if you have it open, and then make the DLL. When you're done restart the COM+ application.

Using a COM Application

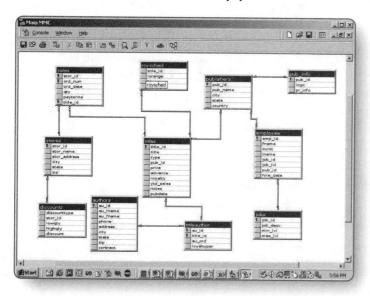

This example makes use of the SQL Server Pubs database. Here is a screen shot of the schema for you to reference during the explanation of the code.

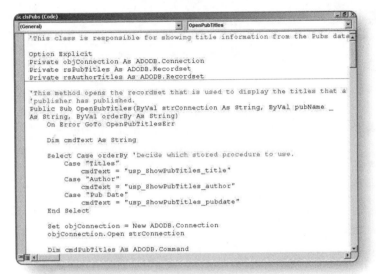

This component was created using Visual Basic 6.0. The code syntax should look familiar to you because Visual Basic is the parent language of VBScript. Remember that VBScript has only one data type, Variant. Visual Basic, on the other hand, has a host of *primitive* data types like String, Boolean, Integer, Date and so on; but it also supports *abstract* data types which can be things like user defined data types or objects.

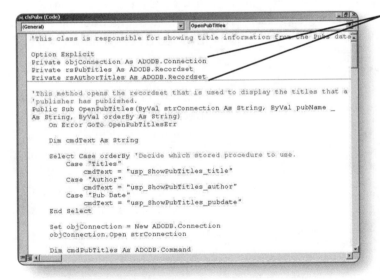

The class `clsPubs` is the main class module in my component. You'll notice that I started by declaring some "private" data members. The `As` keyword is used to specify what data type the variable is. These `Private` variables will be visible only to the procedures in this class. It is not necessary to use the `Class` keyword to create a class in Visual Basic (as we did in VBScript). A module is considered a class.

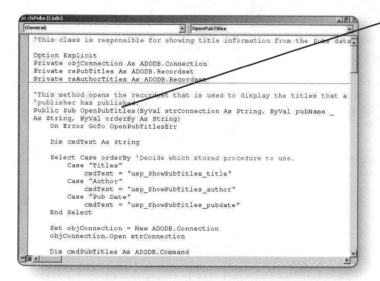

The first procedure in the code is the subroutine OpenPubTitles(). It accepts three String parameters, all of which are passed by value. This subroutine will be used to open a recordset that will contain information about the books that have been published by a particular publishing company.

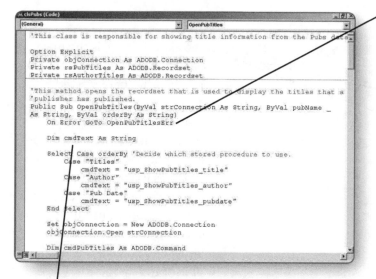

All of the procedures in this class have an On Error GoTo statement at the beginning followed by some error handling at the end. You'll look at the error handler for this sub in a moment. In Visual Basic, you can specify what code should be run if an error occurs in a certain part of the code. In this case, if an error occurs in this procedure the control will be passed to a section of code name OpenPubTitlesErr.

The cmdText variable will be used as the CommandText property of an ADO Command object. The Select Case statement selects a stored procedure to use in the command object based on the value of the "orderBy" parameter passed to the sub. Each of these stored procedures is essentially the same, except for the Order By statement.

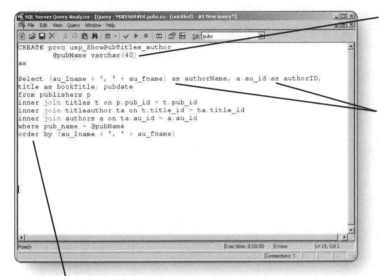

Here is the usp_ShowPubTitles _author stored procedure. It takes the name of a publishing company as a parameter.

The as keyword is used to assign a temporary new name to a column or expression in the Select statement. This stored procedure will return a recordset with four columns: authorName, authorID, BookTitle, and pubdate.

After joining four tables, the recordset (–the Cursor) is ordered by the author names. The only difference between this stored procedure and the other two referred to in the component is the Order By clause.

TIP

It is better to create three different stored procedures than one stored procedure with three Select statements. One reason queries in stored procedures queries run faster than stand-alone queries is that the query can be pre-optimized. If I use conditional logic in the stored procedure (for example, if statements) to determine which Select statement should be run, the stored procedure will not be optimized to the extent it could be. It's better to put the conditional statements in the VB code and let the database be optimized for speed.

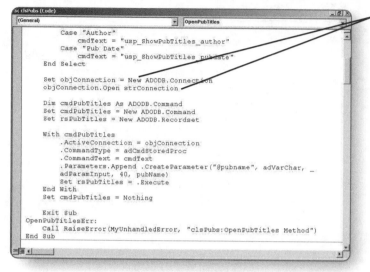

After the `Select Case` statement decides which stored procedure to use as the `CommandType`, you're ready to set up and execute a command object. The first step is to create a connection to the database. I declared the variable `objConnection` to be an ADO Connection in the private data members section at the top of the class. Now I need to actually create the Connection object. In ASP I would have to use the `Server.CreateObject` method.

In VB I can use the `New` keyword to instantiate a Connection object. I open the connection using the connection string specified by the `strConnection` parameter that was passed to the sub.

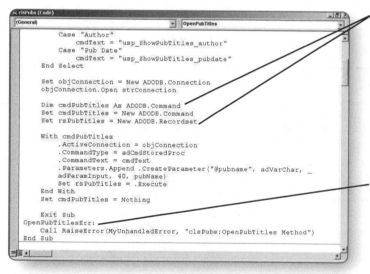

After opening the connection, I create a Command Object and a Recordset Object. The name of the publisher is passed to the stored procedure as a parameter. You've seen this type of code before, so I won't explain it.

Notice the `OpenPubTitlesErr:` that comes at the end of the sub. This is the error-handling segment of code that was specified in the `On Error GoTo` statement at the beginning of the sub. If any errors occur in the procedure at runtime, the code in this error handler will handle the error.

NOTE

I use the Microsoft Visual Modeler to design my components. It's a program that ships with Visual Studio Enterprise Edition. The program allows you to design components visually. After specifying all the methods and properties of a component, the modeler will create the skeleton code for my component in VB. It creates code stubs for every procedure in the component as well as some generic error-handling code. Then all you have to do is fill in the procedure stubs with code. In these examples I just left the generic error-handling code in place. The code calls an error-handling procedure that sends an error message back to the calling code.

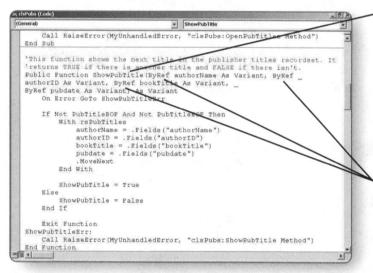

Next comes a function named ShowPubTitle(). This function moves the rsPubTitles recordset forward one record each time it is called. It returns True if the record pointer is not at the end of the recordset and False if it is.

All the parameters passed into the function are passed ByRef. That is because I want the values of the parameters to be changed in the code that called the procedure. You'll see that code when we look at the ASP code later in the chapter.

Notice that I can specify the return type of a function in VB. Since all of these parameters are used in the ASP page, I made them all Variants because that is the only data type that VBScript can use.

The function consists of an If…Else…End If statement. PubTitleBOF and PubTitleEOF are Property Get statements that return the values of rsPubTitles.BOF or rsPubTitles.EOF respectively.

As long as you're not at the end of the recordset, the values of the fields in the recordset are assigned to the parameter variables that were passed to the function. Since these parameters were passed ByRef, the calling code, in this case the ASP code, can use these values.

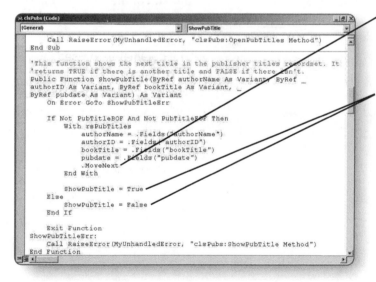

After assigning the values, the record pointer is moved to the next record.

The function returns True if there is another record in the recordset and False if there isn't.

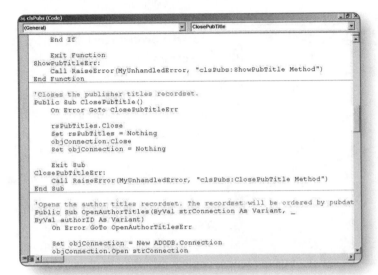

All the `ClosePubTitle()` sub does is close and destroy the `rsPubTitles` recordset and the `objConnection` connection.

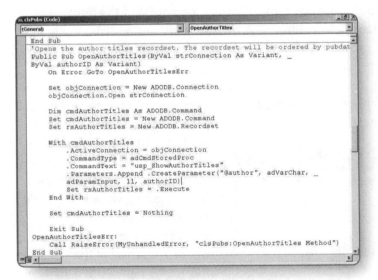

The `OpenAuthorTitles()` subroutine is very similar to the `OpenPubTitles()` sub. It opens a recordset that contains all the books that a particular author has written. I won't explain the code much since it is so similar to what you've already seen.

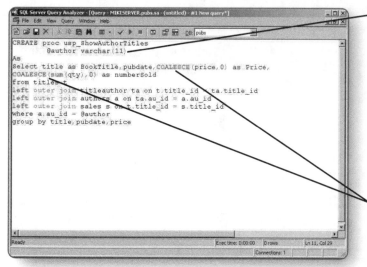

Here is the `usp_ShowAuthorTitles` stored procedure that is used by the command object in this sub. The stored procedure takes one parameter, `@author`, that specifies an `author ID`. It returns a recordset with four columns: `BookTitle`, `pubdate`, `price` and `numberSold`.

The `COALESCE` function is a useful TSQL function. It returns the first non-null value in a comma-separated list of expressions. If all the expressions are null, it returns null. In this `Select` statement I check to see if the `price` column is null; if it is then I replace it with a zero. Likewise, I check to see if the `sum` of the quantity of books sold is null for a particular book (meaning that no copies of the book were sold); if it is then I replace it with a zero. That way the code that's calling the stored procedure will get a recordset back with zeros in it instead of nulls.

These joins use the `Left Outer Join` statement instead of the `Inner Join` statement. The `Inner Join` statement only joins two tables if the join columns are equal. The `Left Outer Join` statement will show all of the columns from the table specified to

the left of the equal sign and return a null value for any missing columns in the recordset if there is no matching value in the table on the right-hand side of the equal sign. I did this because I want to return all of the `titles` in the `Titles` table even if some of them don't have any `authors` or `sales`. Don't get too upset if you don't completely understand. Experiment with the various types of join statements and they will begin to make sense.

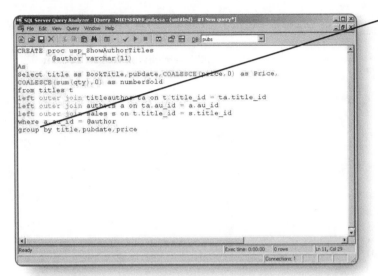

This `Select` statement also uses a `Group By` clause. I used the `Group By` to group the result set by `title`, then by `pubdate`, then by `price`. You have to use a `Group By` statement if you want to use aggregate functions like the `Sum` or `Count` function.

The next procedure is the `ShowAuthorTitle()` function. This function is very similar to the `ShowPubTitle()` function. It is used to move through the author titles recordset and assign values to the parameters that were passed into the function `ByRef`.

```
Else
    ShowAuthorTitle = False
End If

Exit Function
ShowAuthorTitleErr:
    Call RaiseError(MyUnhandledError, "clsPubs:ShowAuthorTitle Method")
End Function

'This closes the author titles recordset.
Public Sub CloseAuthorTitles()
    On Error GoTo CloseAuthorTitlesErr

    rsAuthorTitles.Close
    Set rsAuthorTitles = Nothing
    objConnection.Close
    Set objConnection = Nothing

    Exit Sub
CloseAuthorTitlesErr:
    Call RaiseError(MyUnhandledError, "clsPubs:CloseAuthorTitles Method")
End Sub
Public Function GetPublishers(strConnection) As Variant
    On Error GoTo GetPublishersErr
    Set objConnection = New ADODB.Connection
    objConnection.Open strConnection

    Dim rsPublishers As ADODB.Recordset
```

The `CloseAuthorTitles()` sub is just like the `ClosePubTitles()` sub—it closes the recordset.

```
Exit Sub
CloseAuthorTitlesErr:
    Call RaiseError(MyUnhandledError, "clsPubs:CloseAuthorTitles Method")
End Sub
Public Function GetPublishers(strConnection) As Variant
    On Error GoTo GetPublishersErr
    Set objConnection = New ADODB.Connection
    objConnection.Open strConnection

    Dim rsPublishers As ADODB.Recordset
    Dim cmdPublishers As ADODB.Command
    Set cmdPublishers = New ADODB.Command
    With cmdPublishers
        .ActiveConnection = objConnection
        .CommandType = adCmdStoredProc
        .CommandText = "usp_GetPublishers"
        Set rsPublishers = .Execute
    End With
    Set cmdPublishers = Nothing
    Dim strPublishers
        strPublishers = rsPublishers.GetString(adClipString, , , _
        "<option>")
        strPublishers = "<option>" & Mid(strPublishers, 1, _
        Len(strPublishers) - 8)
        rsPublishers.Close

    Set rsPublishers = Nothing
```

The `GetPublishers()` function returns a string that has a list of the publishers in the database with the `<option>` tag appended to the front of each `pub_name`. This string will become the options in a `<select>` form element. All the stored procedure `usp_GetPublishers` does is get a recordset of sorted publisher names.

```
Public Property Get PubTitleBOF() As Variant
    If rsPubTitles.BOF Then
        PubTitleBOF = True
    Else
        PubTitleBOF = False
    End If
End Property
Public Property Get PubTitleEOF() As Variant
    If rsPubTitles.EOF Then
        PubTitleEOF = True
    Else
        PubTitleEOF = False
    End If
End Property
Public Property Get AuthorTitleBOF() As Variant
    If rsAuthorTitles.BOF Then
        AuthorTitleBOF = True
    Else
        AuthorTitleBOF = False
    End If
End Property
Public Property Get AuthorTitleEOF() As Variant
    If rsAuthorTitles.EOF Then
        AuthorTitleEOF = True
    Else
        AuthorTitleEOF = False
    End If
End Property
```

Finally, we have four `Public Property Get` statements. These properties simply return `True` or `False` depending on whether the `BOF` or `EOF` properties of the underlying recordsets are `True` or `False`. That's it for the code behind the component.

Using a COM/COM+ Component in ASP

Now that you've seen how to create a COM/COM+ component using a tool like Visual Basic you're ready to learn how to use such objects in your ASP applications. This should already be somewhat familiar to you since we've been using ADO since Chapter 8. ADO is made up of COM components.

Creating Objects

There are two methods of instantiating COM/COM+ objects from an active server page. One uses the Server object's `CreateObject` method and the other uses an `<Object>` tag.

Server.CreateObject

To create an object using the `CreateObject` method, use the following syntax:

```
Set myObject = Server.CreateObject("ProjectName.ClassName")
```

This assigns a reference to the object to the variable `myObject`. The `ProjectName` is the name of the Visual Basic project and the `ClassName` is the name of the class (for components created with Visual Basic). Many third party components are identified by the name of the company followed by a period followed by the name of the component.

Objects created using the `CreateObject` method are instantiated as soon as the active server page loads.

<Object>

The `<object>` tag is placed in the HTML code of a page. To create an object using the `<object>` tag, use the following syntax:

```
<Object id = "myObject" Runat = "server" progID = "ProjectName.ClassName">
</Object>
```

The primary difference between the `CreateObject` method and the `<Object>` tag is that the `CreateObject` method will instantiate the object when the page loads. The `<object>` tag will not create the object until the object is referenced in the code. Objects created with the `CreateObject` method can be removed from Application and Session variables since they are part of the Contents collection. Objects created with the `<object>` tag are static objects and cannot be removed from Application or Session objects. I always use the `CreateObject` method to create server-side objects.

Using Components

You've already seen the code for the component, now you're ready for the ASP code that uses the component. Consider the showPublisherTitles.asp active server page.

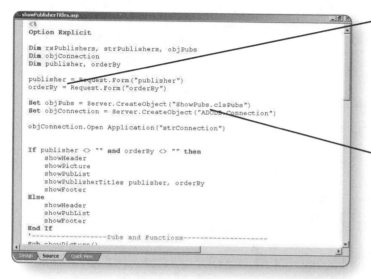

After the variable declarations at the top of the page, I fetch the values of two form elements, `publisher` and `orderBy`. You will take a look at the form further down the page.

Next I create two objects. `objPubs` is an instance of the class I created in Visual Basic, `objConnection` is an ADO connection object. I created these objects here because I will be using them throughout the page. Notice that the `Server.CreateObject` method creates the `objPubs` object by passing in the name of the VB Project, followed by a period, followed by the name of the VB class that contains the definition of the object I want to create. My project is named "`ShowPubs`" and the class is named "`clsPubs`."

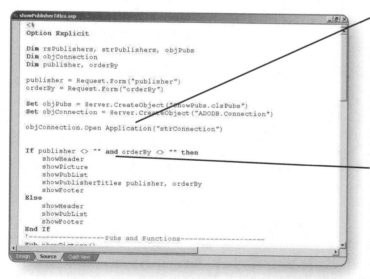

Notice that the connection object I created is opened using the connection string I have saved in the application variable `Application("strConnection")`. This variable is housed in the Global.asa file.

The `If…Else…End If` statement checks to see if the "`publisher`" and "`orderBy`" variables have information in them. If they do, the first series of procedures is called, otherwise the second series is called. This page makes heavy use of procedures. I'll assume that this is the first time I've loaded the page. In that case the "`publisher`" and "`orderBy`" variables will be blank because the form has not been submitted yet. The procedures after the `Else` statement will be run `showHeader()`, `showPubList()` and `showFooter()`. I'll examine those subs now.

```
showPublisherTitles.asp*                                                    _|_|X|
                    & "<td>" & bookTitle & "</td>" _
                    & "<td>" & pubdate & "</td></tr>")
            Loop
            objPubs.ClosePubTitle
            Response.Write ("</table>")
        End If
        Set objPubs = Nothing

End Sub
Sub showHeader()
    Response.Write ("<html><head><title>Show Publisher Titles</title>")
    Response.Write ("<link rel = ""stylesheet"" type = ""text/css""" _
    & "href = ""myStyle.css"">"</head>")
    Response.Write ("<body bgcolor = ""white"">")
    Response.Write ("<h1>Publisher Titles</h1>")
End Sub
Sub showFooter()
    Response.Write ("</body></html>")
End Sub
Sub showPubList()
    'Get list of publishers for <select>
    Dim strPublishers
    strPublishers = objPubs.GetPublishers(Application("strConnection"))

    Response.Write ("<form method = ""post"" name = ""form1""" _
    & " action = ""showPublisherTitles.asp"">")
    Response.Write ("Publisher:<select name = ""publisher""" _
    & " onchange = ""document.form1.submit()"">")
    Response.Write("<option>" & publisher)
```
```
Design   Source   Quick View
```

The showHeader() and showFooter() subs are easy enough—they simply write out the beginning and ending of the HTML page respectively.

—This sub, showPubList(), starts with the declaration of the string strPublishers. I then set this string equal to the return value of the objPubs.GetPublishers()

```
showPublisherTitles.asp                                                    _|_|X|
        Response.Write ("<body bgcolor = ""white"">")
        Response.Write ("<h1>Publisher Titles</h1>")
    End Sub
    Sub showFooter()
        Response.Write ("</body></html>")
    End Sub
    Sub showPubList()
        'Get list of publishers for <select>
        Dim strPublishers
        strPublishers = objPubs.GetPublishers(Application("strConnection"))

        Response.Write ("<form method = ""post"" name = ""form1""" _
        & " action = ""showPublisherTitles.asp"">")
        Response.Write ("Publisher:<select name = ""publisher""" _
        & " onchange = ""document.form1.submit()"">")
        Response.Write ("<option>" & publisher)
        Response.Write (strPublishers)
        Response.Write ("</select>")
        Response.Write (" Order By: <select name = ""orderBy""" _
        & " onchange = ""document.form1.submit()"">")
        Response.Write ("<option>" & orderBy)
        Response.Write ("<option>Titles<option>Author<option>Pub Date")
        Response.Write ("</select>")
        Response.Write ("</form>")
    End Sub
    Set objPubs = Nothing
    Set objConnection = Nothing
%>
```
```
Design   Source   Quick View
```

function. Remember from the VB code that the GetPublishers() function gets the list of publisher names from the Pubs database and sticks an <option> tag in front of each one of them. This string of publisher names is sent back from the function and is stored in the local variable strPublishers.

Notice that I pass in the Application("strConnection") variable to the function. It uses that to establish a connection to the database. I pass in the connection strings to the component rather than hard-coding connection strings in the component. That way I can change the connection string to point at a different database (like a test database) whenever I want.

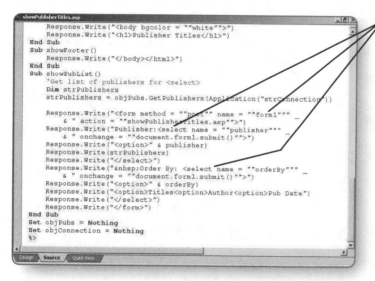

```
- showPublisherTitles.asp                                                    _|8|X|
            Response.Write ("<body bgcolor = ""white"">")
            Response.Write ("<h1>Publisher Titles</h1>")
    End Sub
    Sub showFooter()
            Response.Write ("</body></html>")
    End Sub
    Sub showPubList ()
            'Get list of publishers for <select>
            Dim strPublishers
            strPublishers = objPubs.GetPublishers (Application ("strConnection"))

            Response.Write ("<form method = ""post"" name = ""form1"""  _
                & " action = ""showPublisherTitles.asp"">")
            Response.Write ("Publisher:<select name = ""publisher"""  _
                & " onchange = ""document.form1.submit()"">")
            Response.Write ("<option>" & publisher)
            Response.Write (strPublishers)
            Response.Write ("</select>")
            Response.Write (" Order By: <select name = ""orderBy"""  _
                & " onchange = ""document.form1.submit()"">")
            Response.Write ("<option>" & orderBy)
            Response.Write ("<option>Titles<option>Author<option>Pub Date")
            Response.Write ("</select>")
            Response.Write ("</form>")
    End Sub
    Set objPubs = Nothing
    Set objConnection = Nothing
    %>

   Design   Source   Quick View
```

The code goes on to create a form named form1 with two <select> statements, one named "publisher" and the other named "orderBy". The "publisher" <select> statement gets its <option> tags from the strPublishers variable. I hard-coded the <option> tags for the "orderBy" <select>. Notice that I used the JavaScript onchange event on both <select> tags to cause the form to be resubmitted whenever either of them is changed. That summarizes what would happen when the page is first loaded and the form has not yet been submitted. Here's what the page would look like so far.

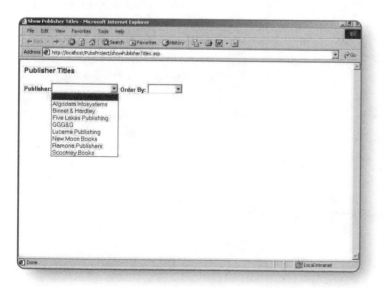

Our page is up and our <select> tag is full of authors. Now we'll look at the code that runs when the form is submitted.

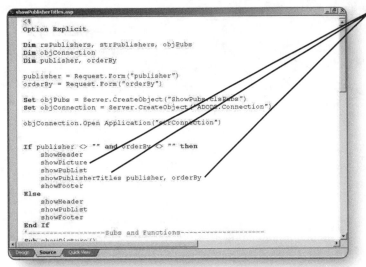

If the form has been submitted and both `publisher` and `orderBy` have values, the top five procedures in the `If...Else...End If` statement will be executed. You've already seen the `showHeader()`, `showPubList()` and `showFooter()` procedures. Now you'll take a look at the `showPicture()` and `showPublisherTitles()` procedures.

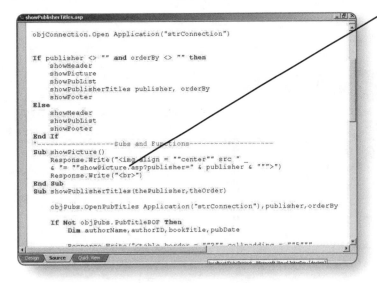

The `showPicture()` sub is easy enough. All it does is write out an image tag. But wait...the `src` attribute of the image tag is different! It's an active server page! Indeed, the source of this picture is showPicture.asp, with the publisher name appended on as a query string. I'll look at that page briefly.

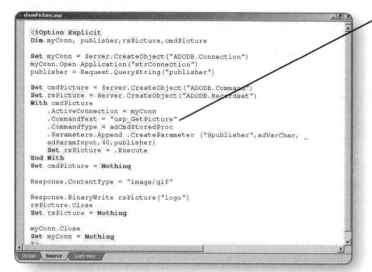

The page is straightforward. It uses a command object to send the `publisher` variable into a stored procedure named `usp_GetPicture`.

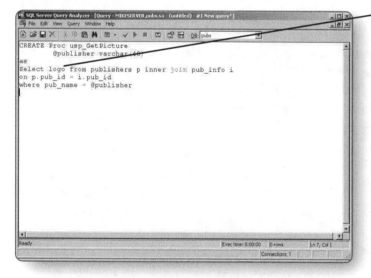

All the `usp_GetPicture` stored procedure does is `Select` the logo column from the `pub_info` table that corresponds to the publisher name that was passed in as a parameter.

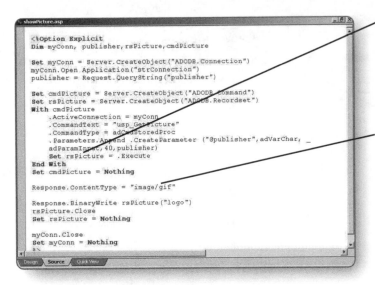

```
showPicture.asp
<%Option Explicit
Dim myConn, publisher, rsPicture, cmdPicture

Set myConn = Server.CreateObject("ADODB.Connection")
myConn.Open Application("strConnection")
publisher = Request.QueryString("publisher")

Set cmdPicture = Server.CreateObject("ADODB.Command")
Set rsPicture = Server.CreateObject("ADODB.Recordset")
With cmdPicture
    .ActiveConnection = myConn
    .CommandText = "usp_GetPicture"
    .CommandType = adCmdStoredProc
    .Parameters.Append .CreateParameter ("@publisher", adVarChar, _
    adParamInput, 40, publisher)
    Set rsPicture = .Execute
End With
Set cmdPicture = Nothing

Response.ContentType = "image/gif"

Response.BinaryWrite rsPicture("logo")
rsPicture.Close
Set rsPicture = Nothing

myConn.Close
Set myConn = Nothing
%>
Design   Source   Quick View
```

The recordset that comes back from the command object is put in the rsPicture recordset. There should only be one picture in the recordset.

Next, I set the page content type equal to "image/gif" since the logo is a .gif file.

NOTE

This example uses image files that are stored in the database. Storing images in databases is not as efficient as storing them in directories in the file system. In most cases your best off to store images in the file system and just store the name of the image file in the database. You can then retrieve the name of the image file from the database and use that as the src of an <img> tag.

```
showPicture.asp
<%Option Explicit
Dim myConn, publisher, rsPicture, cmdPicture

Set myConn = Server.CreateObject("ADODB.Connection")
myConn.Open Application("strConnection")
publisher = Request.QueryString("publisher")

Set cmdPicture = Server.CreateObject("ADODB.Command")
Set rsPicture = Server.CreateObject("ADODB.Recordset")
With cmdPicture
    .ActiveConnection = myConn
    .CommandText = "usp_GetPicture"
    .CommandType = adCmdStoredProc
    .Parameters.Append .CreateParameter ("@publisher", adVarChar, _
    adParamInput, 40, publisher)
    Set rsPicture = .Execute
End With
Set cmdPicture = Nothing

Response.ContentType = "image/gif"

Response.BinaryWrite rsPicture("logo")
rsPicture.Close
Set rsPicture = Nothing

myConn.Close
Set myConn = Nothing
%>
Design   Source   Quick View
```

Finally, I use the Response.BinaryWrite method of the Response Object to write the picture out to the client. I'm showing you this because I promised that I would way back in the beginning of the book.

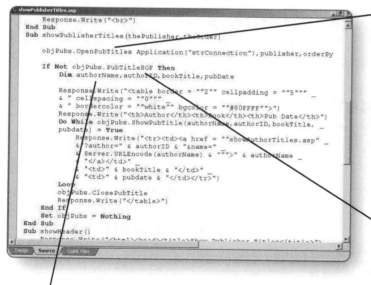

```
showPublisherTitles.asp
objConnection.Open Application("strConnection")

If publisher <> "" and orderBy <> "" then
    showHeader
    showPicture
    showPubList
    showPublisherTitles publisher, orderBy
    showFooter
Else
    showHeader
    showPubList
    showFooter
End If
'------------------Subs and Functions--------------------
Sub showPicture()
    Response.Write("<img align = ""center"" src "
    & "= ""showPicture.asp?publisher=" & publisher & """>")
    Response.Write("<br>")
End Sub
Sub showPublisherTitles(thePublisher,theOrder)

    objPubs.OpenPubTitles Application("strConnection"),publisher,orderBy

    If Not objPubs.PubTitleBOF Then
        Dim authorName,authorID,bookTitle,pubDate
```

That takes care of the showPicture() sub. Now I'll consider the showPublisherTitles() procedure. Before you leave this screen shot, notice that I pass the publisher and orderBy variables into the sub as arguments.

```
showPublisherTitles.asp
    Response.Write("<br>")
End Sub
Sub showPublisherTitles(thePublisher,theOrder)

    objPubs.OpenPubTitles Application("strConnection"),publisher,orderBy

    If Not objPubs.PubTitleBOF Then
        Dim authorName,authorID,bookTitle,pubDate

        Response.Write("<table border = ""2"" cellpadding = ""5"""
    & " cellspacing = ""0"""
    & " bordercolor = ""white"" bgcolor = ""#80FFFF"">")
        Response.Write("<th>Author</th><th>Book</th><th>Pub Date</th>")
        Do While objPubs.ShowPubTitle(authorName,authorID,bookTitle,
    pubdate) = True
            Response.Write("<tr><td><a href = ""showAuthorTitles.asp"""
    & "?author=" & authorID & "&name="
    & Server.URLEncode(authorName) & """>" & authorName
    & "</a></td>"
    & "<td>" & bookTitle & "</td>"
    & "<td>" & pubdate & "</td></tr>")
        Loop
        objPubs.ClosePubTitle
        Response.Write("</table>")
    End If
    Set objPubs = Nothing
End Sub
Sub showHeader()
    Response.Write("<html><head><title>Show Publisher Titles</title>")
```

This sub builds a table that contains information about the books that a particular publisher has published. The procedure starts by calling the component's OpenPubTitles() procedure, which takes three arguments: a connection string, a publisher name and an order by specification.

I next check the PubTitleBOF property of the object to see if the recordset that was opened has any records in it.

If there are records in the recordset, I declare four variables: authorName, authorID, bookTitle and pubDate.

```
showPublisherTitles.asp
          Response.Write ("<br>")
     End Sub
     Sub showPublisherTitles(thePublisher,theOrder)

          objPubs.OpenPubTitles Application("strConnection"),publisher,orderBy

          If Not objPubs.PubTitleBOF Then
               Dim authorName,authorID,bookTitle,pubDate

               Response.Write("<table border = ""2"" cellpadding = ""5""" _
               & " cellspacing = ""0""" _
               & " bordercolor = ""white"" bgcolor = ""#80FFFF"">")
               Response.Write("<th>Author</th><th>Book</th><th>Pub Date</th>")
               Do While objPubs.ShowPubTitle(authorName,authorID,bookTitle, _
               pubdate) = True
                    Response.Write("<tr><td><a href = ""showAuthorTitles.asp" _
                    &"?author=" & authorID & "&name=" _
                    & Server.URLEncode(authorName) & """>" & authorName _
                    & "</a></td>" _
                    & "<td>" & bookTitle & "</td>" _
                    & "<td>" & pubdate & "</td></tr>")
               Loop
               objPubs.ClosePubTitle
               Response.Write("</table>")
          End If
          Set objPubs = Nothing
     End Sub
     Sub showHeader()
          Response.Write("<html><head><title>Show Publisher Titles</title>")
```

After that I write out the opening `<table>` tag and some table headings, `<th>`.

Next comes the "power code" of the page. I create a loop that loops as long as the objPubs function ShowPubTitle() returns true. Recall that in the VB code where the component is defined that this procedure takes four arguments passed ByRef. I pass in the four variables that I created. The values of these variables will be changed by the VB function in the component because they are passed ByRef.

```
showPublisherTitles.asp
          Response.Write ("<br>")
     End Sub
     Sub showPublisherTitles(thePublisher,theOrder)

          objPubs.OpenPubTitles Application("strConnection"),publisher,orderBy

          If Not objPubs.PubTitleBOF Then
               Dim authorName,authorID,bookTitle,pubDate

               Response.Write("<table border = ""2"" cellpadding = ""5""" _
               & " cellspacing = ""0""" _
               & " bordercolor = ""white"" bgcolor = ""#80FFFF"">")
               Response.Write("<th>Author</th><th>Book</th><th>Pub Date</th>")
               Do While objPubs.ShowPubTitle(authorName,authorID,bookTitle, _
               pubdate) = True
                    Response.Write("<tr><td><a href = ""showAuthorTitles.asp" _
                    &"?author=" & authorID & "&name=" _
                    & Server.URLEncode(authorName) & """>" & authorName _
                    & "</a></td>" _
                    & "<td>" & bookTitle & "</td>" _
                    & "<td>" & pubdate & "</td></tr>")
               Loop
               objPubs.ClosePubTitle
               Response.Write("</table>")
          End If
          Set objPubs = Nothing
     End Sub
     Sub showHeader()
          Response.Write("<html><head><title>Show Publisher Titles</title>")
```

Then all I have to do is write out a `<tr>` tag with the values of the variables displayed in the appropriate places. The values will change as the ShowPubTitle() method moves through the recordset it is using. When it reaches the end of the recordset, the function will return False and the loop will end. At that point I can close the object, close the table, and finish off the sub. Let's see what this code looks like in action.

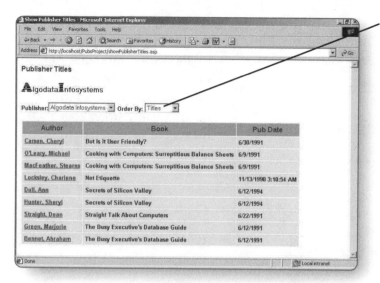

Voilà! Notice that the publisher's logo was successfully extracted from the database and displayed on the page. Furthermore, the table shows all of the books that the publisher has published. In this case they are ordered by "Titles."

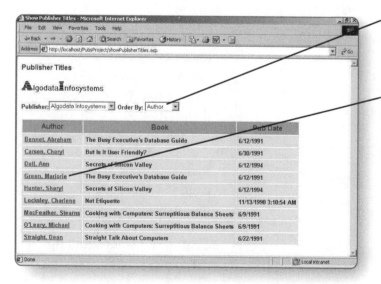

Just to show you that it works, the same information is now ordered by "Author."

You'll notice that I made all of the authors' names hyperlinks. This takes us to the final code in this example.

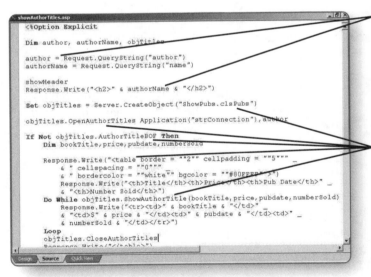

```
showPublisherTitles.asp
        Response.Write("<br>")
End Sub
Sub showPublisherTitles(thePublisher,theOrder)

    objPubs.OpenPubTitles Application("strConnection"),publisher,orderBy

    If Not objPubs.PubTitleBOF Then
        Dim authorName, authorID, bookTitle, pubDate

        Response.Write("<table border = ""2"" cellpadding = ""5""" _
        & " cellspacing = ""0"""
        & " bordercolor = ""white"" bgcolor = ""#80FFFF"">")
        Response.Write("<th>Author</th><th>Book</th><th>Pub Date</th>")
        Do While objPubs.ShowPubTitle(authorName,authorID,bookTitle, _
        pubdate) = True
            Response.Write("<tr><td><a href = ""showAuthorTitles.asp" _
            &"?author=" & authorID & "&name="
            & Server.URLEncode(authorName) & """>" & authorName _
            & "</a></td>" _
            & "<td>" & bookTitle & "</td>" _
            & "<td>" & pubdate & "</td></tr>")
        Loop
        objPubs.ClosePubTitle
        Response.Write("</table>")
    End If
    Set objPubs = Nothing
End Sub
Sub showHeader()
    Response.Write("<html><head><title>Show Publisher Titles</title>")
```

As you can see, the author name is used as a hyperlink that points to the showAuthorTitles.asp page. The `authorID` and `authorName` are passed to the page as query string elements. Here's the showAuthorTitles.asp page.

```
showAuthorTitles.asp
<%Option Explicit

Dim author, authorName, objTitles

author = Request.QueryString("author")
authorName = Request.QueryString("name")

showHeader
Response.Write("<h2>" & authorName & "</h2>")

Set objTitles = Server.CreateObject("ShowPubs.clsPubs")

objTitles.OpenAuthorTitles Application("strConnection"),author

If Not objTitles.AuthorTitleBOF Then
    Dim bookTitle,price,pubdate,numberSold

    Response.Write("<table border = ""2"" cellpadding = ""5""" _
    & " cellspacing = ""0"""
    & " bordercolor = ""white"" bgcolor = ""#80FFFF"">")
    Response.Write("<th>Title</th><th>Price</th><th>Pub Date</th>" _
    & "<th>Number Sold</th>")
    Do While objTitles.ShowAuthorTitle(bookTitle,price,pubdate,numberSold)
        Response.Write("<tr><td>" & bookTitle & "</td>" _
        & "<td>$" & price & "</td><td>" & pubdate & "</td><td>" _
        & numberSold & "</td></tr>")
    Loop
    objTitles.CloseAuthorTitles
    Response.Write("</table>")
```

The query string elements are retrieved into local variables. Next the `showHeader()` procedure writes the top of the HTML page. The `authorName` is then written to the page.

The rest of the code uses the same technique as the last page so I won't spend a lot of time explaining it. First, an instance of the VB class is created and assigned to the variable `objTitles`. The `OpenAuthorTitles()` method opens the author titles recordset. After checking the `AuthorTitleBOF` property to see if the recordset has data, I write out a table using the `ShowAuthorTitle()` method of the class. When all's done, I close everything out.

```
showAuthorTitles.asp
                & " bordercolor = ""white"" bgcolor = ""#80FFFF"">")
        Response.Write("<th>Title</th><th>Price</th><th>Pub Date</th>" _
                & "<th>Number Sold</th>")
    Do While objTitles.ShowAuthorTitle(bookTitle,price,pubdate,numberSold)
        Response.Write("<tr><td>" & bookTitle & "</td>" _
        & "<td>$" & price & "</td><td>" & pubdate & "</td><td>" _
        & numberSold & "</td></tr>")
    Loop
    objTitles.CloseAuthorTitles
    Response.Write("</table>")
Else
        Response.Write("<h2>This author doesn't have any titles.</h2>")
End If
Set objTitles = Nothing
showFooter
'-----------------Procedures------------------
Sub showHeader()
    Response.Write("<html><head><title>Show Author Titles</title>")
    Response.Write("<link rel = ""stylesheet"" type = ""text/css""" _
    & "href = ""myStyle.css"">")</head>")
    Response.Write("<body bgcolor = ""white"">")
    Response.Write("<h1>Author Titles</h1>")
End Sub
Sub showFooter()
    Response.Write("<br><a href = ""javascript:history.back()"">Back</a>")
    Response.Write("</body></html>")
End Sub
%>
```

Here's the bottom of the page for your viewing pleasure.

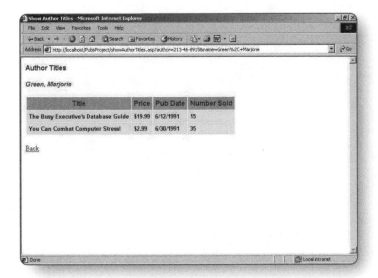

This page is displayed whenever you click on one of the author's names in the showPublisherTitles.asp page.

12

Transactional COM+ Components

You've already seen some examples of stored procedures that use transactions. Recall that a transaction is simply a series of changes (usually to a database) that either succeed or fail as a group. If every change in the group is made successfully, the transaction commits. If any one change fails, all the changes made by the group are rolled back. COM+ Services allows you to create transactions that involve one or more components as well as one or more active server pages (by using `Server.Execute` or `Server.Transfer`). In this chapter, you'll learn how to:

- Create a transactional component in Visual Basic
- Add the component to a COM+ application
- Use the transactional component in an ASP application

Creating a Transactional Component in Visual Basic

A transactional component can participate in COM+ transactions. As such, any changes made to a data source by a transactional component can be committed or rolled back by COM+ services depending on whether the transaction succeeded or failed. Here's how to make a transactional component.

Project Settings

There are a few additional project settings that you'll have to make if you are going to make a component transactional.

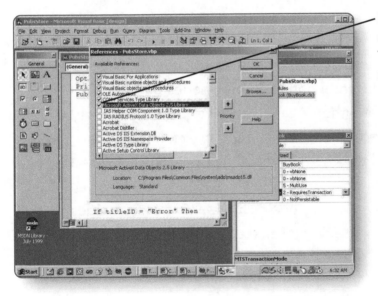

First, you need to include a reference to the COM+ Services Type Library in addition to referencing ADO.

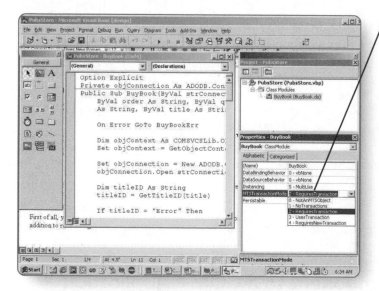

The second thing you have to do is set the MTS Transaction Mode for the class to Requires Transaction. Remember that COM+ Services used to be called "Microsoft Transaction Server (MTS)". I'm sure that the new terminology will be reflected in the next release of Visual Studio.

Transactional Code

There's really not much additional code required to make a component transactional. It only requires that you add one object to the equation, the ObjectContext Object. The ObjectContext Object allows a component to participate in a COM+ Services transaction. It's a good idea to put an instance of the ObjectContext Object in every method in a transactional class. Here are the steps you need to take to create and use the ObjectContext Object.

1. Declare a variable that will reference the object. This is done by declaring a variable that is of type COMSVCSLib.ObjectContext.

```
Dim objContext As COMSVCSLib.ObjectContext
```

2. Use the GetObjectContext() method to obtain an ObjectContext object from COM+. Make the ObjectContext variable you created reference an ObjectContext object.

```
Set objContext = GetObjectContext()
```

3. Vote on the outcome of the transaction using `SetComplete` or `SetAbort`. If everything worked in the method it should vote for the transaction to commit, otherwise it should vote for a rollback of the transaction.

```
objContext.SetComplete 'Vote for commit
```

Or

```
objContext.SetAbort 'Vote for rollback
```

4. Destroy the ObjectContext object.

```
Set objContext = Nothing
```

Adding the Component to a COM+ Application

You've already seen how to add a component to a COM+ application. Adding a transactional component is done in the same way. After you've added the component, however, there are a few property changes that you need to make.

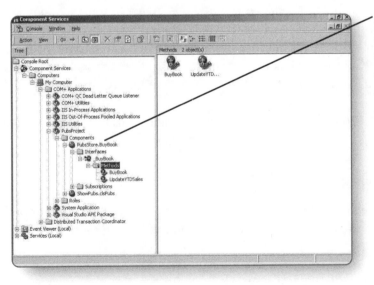

As you can see, I've already added the component that I created in the example for this chapter to the PubsProject COM+ application.

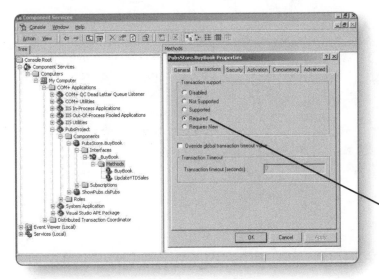

Here are the transactional properties of the PubsStore.BuyBook component that I created. I got to this property page by right clicking on the component and clicking on Properties. Then I clicked on the Transactions tab on the property window.

Notice that the Transaction support is set to Required. COM+ automatically set this when I added the component to the application.

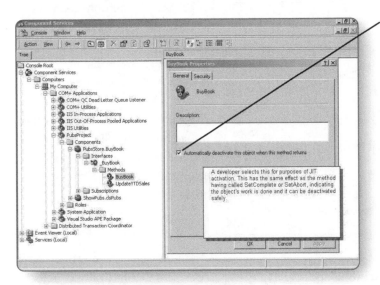

If you look at the Properties for one of the methods, you'll see a check box that says Automatically deactivate this object when this method returns. Clicking on this check box will make the method participate in the transaction even if you don't call the SetComplete or SetAbort methods in the procedure. It doesn't hurt to check this box in case you forget to explicitly put the code in all of your procedures.

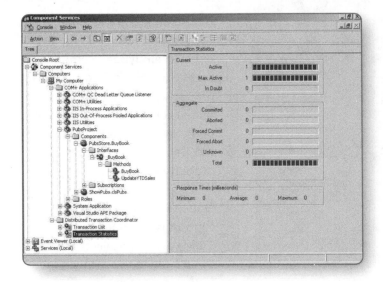

Here is a screen shot of the transaction statistics while my component was involved in a transaction. These statistics can be seen by clicking on "Transaction Statistics" in the Distributed Transaction Coordinator folder.

Using Transactional Code

This Visual Basic class is named BuyBook. It is the only class in my project named "PubsStore". This class has one public method, two private methods, and a private ADO connection object.

```vb
Option Explicit
Private objConnection As ADODB.Connection
Public Sub BuyBook(ByVal strConnection As String, ByVal store As String, _
    ByVal order As String, ByVal quantity As Integer, ByVal payterms _
    As String, ByVal title As String)

    On Error GoTo BuyBookErr

    Dim objContext As COMSVCSLib.ObjectContext
    Set objContext = GetObjectContext()

    Set objConnection = New ADODB.Connection
    objConnection.Open strConnection

    Dim titleID As String
    titleID = GetTitleID(title)

    If titleID = "Error" Then
        Err.Raise vbObjectError + 603
    End If
    Dim cmdBuy As ADODB.Command
    Set cmdBuy = New ADODB.Command
    With cmdBuy
        .ActiveConnection = objConnection
        .CommandType = adCmdStoredProc
        .CommandText = "usp_PurchaseBook"
        .Parameters.Append .CreateParameter("Return_value", adInteger _
        , adParamReturnValue)
```

The BuyBook() subroutine is the public method called from an active server page. It has six arguments, all of which are passed in ByVal.

Every method in the class uses an ObjectContext object. The ObjectContext object enables the method to participate in a transaction. After declaring an ObjectContext variable named objContext, I make it reference an ObjectContext object by calling the GetObjectContext() function that returns an ObjectContext object.

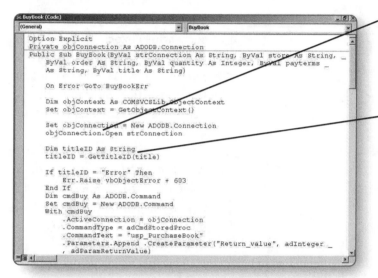

Next I open the `objConnection` connection object using the connection string that was passed to the subroutine.

The `title` argument that was passed to the sub contains the title of a book. I wrote the `GetTitleID()` function to get the `titleID` of the book.

Here's the function.

This method also creates an ObjectContext object named `objContext`. It's OK for me to name the objects the same thing in each procedure because they are local variables that can only be used within the procedure in which they are declared.

This function creates a command object and passes in the `title` as a parameter. The output parameter will be the book's `titleID`, although I named the parameter "@theID". The output parameter is assigned to the `titleID` variable.

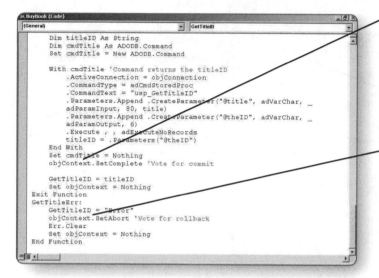

```
M. BuyBook (Code)
(General)                                    ▼ GetTitleID

    Dim titleID As String
    Dim cmdTitle As ADODB.Command
    Set cmdTitle = New ADODB.Command

    With cmdTitle 'Command returns the titleID
        .ActiveConnection = objConnection
        .CommandType = adCmdStoredProc
        .CommandText = "usp_GetTitleID"
        .Parameters.Append .CreateParameter("@title", adVarChar, _
        adParamInput, 80, title)
        .Parameters.Append .CreateParameter("@theID", adVarChar, _
        adParamOutput, 6)
        .Execute , , adExecuteNoRecords
        titleID = .Parameters("@theID")
    End With
    Set cmdTitle = Nothing
    objContext.SetComplete 'Vote for commit

    GetTitleID = titleID
    Set objContext = Nothing
Exit Function
GetTitleErr:
    GetTitleID = "Error"
    objContext.SetAbort 'Vote for rollback
    Err.Clear
    Set objContext = Nothing
End Function
```

If the command object was successfully executed, I call the objContext.SetComplete method to cast a vote to commit the transaction and return the titleID to the calling procedure.

If there was an error along the way, I set the functions return value equal to "Error" and call the objContext.SetAbort method to vote for a rollback of the transaction.

NOTE

COM+ keeps track of all of the "voters" in a transaction. By "voters" I mean components or active server pages that are participating in a transaction. Each participant (even each method in a component) needs to submit a vote for the transaction to commit or abort by calling SetComplete or SetAbort. Once all of the votes are tallied by COM+ services, then it will commit or rollback the transaction based on the votes. If any voters call SetAbort then the transaction will be rolled back.

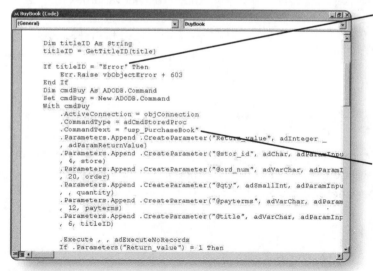

```
M. BuyBook (Code)
(General)                                    ▼ BuyBook

    Dim titleID As String
    titleID = GetTitleID(title)

    If titleID = "Error" Then
        Err.Raise vbObjectError + 603
    End If
    Dim cmdBuy As ADODB.Command
    Set cmdBuy = New ADODB.Command
    With cmdBuy
        .ActiveConnection = objConnection
        .CommandType = adCmdStoredProc
        .CommandText = "usp_PurchaseBook"
        .Parameters.Append .CreateParameter("Return_value", adInteger _
        , adParamReturnValue)
        .Parameters.Append .CreateParameter("@stor_id", adChar, adParamInpu
        , 4, store)
        .Parameters.Append .CreateParameter("@ord_num", adVarChar, adParamI
        , 20, order)
        .Parameters.Append .CreateParameter("@qty", adSmallInt, adParamInpu
        , , quantity)
        .Parameters.Append .CreateParameter("@payterms", adVarChar, adParam
        , 12, payterms)
        .Parameters.Append .CreateParameter("@title", adVarChar, adParamInp
        , 6, titleID)

        .Execute , , adExecuteNoRecords
        If .Parameters("Return_value") = 1 Then
```

After control returns to the BuyBook() sub, I check to see if the return value was "Error." If it was, I raise an error that sends control to the sub's error-handler. I'll look at the error-handler momentarily.

If there was no error I create a command object and send in a bunch of parameters to a stored procedure called "usp_PurchaseBook".

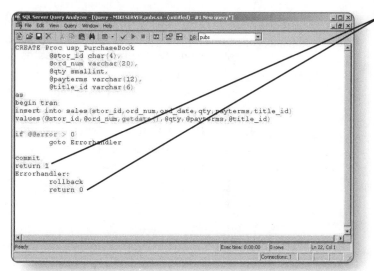

```
CREATE Proc usp_PurchaseBook
        @stor_id char(4),
        @ord_num varchar(20),
        @qty smallint,
        @payterms varchar(12),
        @title_id varchar(6)
as
begin tran
insert into sales(stor_id,ord_num,ord_date,qty,payterms,title_id)
values (@stor_id, @ord_num, getdate(), @qty, @payterms, @title_id)

if @@error > 0
        goto Errorhandler

commit
return 1
Errorhandler:
        rollback
        return 0
```

The procedure inserts a row into the Sales table of the Pubs database. If the Insert was successful I return 1, otherwise I rollback the transaction (in this procedure) and send back a 0.

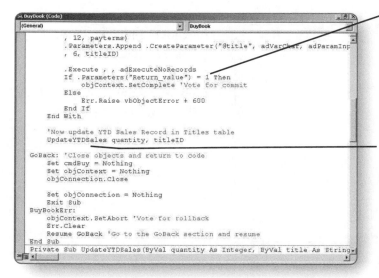

```
        , 12, payterms)
        .Parameters.Append .CreateParameter("@title", adVarChar, adParamInp
        , 6, titleID)

        .Execute , , adExecuteNoRecords
        If .Parameters("Return_value") = 1 Then
                objContext.SetComplete 'Vote for commit
        Else
                Err.Raise vbObjectError + 600
        End If
    End With

    'Now update YTD Sales Record in Titles table
    UpdateYTDSales quantity, titleID

GoBack: 'Close objects and return to code
    Set cmdBuy = Nothing
    Set objContext = Nothing
    objConnection.Close

    Set objConnection = Nothing
    Exit Sub
BuyBookErr:
    objContext.SetAbort 'Vote for rollback
    Err.Clear
    Resume GoBack 'Go to the GoBack section and resume
End Sub
Private Sub UpdateYTDSales(ByVal quantity As Integer, ByVal title As String
```

After executing the command object I check to see if the return value is 1. If it is, then this method votes that the transaction be committed. Otherwise, I raise an error.

Next I have to update the ytd_sales column in the Titles table to reflect the additional sales. Of course, I could have done this all in one stored procedure, but don't worry about that for now. This was done for demonstration purposes. To update the ytd_sales I call the UpdateYTDSales() sub and send in the quantity and titleID.

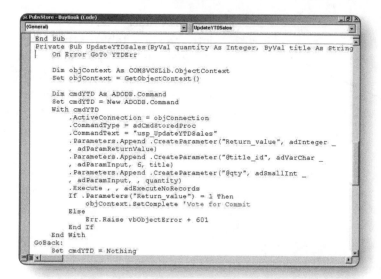

```
PubsStore - BuyBook (Code)
(General)                                    UpdateYTDSales
    End Sub
    Private Sub UpdateYTDSales(ByVal quantity As Integer, ByVal title As String
        On Error GoTo YTDErr

        Dim objContext As COMSVCSLib.ObjectContext
        Set objContext = GetObjectContext()

        Dim cmdYTD As ADODB.Command
        Set cmdYTD = New ADODB.Command
        With cmdYTD
            .ActiveConnection = objConnection
            .CommandType = adCmdStoredProc
            .CommandText = "usp_UpdateYTDSales"
            .Parameters.Append .CreateParameter("Return_value", adInteger _
            , adParamReturnValue)
            .Parameters.Append .CreateParameter("@title_id", adVarChar _
            , adParamInput, 6, title)
            .Parameters.Append .CreateParameter("@qty", adSmallInt _
            , adParamInput, , quantity)
            .Execute , , adExecuteNoRecords
            If .Parameters("Return_value") = 1 Then
                objContext.SetComplete 'Vote for Commit
            Else
                Err.Raise vbObjectError + 601
            End If
        End With
GoBack:
        Set cmdYTD = Nothing
```

Here is the UpdateYTDSales() sub. It is similar to the BuyBook() sub in that it creates an objContext object, runs a command object, and then votes on the outcome of the transaction based on the return value that comes back from a stored procedure.

```
SQL Server Query Analyzer - [Query - MIKESERVER.pubs.sa - (untitled) - #1 New query*]
File  Edit  View  Query  Window  Help
                                                        DB: pubs
CREATE proc usp_UpdateYTDSales
        @title_id varchar(6),
        @qty smallint
as
begin tran
update titles set ytd_sales = (ytd_sales + @qty)
where title_id = @title_id

if @@error > 0
        goto Errorhandler

commit
return 1
Errorhandler:
        rollback
        return 0
```

The usp_UpdateYTDSales stored procedure simply updates the ytd_sales column of the appropriate record in the titles table with a new ytd_sales that includes the latest purchase.

After the command is run, the vote is cast for a commit if the procedure returned 1. An error is raised if the procedure returned 0.

If an error occurred anywhere along the way then the `objContext.SetAbort` method is used to vote for a rollback of the transaction.

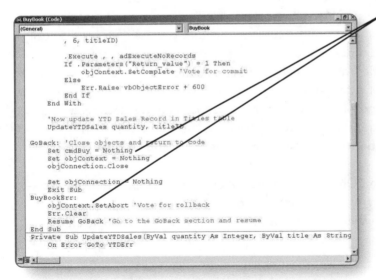

If everything went smoothly, the `BuyBook()` method will close any open objects and send control back to the active server page. If an error occurred, a vote would be cast for a rollback of the transaction prior to returning to the ASP page.

Using Transactional Components in ASP

Now that you've learned how to create transactional components using Visual Basic you're ready to see how to use transactional components in an active server page.

Transactional ASP Code

There are only a few pieces of code to add to your active server page to make it transactional.

1. Put transaction directive: Make the page require a transaction by putting the transactional directive at the top of the page.

```
<% @TRANSACTION=Required %>
```

2. Create and use transactional components: Next you create and use instances of one or more transactional COM+ components. Since the page has been declared as transactional, COM+ will be listening for SetComplete or SetAbort from every method in every instance of the components that you use. You can also call the ObjectContext.SetComplete or ObjectContext.SetAbort methods from your ASP page if you do some transactional processing in it. COM+ waits until all of the "votes" are in from your active server page and from any transactional components you used before deciding whether to commit or rollback the transaction. If all of the "members" of the transaction vote SetComplete then the transaction is completed. If any member votes SetAbort then the transaction is rolled back.

3. Put code in the two COM+ event subroutines: The OnTransactionCommit event is fired when COM+ commits a transaction and the OnTransactionAbort event is fired when a transaction fails. You can put code in these events to handle either outcome.

```
Sub OnTransactionCommit
       ...Some Code
End Sub
Sub OnTransactionAbort
       ...Some Code
End Sub
```

An example should help at this point.

```
showPublisherTitles2.asp                                    _ |&|×|
End Sub
Sub showPublisherTitles(thePublisher,theOrder)

   objPubs.OpenPubTitles Application("strConnection"),publisher,orderBy

   If Not objPubs.PubTitleBOF Then
      Dim authorName,authorID,title,pubDate

      Response.Write("<table border = ""2"" cellpadding = ""5""" _
      & " cellspacing = ""0""" _
      & " bordercolor = ""white"" bgcolor = ""#80FFFF""")
      Response.Write("<th>Author</th><th>Book</th><th>Pub Date</th>" _
      & "<th>Purchase</th>")
      Do While objPubs.ShowPubTitle(authorName,authorID,title, _
      pubdate) = True
         Response.Write("<tr><td><a href = ""showAuthorTitles.asp" _
         &"?author=" & authorID & "&name="
         & Server.URLEncode(authorName) & """>" & authorName _
         & "</a></td>" _
         & "<td>" & title & "</td>" _
         & "<td>" & pubdate & "</td>" _
         & "<td><a href = ""prepareOrder.asp?title=" _
         & Server.URLEncode(title) & """>Order</a></tr>")
      Loop
      objPubs.ClosePubTitle
      Response.Write("</table>")
   End If
   Set objPubs = Nothing
End Sub
Design   Source   Quick View
```

I created a new version of the showPublisherTitles.asp page called showPublisherTitles2.asp. The only difference between the two pages is that the new version adds an extra column to the table that shows information about the books that a particular publishing company has published. The column is a hyperlink that sends a book title as a query string element to the prepareOrder.asp page. The hyperlink reads "Order" on the showPublisherTitles2.asp page.

```
prepareOrder.asp                                            _ |&|×|
<% Option Explicit
Dim title

title = Request.QueryString("title")

%>
<html>
<head>
<title>Prepare Order</title>
<link rel = "stylesheet" type = "text/css" href = "myStyle.asp">
</head>
<body bgcolor = "white">
<h1>Pubs Store</h1>
<h2>Order Confirmation</h2>
<blockquote>
   <form method = "post" action = "placeOrder.asp">
      How many copies of <i><%=title%></i> would
      you like to purchase?
      <input type = "text" name = "quantity" size = "7"><br>
      Enter an Order Number:
      <input type = "text" name = "ord_num" size = "10"><br>
      Enter your Store ID:
      <input type = "text" name = "storeID" size = "4"><br>
      Please select a billing option:
      <select name = "billing">
         <option>Net 30
         <option>Net 60
         <option>ON Invoice
      </select><br>
Design   Source   Quick View
```

The prepareOrder.asp page simply takes the book title and incorporates it into an HTML form that posts information to the placeOrder.asp page. All the information gathered in this form is information required to insert a row into the Sales table in the Pubs database.

```
prepareOrder.asp
</head>
<body bgcolor = "white">
<h1>Pubs Store</h1>
<h2>Order Confirmation</h2>
<blockquote>
    <form method = "post" action = "placeOrder.asp">
        How many copies of <i><%=title%></i> would
        you like to purchase?
        <input type = "text" name = "quantity" size = "7"><br>
        Enter an Order Number:
        <input type = "text" name = "ord_num" size = "10"><br>
        Enter your Store ID:
        <input type = "text" name = "storeID" size = "4"><br>
        Please select a billing option:
        <select name = "billing">
            <option>Net 30
            <option>Net 60
            <option>ON Invoice
        </select><br>
        <br>
        <input type = "hidden" name = "title" value = "<%=title%>">
        <input type = "submit" value = "Place Order"> 
        <input type = "button" value = "Cancel"
        onclick = "javascript:history.back()">
    </form>
</blockquote>
</body>
</html>
```

Here's the bottom of the prepareOrder.asp page. Notice that the "title" is also passed along as a "hidden" form element.

```
placeOrder.asp
<%@ Transaction = Required %>
<% Option Explicit

Dim title, storeID, quantity, billing,ord_num
title = Request.Form("title")
storeID = Request.Form("storeID")
quantity = Request.Form("quantity")
billing = Request.Form("billing")
ord_num = Request.Form("ord_num")

Dim objBuyBook
'Buy the Book
Set objBuyBook = Server.CreateObject("PubsStore.BuyBook")
objBuyBook.BuyBook Application("strConnection"),storeID,ord_num, _
quantity,billing,title

Set objBuyBook = Nothing

Sub OnTransactionCommit
    showHeader
    Response.Write("<h1>Your order has been processed.</h1>")
    Response.Write("<h2>Thank you for your business.</h2>")
    showFooter
End Sub
Sub OnTransactionAbort
    showHeader
    Response.Write("<h1>An error occurred processing your request.</h1>")
    Response.Write("<h2>Please try again later</h2>")
    showFooter
```

Finally we get to the placeOrder.asp page. The big thing to notice on this page is the @Transaction = Required directive at the top. That means that this page will enlist COM+ Services to make sure that a transaction is carried out on the page.

After gathering the necessary information from the form that was filled out, it's time to buy the book. We create an instance of a PubsStore.BuyBook object and send the form information to the BuyBook() method.

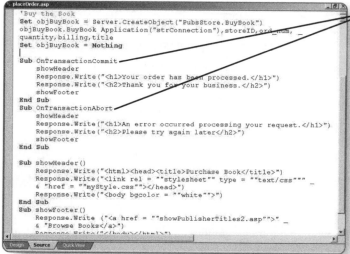

```
placeOrder.asp
'Buy the Book
Set objBuyBook = Server.CreateObject("PubsStore.BuyBook")
objBuyBook.BuyBook Application("strConnection"),storeID,ord_num, _
quantity,billing,title
Set objBuyBook = Nothing

Sub OnTransactionCommit
    showHeader
    Response.Write("<h1>Your order has been processed.</h1>")
    Response.Write("<h2>Thank you for your business.</h2>")
    showFooter
End Sub
Sub OnTransactionAbort
    showHeader
    Response.Write("<h1>An error occurred processing your request.</h1>")
    Response.Write("<h2>Please try again later</h2>")
    showFooter
End Sub

Sub showHeader()
    Response.Write("<html><head><title>Purchase Book</title>")
    Response.Write("<link rel = ""stylesheet"" type = ""text/css""" _
    & "href = ""myStyle.css""></head>")
    Response.Write("<body bgcolor = ""white"">")
End Sub
Sub showFooter()
    Response.Write ("<a href = ""showPublisherTitles2.asp"">" _
    & "Browse Books</a>")
    Response.Write("</body></html>")
```

Because a transaction is required on this page, the ASP page is listening for news from COM+ Services that the transaction was either committed or aborted. If the transaction was successfully completed, the `OnTransactionCommit` event sub will be called. Likewise, if the transaction fails, the `OnTransactionAbort` event will be run. The two events simply create an HTML page that displays an appropriate message. Now let's see if it works.

Here's the showPublisherTitles2.asp page in action.

Author	Book	Pub Date	Purchase
Green, Marjorie	You Can Combat Computer Stress!	6/30/1991	Order
Locksley, Charlene	Emotional Security: A New Algorithm	6/12/1991	Order
Ringer, Albert	Is Anger the Enemy?	6/15/1991	Order
Ringer, Albert	Life Without Fear	10/5/1991	Order
Ringer, Anne	Is Anger the Enemy?	6/15/1991	Order
White, Johnson	Prolonged Data Deprivation: Four Case Studies	6/12/1991	Order

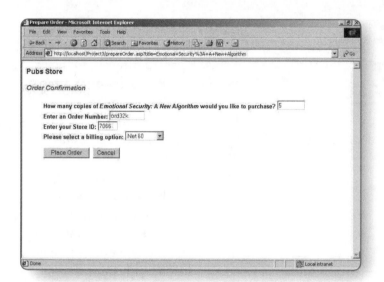

Getting closer—this is the prepareOrder.asp page. I put in a valid `storeID` value so this transaction should work.

After a few moments of silence the votes are in and we own some new books! We'll check the database just to make sure.

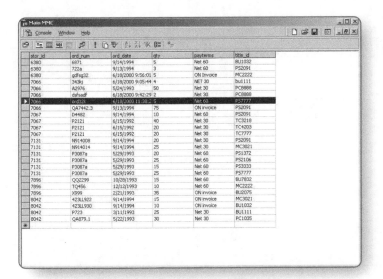

There it is! Trust me that the update of the ytd_sales also took place in the Titles table. Now I'll try again with an invalid storeID.

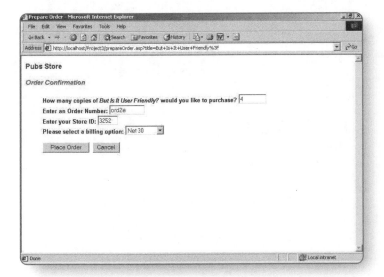

This one shouldn't work because it is an invalid storeID that would conflict with a foreign key relationship in the database between the Stores table and the Sales table.

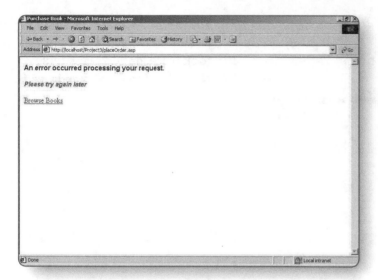

Beautiful, it failed miserably just as we had hoped!

13

Components That Ship with IIS/Windows 2000

There are several COM components that come with IIS and Windows 2000 that can be used in your active server pages. Of course, you've already looked at ADO, one of the sets of COM objects that ship with IIS. In this chapter you'll look at the Scripting Runtime Library components, ASP Installable components, and some Windows 2000 components. You'll see examples at the end of the chapter of how to use three of the components. In this chapter, you'll learn about:

- The components associated with the Scripting Runtime Library
- The ASP Installable Components that come with IIS
- Some Windows Components
- Using the Ad Rotator, Browser Capabilities, and CDONTS components
- Setting up Microsoft's SMTP Service

Scripting Runtime Library Components

Three objects come with the Scripting Runtime Library. This library is automatically installed with ASP, and it provides the VBScript and JScript engines. The three objects are the Dictionary Object, the FileSystemObject, and the TextStream Object.

Dictionary Component

The Dictionary component allows you to create your own collections. You've seen several examples of collections already in this book. A collection is similar to an array. Consider the Request Object's Forms collection for a moment. This collection contains all the information that was submitted by an HTML form (when the POST method was used). Each element of the form is identified by a name and has a value associated with it. You can iterate through the Forms collection and retrieve all the names and values associated with a particular form. The Dictionary object also allows you to create keys and items. *Keys* are like the name of an element in the Forms collection and *items* are like the value of an element. You can Add and Remove keys and items to or from a Dictionary object. To create a Dictionary object, use the following syntax:

```
Set objDictionary = Server.CreateObject("Scripting.Dictionary")
```

To Add a key/item to the object, use:

```
objDictionary.Add "aKey","an Item"
```

You can remove an item from the dictionary by referencing its key in the Remove method:

```
objDictionary.Remove ("aKey")
```

FileSystemObject Component

The FileSystemObject allows you to access the drives, folders, and files on the server from your script. The object model for the FileSystemObject can be summarized as follows: the FileSystemObject has a collection of Drives, a Drives object has a collection of Folders, and a Folder object has a collection of Files. To create an instance of the FileSystemObject use the following syntax:

```
Set objFileSystemObject = Server.CreateObject("Scripting.FileSystemObject")
```

TextStream Component

The TextStream component works with the FileSystemObject and allows you to create and open text files. A TextStream object can only be instantiated with a FileSystemObject object. Here's an example of how to create a text file with the TextStream object:

```
Set objFileSystem = Server.CreateObject("Scripting.FileSystemObject")
Set objText = objFileSystem.CreateTextFile("C:\myTextFile.txt")
```

The component also has a method called OpenTextFile() that can open a text file for reading, for writing, or for appending. There is also an OpenAsTextStream() method that is similar to the OpenTextFile() method, but it works with a File object rather than a FileSystemObject.

ASP Installable Components

There are several components that are installed with IIS (even though they're called "installable"). The components and files associated with them are found in the Winnt\System32\inetsrv\ directory. I'll look briefly at several of them. You can find more about any of these components by looking at the IIS documentation at http://localhost/iishelp.

Ad Rotator

The Ad Rotator component can be used to rotate banner advertisements on your Web site. You can specify the percentage of time that a particular ad is shown. You need to create two additional files for this component to work correctly. One file is a text file that specifies information about the ads to be rotated. The other file is an active server page that redirects the client to a specified Web site when the user clicks on an ad. You'll see an example of this component in action at the end of the chapter. Here's the syntax for instantiating this component:

```
Set objRotator = Server.CreateObject( "MSWC.AdRotator" )
```

Browser Capabilities

The Browser Capabilities component is used to determine what browser a client is using to view your Web site and what capabilities the browser has. It can tell you whether the browser supports frames, tables, JavaScript, Java, VBScript, cookies, and the like. This kind of information can be useful for determining what content to show a client. If their browser won't support a certain feature, you can send them a page that doesn't contain that feature. The component works by reading the browscap.ini file located in the \inetsrv directory. This file contains a list of browsers and their capabilities. It obviously becomes outdated as new browsers are released. You should periodically get the latest version of the file by downloading it from http://www.cyscape.com/browscap/ or http://www.asptracker.com/. You will see an example of this component in action at the end of the chapter. Here's how to instantiate the component:

```
Set objBrowser = Server.CreateObject("MSWC.BrowserType")
```

Content Linking

The Content Linking component can be used to link together several pages in your Web site. It works by looking at a text file that contains a list of links to pages in your site. The links in the text file are in a specified order and contain a description of the page. If you use the Content Linking component in your site, people will be able to navigate forward, backward, or to a specified page by clicking on links generated by a content linking object. If you add or remove pages to your site, you have only to change the list of links in the text file and all of the links in your site will still work. This component provides an easy way to manage links in your Web site. To create an instance of this object use the following syntax:

```
Set objLink = Server.CreateObject( "MSWC.NextLink" )
```

Content Rotator

The Content Rotator component is similar to the Ad Rotator component. However, instead of rotating ads it rotates HTML content. The component relies on a text file that contains different pieces of HTML code along with a number that specifies the relative amount of time that the content should be shown. By using this component on a Web page users will see different content each time they view the page. To create the object use the following syntax:

```
Set objContent = Server.CreateObject( "MSWC.ContentRotator" )
```

Counters

The Counters component can be used to keep count things on your Web site. You can create as many counter objects as you want. Each counter will have a unique name. You can create a counter by using the Set(counterName,number) method and passing in the name of the counter and a starting value. The Get(counterName) method will retrieve the current value of the specified counter. The Increment(counterName) method will increment the specified counter by one and the Remove(counterName) method will remove the specified counter. The values of all of the counters are kept in a text file named counters.txt in the \inetsrv directory. Since there is only one copy of the counters.txt file that must be shared by every instance of this object, you should only create one instance and share it throughout the application. You can do this by specifying the following in your global.asa file:

```
<OBJECT RUNAT="Server" SCOPE="Application" ID="objCounter"
PROGID="MSWC.Counters"></OBJECT>
```

Logging Utility

The Logging Utility component can be used to add information to or extract information from the IIS Log files. This component can be used to create a useful analysis page for you to analyze traffic on your Web site. To make this component work, you must turn off anonymous access for the pages that use the component. You can do this from IIS by right-clicking on the page and clicking on properties. Click on the File Security tab. From there click on the Edit button next to the anonymous access and authentication information. Uncheck the box that says "Anonymous access." Users visiting this page will be allowed to see only it if they have administrative privileges. Create a Logging Utility object using:

```
Set objLog = Server.CreateObject( MSWC.IISLog )
```

Page Counter

You can use the Page Counter component to keep track of hits on your Web site. Count information can be kept on each page on which you create an instance of the Page Counter component. The page count information is stored in a text file. To record a hit, use the `PageHit()` method. To retrieve the number of hits for a specified page, use the `Hits(page)` method and specify the path and page name of the Web page. The `Reset(page)` method resets the counter for the page specified. To create an instance of the Page Counter object use the following syntax:

```
Set objPageCounter = Server.CreateObject( "MSWC.PageCounter" )
```

Permission Checker

The Permission Checker component can be useful for controlling access to pages in an intranet environment. The component checks to see if a user has permission to access a specified resource. This component requires that anonymous access be turned off. To create an instance, use the following syntax:

```
Set objPermission = Server.CreateObject( "MSWC.PermissionChecker" )
```

Tools

The Tools component provides an assortment of functionality. Use the `FileExists(file)` method to determine whether or not the specified file exists. The `Random()` method returns a random number. The `ProcessForm()` method processes information from a submitted HTML form and saves the information to a file in a specified format. To create a Tools object, use the following syntax:

```
Set objTools = Server.CreateObject("MSWC.Tools")
```

Windows Components

I want to mention a few Windows components that can be very useful in ASP development. The CDO (*Collaboration Data Objects*) component . works either with Microsoft Exchange Server or the Windows NT or 2000 SMTP service. CDO provides the ability to send and receive email, work with calendars, contacts, notes, public folders, and so on. It is a very powerful messaging component that can be used to create powerful intranet applications. Outlook Web Access uses the CDO Library. A scaled down version of the CDO Library is the CDONTS Library of objects. CDONTS stands for Collaboration Data Objects for NT Server. The cdonts.dll is installed with the Microsoft SMTP service, an installation option on the Windows CD. CDONTS is a great tool for sending email from your Web site. You'll see an example that uses CDONTS at the end of the chapter.

Using Components

Here are a few examples that show how to use some of the components discussed above. If you want learn more about an individual component search for the components name in the MSDN library (if you have it) or the MSDN Online Library at http://msdn.microsoft.com.

Using the Ad Rotator

I created a simple example that makes use of the Ad Rotator component.

At the top of the page I create a variable named `objRotator` and assign it a reference to an Ad Rotator object.

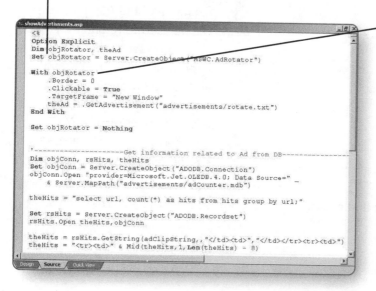

Next I set all of the properties of the object. Because I don't want a border around the ads, I set the `Border` property to 0. The `Clickable` property specifies whether or not the ad will be a hyperlink. I want mine to be hyperlinks, so I set the property to `True`. The `TargetFrame` property specifies in which frame the ad URL should be opened. I want it to open in a new window that I titled `Advertisements`.

```
showAdvertisments.asp
<%
Option Explicit
Dim objRotator, theAd
Set objRotator = Server.CreateObject("MSWC.AdRotator")

With objRotator
    .Border = 0
    .Clickable = True
    .TargetFrame = "New Window"
    theAd = .GetAdvertisement("advertisements/rotate.txt")
End With

Set objRotator = Nothing


'----------------------Get information related to Ad from DB-----------------
Dim objConn, rsHits, theHits
Set objConn = Server.CreateObject("ADODB.Connection")
objConn.Open "provider=Microsoft.Jet.OLEDB.4.0; Data Source=" _
    & Server.MapPath("advertisements/adCounter.mdb")

theHits = "select url, count(*) as hits from hits group by url;"

Set rsHits = Server.CreateObject("ADODB.Recordset")
rsHits.Open theHits, objConn

theHits = rsHits.GetString(adClipString,,"</td><td>","</td></tr><tr><td>")
theHits = "<tr><td>" & Mid(theHits,1,Len(theHits) - 8)
```

Design   Source   Quick View

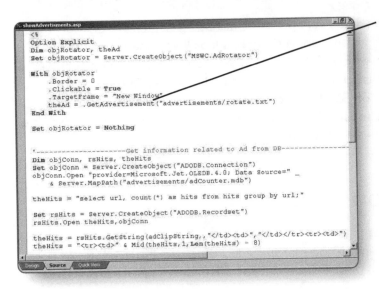

```
showAdvertisments.asp
<%
Option Explicit
Dim objRotator, theAd
Set objRotator = Server.CreateObject("MSWC.AdRotator")

With objRotator
    .Border = 0
    .Clickable = True
    .TargetFrame = "New Window"
    theAd = .GetAdvertisement("advertisements/rotate.txt")
End With

Set objRotator = Nothing


'--------------------Get information related to Ad from DB--------------
Dim objConn, rsHits, theHits
Set objConn = Server.CreateObject("ADODB.Connection")
objConn.Open "provider=Microsoft.Jet.OLEDB.4.0; Data Source=" _
    & Server.MapPath("advertisements/adCounter.mdb")

theHits = "select url, count(*) as hits from hits group by url;"

Set rsHits = Server.CreateObject("ADODB.Recordset")
rsHits.Open theHits, objConn

theHits = rsHits.GetString(adClipString,,"</td><td>","</td></tr><tr><td>")
theHits = "<tr><td>" & Mid(theHits,1,Len(theHits) - 8)
```

Design   Source   Quick View

I declared another variable named theAd. I use this variable to get the HTML string returned from the objRotator. GetAdvertisement() method. Notice that I pass in the relative path to my advertisement text file named rotate.txt. You can create as many advertisement text files as you want and name them whatever you want to. All that the GetAdvertisement() method does is get advertisement information from the specified text file and create an HTML hyperlink statement out of it.

```
advertisements\rotate.txt
REDIRECT advertisements/sendEm.asp
HEIGHT 170
WIDTH 170
*
advertisements/prima.gif
http://www.prima-tech.com/
Books by Prima Tech
5
advertisements/chili.gif
http://www.chilisoft.com
Get platform independant ASP
2
advertisements/vi.gif
http://msdn.microsoft.com/vinterdev/wsk/default.asp
Get a 90 day trial of Visual InterDev
3
```

At the top of the text file is a list of properties that will apply to all of the advertisements in the file. The REDIRECT property specifies the relative path and file name of the ASP page that will be used to redirect the client browser to the appropriate URL. The HEIGHT and WIDTH properties specify the height and width of the advertisement picture. You could also specify the BORDER size here if you wanted to.

Next comes an asterisk that separates the properties from the advertisements.

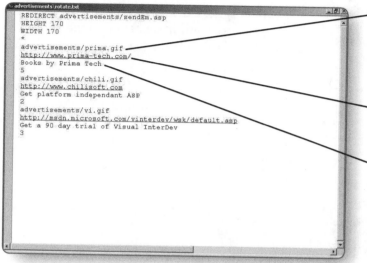

The first line in each advertise-ment specification tells the relative path and file name of the picture to be used for the ad.

Next comes the URL of the company that the ad represents.

After that is a description of the ad. This description will become the alt text of the hyperlink image.

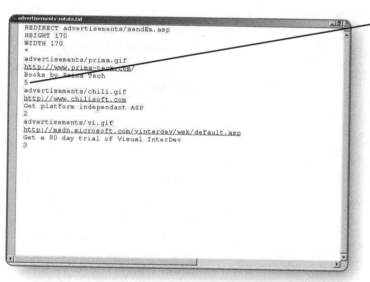

Finally comes a "weighting" number. This number specifies the number of times that this particular ad should be show relative to the other ads in the list. If you do the math, you'll figure out that the first ad will show 50% of the time, the second ad 20% of the time and the last ad 30% of the time.

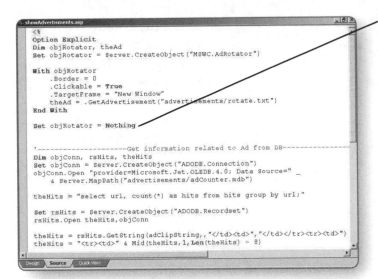

After I've gotten the advertisement into the `theAd` variable, I can destroy the object.

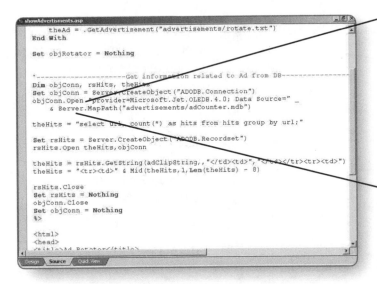

I decided to create a little Access database (`adCounter.mdb`) to keep track of how many hits each one of my advertisers gets. I just put the database in the advertisements folder (sure, someone could download it, but that's OK).

Notice that I used the `Server.MapPath` method to specify the path to the `Data Source` in the connection string. The `Server.MapPath` method returns the full physical path to the specified file. If you put a slash (either / or \) in front of the path you pass to the method, the `MapPath` method will assume that you are providing the full virtual path to the file. If you don't put a slash mark first, it assumes that you are specifying a relative virtual path to the specified file from the current file. In this case I am specifying the relative path to my database.

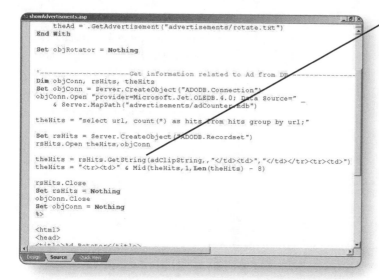

```
        theAd = . GetAdvertisement ("advertisements/rotate.txt")
End With

Set objRotator = Nothing


'---------------------Get information related to Ad from DB--------------
Dim objConn, rsHits, theHits
Set objConn = Server.CreateObject ("ADODB.Connection")
objConn.Open "provider=Microsoft.Jet.OLEDB.4.0; Data Source=" _
    & Server.MapPath ("advertisements/adCounter.mdb")

theHits = "select url, count (*) as hits from hits group by url;"

Set rsHits = Server.CreateObject ("ADODB.Recordset")
rsHits.Open theHits,objConn

theHits = rsHits.GetString(adClipString,,"</td><td>","</td></tr><tr><td>")
theHits = "<tr><td>" & Mid(theHits,1,Len(theHits) - 8)

rsHits.Close
Set rsHits = Nothing
objConn.Close
Set objConn = Nothing
%>

<html>
<head>
<title>Ad Rotator</title>
```

The rest of the ASP code selects the URL and hit count for each of the advertisers in my database. I used the `Recordset.GetString()` method to create `<tr>` tags from the information and assign the resulting HTML string to a variable named `theHits`.

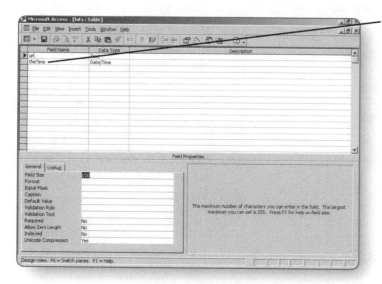

I have only one table named `hits` in this database. The table has two columns: `url` is the URL of the advertiser and `theTime` is the time of the hit.

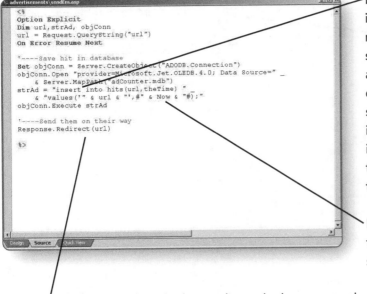

```
showAdvertisements.asp
    theHits = rsHits.GetString(adClipString,,"</td><td>","</td></tr><tr><td>")
    theHits = "<tr><td>" & Mid(theHits,1,Len(theHits) - 8)

    rsHits.Close
    Set rsHits = Nothing
    objConn.Close
    Set objConn = Nothing
    %>

    <html>
    <head>
    <title>Ad Rotator</title>
    <link rel = "stylesheet" type = "text/css" href = "myStyle.css">
    </head>
    <body bgcolor = "white">
    <div align = "center">
        <h1>Ad of the Day</h1>

        <%=theAd%>
        <h2>Visits to our sponsors</h2>
        <table border = "1" bordercolor = "black" cellpadding = "5"
        cellspacing = "0">
        <th>Ad URL</th><th>Hits</th>
        <%=theHits%>
        </table>
    </div>
    </body>
    </html>

 Design  Source  Quick View
```

Here is the HTML part of the page. I display theAd variable that will have the ad image and hyperlink. Under that I display a table that shows how many times each of the advertisements has been hit.

```
advertisements\sendEm.asp
    <%
    Option Explicit
    Dim url,strAd, objConn
    url = Request.QueryString("url")
    On Error Resume Next

    '----Save hit in database
    Set objConn = Server.CreateObject("ADODB.Connection")
    objConn.Open "provider=Microsoft.Jet.OLEDB.4.0; Data Source=" _
        & Server.MapPath("adCounter.mdb")
    strAd = "insert into hits(url,theTime) " _
        & "values('" & url & "',#" & Now & "#);"
    objConn.Execute strAd

    '----Send them on their way
    Response.Redirect(url)

    %>

 Design  Source  Quick View
```

Before I show you the page in action I better explain the redirection page. When someone clicks on one of the ads it will send the url as a query string to this page, sendEm.asp. On the page I insert a row into the hits table in my database that specifies the URL that was hit and the time the hit occurred.

Notice that in Access you have to enclose dates in pound (#) signs.

After recording the hit I redirect the browser to the appropriate site.

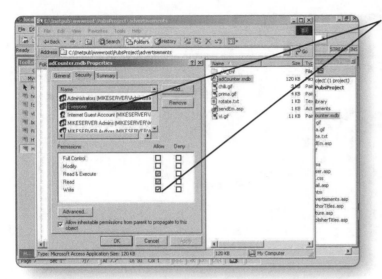

Because this page inserts into the database, you need to make sure that Everyone or the IUSR_machinename user has "write" permissions to the database.

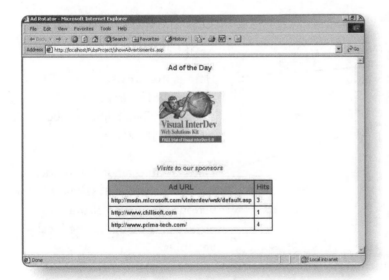

Here is the page in action. Every time the page is loaded a different ad will be displayed according to the weighting you specified.

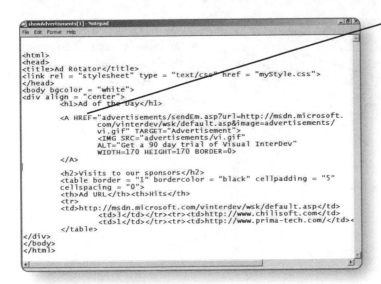

When you view the HTML source, you'll notice that the URL of the advertisement was automatically inserted into the HTML where I placed `theAd` variable.

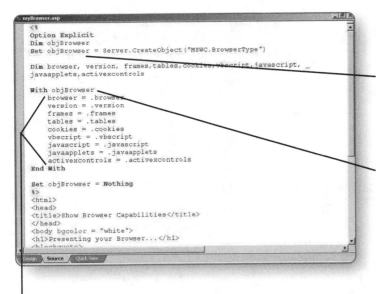

Using Browser Capabilities

Here is the Browser Capabilities component example. I created a Browser Capabilities object named `objBrowser`.

I also created a number of local variables and then assigned various properties of the `objBrowser` object to the local variables.

These are just some of the Browser Capabilities object properties that you can use. The information returned by the properties reflects the capabilities of the browser viewing the page.

```
End With

Set objBrowser = Nothing
%>
<html>
<head>
<title>Show Browser Capabilities</title>
</head>
<body bgcolor = "white">
<h1>Presenting your Browser...</h1>
<blockquote>
    <h2>Your browser is <%=browser%> version <%=version%>.</h2>
    Here's what your browser can and cannot do:
    <blockquote>
    <table border = "1" cellpadding = "5" cellspacing = "0" bordercolor = '
    <th>Feature</th><th>Capability</th>
    <tr><td>Frames:</td><td><%=frames%></td></tr>
    <tr><td>Tables:</td><td><%=frames%></td></tr>
    <tr><td>Cookies:</td><td><%=frames%></td></tr>
    <tr><td>VB Script:</td><td><%=frames%></td></tr>
    <tr><td>Java Script:</td><td><%=frames%></td></tr>
    <tr><td>Java Applets:</td><td><%=frames%></td></tr>
    <tr><td>ActiveX Controls:</td><td><%=frames%></td></tr>
    </table>
    </blockquote>
</blockquote>
</body>
</html>
```

At the bottom of the page I just show an HTML table that displays the browser information.

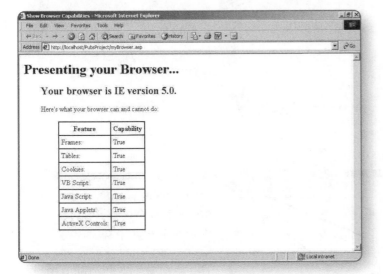

Here's the page viewed with IE 5.

CDONTS

I created a simple example that uses the CDONTS NewMail Object to send an email. Before looking at any code, you need to see how to set up the Microsoft SMTP service because it is required for CDONTS to work. SMTP is one of the optional features in the Windows installation. If you don't have it installed, go back to Chapter 1, "Getting Started with Visual InterDev," and follow the instructions for installing IIS. SMTP is one of the optional features of IIS. To get to the SMTP service, follow these instructions:

1. Click on Start, Settings, Control Panel.

2. Double-click on Administrative Tools.

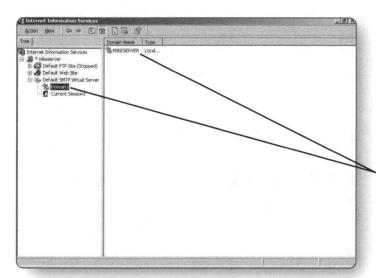

3. Double-click on Internet Services Manager.

4. Expand the plus (+) signs next to your server until you find the "Default SMTP Virtual Server."

5. If you click on Domains, you should have one domain that is named after your computer. This is your local domain.

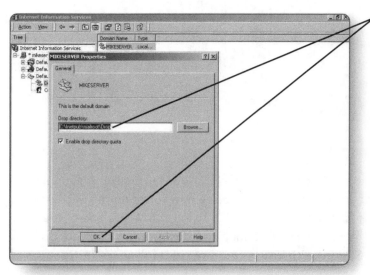

6. If you double-click on the domain, you'll see the properties. Notice that by default the drop directory is C:\Inetpub\mailroot\Drop. This is where all incoming mail will be dropped. Click on OK.

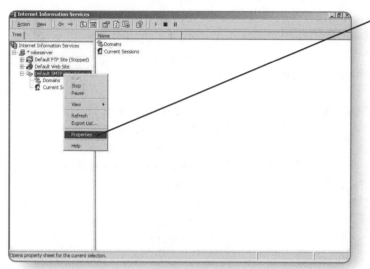

7. Right-click on Default SMTP Virtual Server and click on Properties.

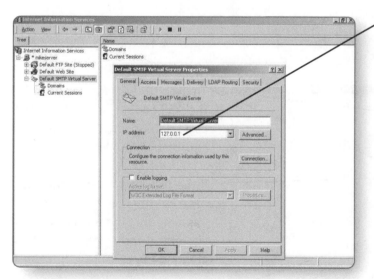

8. You can specify what IP address to use for your SMTP server. Leave all of the settings with the defaults for now.

You can make sure that your SMTP service is started by right-clicking on the Virtual Server. If Start is grayed out then the service is started, if it's not then click on Start.

We're now ready to get into the code.

```
             End If
     End If

     %>
     <html>
     <head>
     <title>Online Mailer</title>
     </head>
     <body bgcolor = "white">
     <h1>Online E-mail Maker</h1>
     <blockquote>
         <form method = "post" action = "OnlineMail.asp">
         From: <input type = "text" name = "from"><br>
         To: <input type = "text" name = "to"><br>
         CC: <input type = "text" name = "cc"><br>
         BCC: <input type = "text" name = "bcc"><br>

         <br>
         Subject:<input type = "text" name = "subject"><br>
         Message:<br>
         <textarea rows = "10" cols = "50" name = "message"></textarea><br><br>

         <input type = "submit" value = "Send"> 
         <input type = "reset" value = "Clear">
         </form>
     </blockquote>
     </body>
     </html>
```

Here is the lower half of OnlineMail.asp. This is the HTML form that collects all the information for a simple email message. You can also set the importance of the message and add attachments using CDONTS.

```
     <%Option Explicit
     Dim mailTo, cc, bcc, from, subject, message

     mailTo = Request.Form("to")
     from = Request.Form("from")
     cc = Request.Form("cc")
     bcc = Request.Form("bcc")
     subject = Request.Form("subject")
     message = Request.Form("message")
     If from <> "" and mailto <> "" Then
         Dim objMail
         Set objMail = Server.CreateObject("CDONTS.NewMail")
         On Error Resume Next
         With objMail
             .From = from
             .To = mailto
             .Cc = cc
             .Bcc = bcc
             .Subject = subject
             .Body = message
             .Send
         End With
         If Err.number > 0 Then
             Response.Write("<h2>Error sending message</h2>")
         Else
             Response.Write("<h2>Message sent!</h2>")
         End If
     End If
```

The top of the page has all of the ASP code. The first thing the code does is fetch all the form information into local variables.

If the from and mailto variables have information in them, then I assume that the form has been submitted and commence with creating the email.

The first step is to create a CDONTS.NewMail object. I assigned such an object to the variable "objMail."

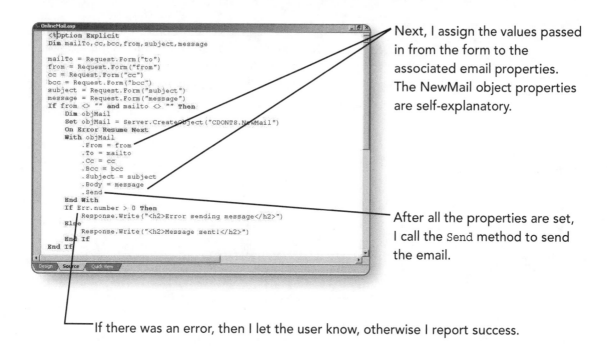

```
OnlineMail.asp
<%Option Explicit
Dim mailTo,cc,bcc,from,subject,message

mailTo = Request.Form("to")
from = Request.Form("from")
cc = Request.Form("cc")
bcc = Request.Form("bcc")
subject = Request.Form("subject")
message = Request.Form("message")
If from <> "" and mailto <> "" Then
    Dim objMail
    Set objMail = Server.CreateObject("CDONTS.NewMail")
    On Error Resume Next
    With objMail
        .From = from
        .To = mailto
        .Cc = cc
        .Bcc = bcc
        .Subject = subject
        .Body = message
        .Send
    End With
    If Err.number > 0 Then
        Response.Write("<h2>Error sending message</h2>")
    Else
        Response.Write("<h2>Message sent!</h2>")
    End If
End If

Design   Source   Quick View
```

Next, I assign the values passed in from the form to the associated email properties. The NewMail object properties are self-explanatory.

After all the properties are set, I call the Send method to send the email.

If there was an error, then I let the user know, otherwise I report success.

```
Online Mailer - Microsoft Internet Explorer
File  Edit  View  Favorites  Tools  Help
Back  →  ⊗ ⊗ ⊗  ⊗Search  ⊗Favorites  ⊗History  ⊗ ⊗ ⊗ ⊗
Address  http://localhost/PubsProject/OnlineMail.asp                    Go

Online E-mail Maker

    From: Mike@here.com
    To: Brian@there.com
    CC:
    BCC:

    Subject: Hello!
    Message:
    Hello Brian,

    Isn't CDONTS great!

    Mike



    Send   Clear

Done                                              Local intranet
```

Now I'll giv'er a shot!

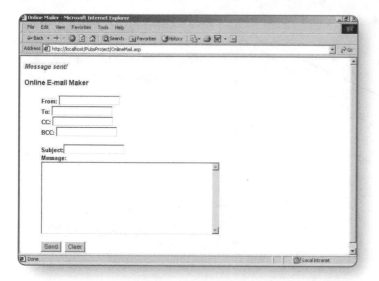

Well, it says it worked. If I had been connected to the Internet then the message would have gone to wherever "there.com." is. However...

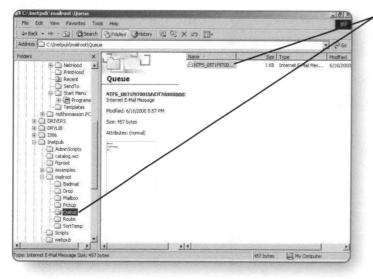

I wasn't connected to the Internet so the message is waiting in the Queue until the next time I connect (of course I'll delete it before then).

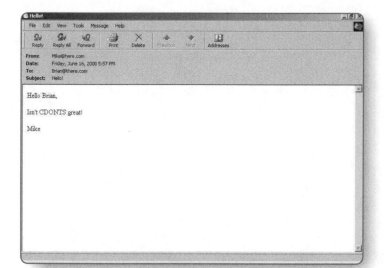

Here's the message!

14

Testing Your Web Application

You've got your active server pages all prettied up, your back-end database is chock full of stored procedures, you've created a full range of middle-tier COM+ components—now is the moment of truth: What can this thing do? Before you actually release a production Web application into the Wild Wild Web, you should put it through some stress tests to see how it will perform when the pressure's on. There are several tools available that allow you to test your Web application's performance under pressure by simulating multiple concurrent hits to your site. This chapter will cover how to effectively use the Windows Performance Monitor and the Microsoft Web Application Stress Tool to stress test a Web application. In this chapter, you'll learn how to:

- Use the Windows Performance Monitor
- Use the Web Application Stress Tool
- Analyze the results of your stress test

Using Performance Monitor

Window NT and Windows 2000 ship with a tool called Performance Monitor. This tool can be used to analyze many aspects of a machine's performance. The performance metrics tracked with the Performance Monitor can be viewed graphically, in report format, or saved in log files to be analyzed later. Becoming familiar with the Performance Monitor (Perfmon) will be help you maximize the performance of your Web application by helping you find performance bottlenecks. One easy way to open Perfmon is simply to click on Start, Run, and type perfmon in the text box. Another way is to click on Start, Settings, Control Panel. Double-click on Administrative Tools, and then double-click on Performance.

Here's what Performance Monitor looks like when you first open it.

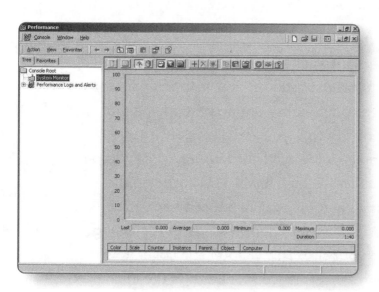

Adding Counters

To add some counters to the Perfmon graph click on the + sign on the toolbar.

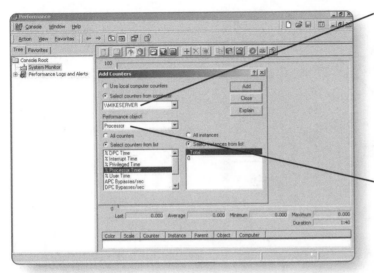

Select the computer that you want to gather information for. You can gather performance metrics from more than one computer on the same graph. In this case I will gather information from my computer, "MIKESERVER."

Next you select the Performance object. This is the category of information that you want to gather. The currently selected category is Processor. That means that all of the counters in the list below have to do with the selected computer's processor(s).

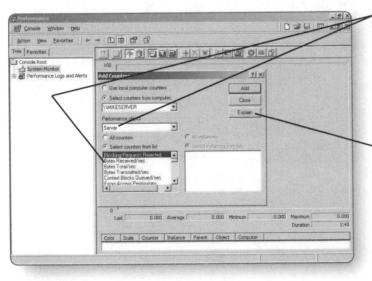

Notice that if I change the Performance object, the list of counters changes to reflect the counters available for the selected object. I changed the object to Server.

To find out what a particular counter in the list counts, click on the counter and then click on the Explain button.

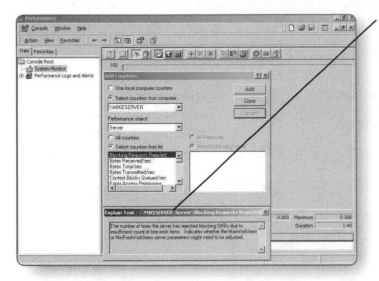

An explanation of the selected counter will appear in a small window.

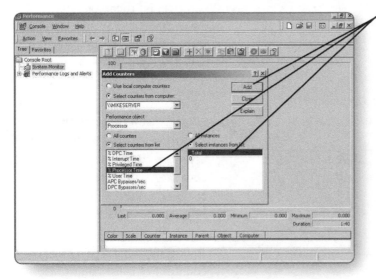

When you want to add a counter to the graph, click on the counter in the counters list and then click on the Add button. I'll add the Processor object's % Processor Time metric. If I had multiple processors in this machine, I could click on the All Instances radio button to the right to get the percentage for all of the processors. Alternatively, I could select an individual processor by clicking on it in the list.

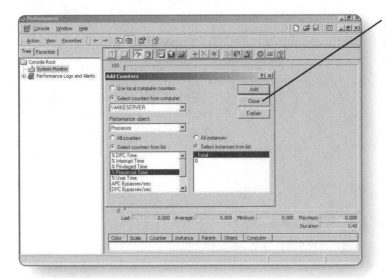

After I've added all of the counters that I want on the graph, I can click on Close.

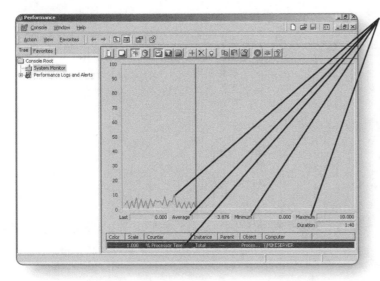

Notice that the graph will begin to show the counters you've selected. Since I only selected one counter, that's all it shows. The name of the counter shows up in the list at the bottom. Notice that I can also see the Average, Minimum, and Maximum values that this counter has had since the monitoring began.

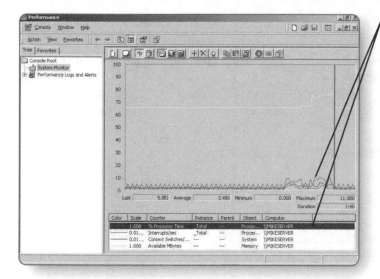

I've added some more counters so you can get a better idea how the tool works. If you double-click on one of the lines in the graph, the corresponding counter will be highlighted in the counter list below.

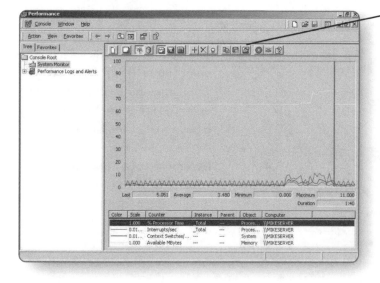

To change the Properties of the graph, click on the Properties button on the toolbar.

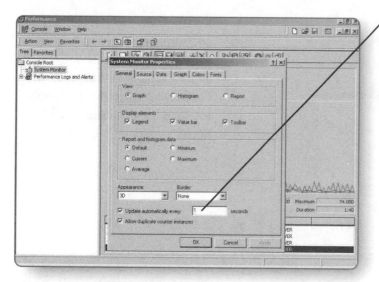

I'll point out a few helpful properties. On the General tab you might want to change the counter interval from one second to something else.

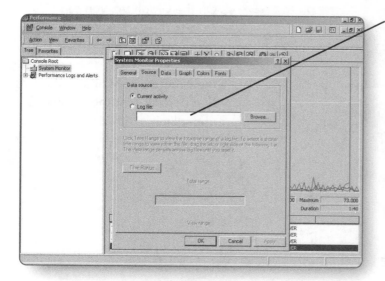

On the Source tab you can specify whether the graph should be made from current activity or from a log file. You can record all of the activity for a day in a log. Then you can browse through the log to look for anything interesting.

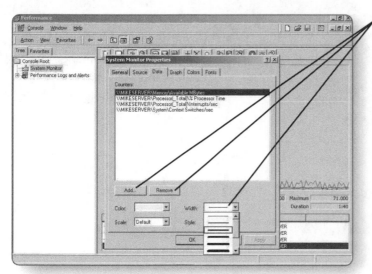

On the Data tab you can add and remove counters. You can also specify the color and line width of the lines on the graph. I usually increase the line width to make the lines stand out better.

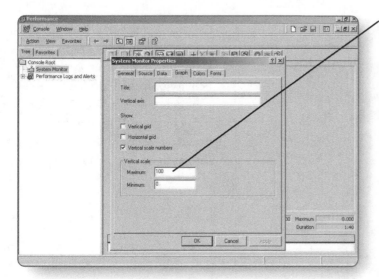

On the Graph tab you can change the vertical access range on the graph. This is often helpful because many of the counters have high numbers that go well over the default upper limit of 100.

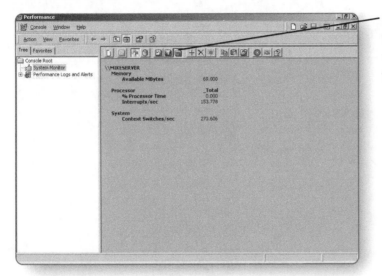

If you click on the Report button on the toolbar, you'll be able to view a textual representation of the counters.

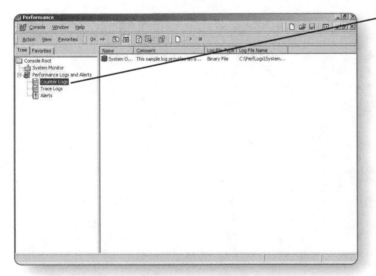

To create a log that will record counters for a specified period of time, expand the (+) sign next to Performance Logs and Alerts. Next, right-click on Counter Logs and click on New Log Settings.

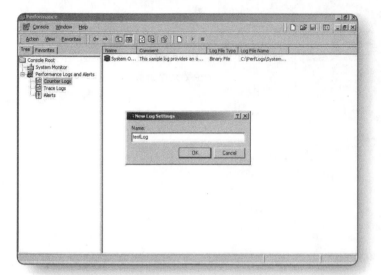

Type a name for the log file and click on OK.

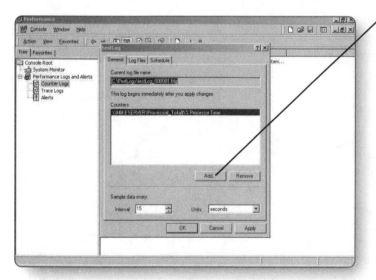

Add counters to the log by clicking on Add and choosing the counters you want.

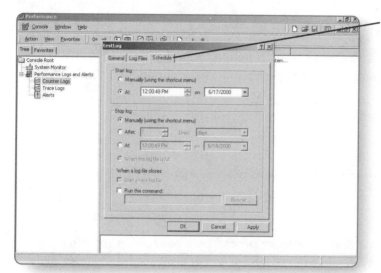

Click on the Schedule tab to establish when the log should start recording the specified counters as well as when it should stop recording.

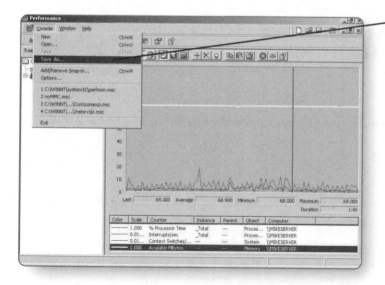

To save a particular Perfmon setup, click on Console and then Save As.

Some Useful Counters

There are many counters to choose from. Here are some that are particularly useful when it comes to analyzing your Web application. I've grouped the counters by "Performance object."

Processor

The Processor object references the server's processor(s).

% Processor Time

This is the amount of time that a particular processor is busy doing something. If the processors on your Web server or database server are consistently busy more than 75%—80% of the time, they are too busy. Consider adding more servers and creating a server cluster using something like the Windows Load Balancing Service.

Memory

This object references the server's memory.

Available MBytes

This is the number of megabytes of physical memory available at a particular time.

Process

This object contains the various server Processes that are running on the server. These are basically the programs that the server is running.

Private Bytes

Select the Process object in the Performance objects list. Then select the Private Bytes counter from the counters list. Select the "inetinfo" process from the instances list. This counter will tell you how many bytes of memory IIS is using at the time. If the number of bytes being used begins to creep up as time goes by, then you may have a memory leak in one of your COM components.

WebService

This object has all of the metrics having to do with the IIS Web service.

Get Requests/Sec

Select Get Requests/Sec from the counters list and select your Web site in the instances list. This counter lets you know how many Get method requests are being filled per second for your site.

Post Requests/Sec

Select Post Requests/Sec from the counters list and select your Web site in the instances list. This counter lets you know how many Post method requests are being filled per second for your site.

Active Server Pages

This object contains metrics about active server pages running on the server.

Requests Per Second

This is the number of requests successfully processed per second by the ASP interpreter. This metric is usually used to benchmark an application's performance. The more requests per second that the server can process the higher the performance of your Web application.

Requests Queued

When the ASP processor is busy processing other requests, ASP requests are put into a request queue. As the processor becomes available, requests are processed from the queue. If the ASP queue fluctuates a lot, the processor might be hung up waiting for a particular COM object or database process to complete.

Requests Timed Out

This is the number of ASP requests that timed out waiting in the queue. When a script times out, the server will return an ugly timeout message to the client. You can change the amount of time allowed to pass before a script times out in the IIS administration console.

Template Cache Hit Rate

This is the number of ASP requests that were satisfied by pulling already run script pages from the cache. Obviously, pages pulled from cache will be returned more quickly than pages that have to be freshly processed.

SQLServer:CacheManager

This object contains information about how SQL Server caches information in memory.

Cache Hit Ratio

This is the ratio of the number of database requests satisfied from cache verses those that had to look up data on the disk. The higher the number, the better the performance.

Using the Web Application Stress Tool

Microsoft has a free stress tool that you can download and use to stress test your Web application. The Web Application Stress tool (WAS) is provided for you on the CD that came with this book. There is valuable information about the WAS tool on the WAS Web site at http://webtool.rte.microsoft.com. We'll learn the basics about using this tool to test your Web application in this section.

Installation

The installation of the tool is easy. Just double-click on the "Click here to Install" link from the Prima Tech CD ROM interface and follow the directions. One thing to note, however, is that this tool should not be installed on the Web server. The tool should be installed on client computers. You can have several client computers participate in a stress test. Each of them can simulate the effect of hundreds of users hitting a Web site.

Creating a Test Script

Open the Web Application Stress Tool.

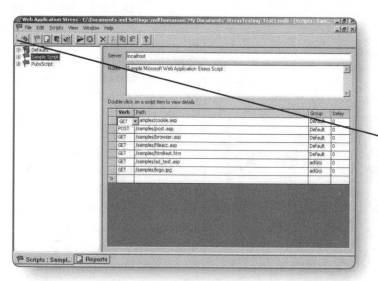

You should have a sample script in the left-hand window. I've created another script called the PubsScript that I'll look at in a minute.

You probably had a pop-up window with four buttons on it when you opened the program. If you closed that window, then click on the far left button on the tool bar to see it again.

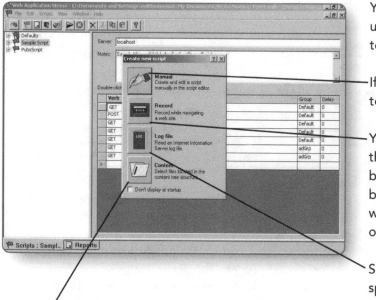

You can create a new test script using one of these four techniques.

If you choose Manual, you have to manually design a test script.

You can Record a script. Using this method you will be able to browse your Web site in a Web browser. Every page that you hit will be recorded and made part of the test script.

Scripts can be created by specifying a Web server log file.

Finally, test scripts can be created by clicking on the Content button and identifying Web pages in a virtual directory that should be included in a script.

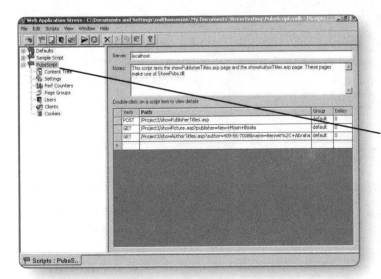

You'll be looking at the PubsScript example that I created. This script is simple, but it demonstrates the basic principles of stress testing.

By clicking on the name of the script, you can see the script items in the frame on the right. In my script, I have three script items that consist of three active server pages. These are the pages where I use the COM component I created.

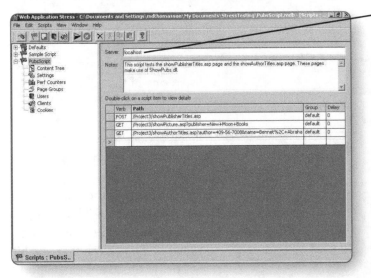

Notice that you put the name of the Web server at the top of the script items page. Normally, you wouldn't put "localhost." You're not supposed to run WAS on the Web server itself because the results will be skewed. In this case I'm not connected to a network so my machine will have to suffice as both client and server.

CAUTION

You shouldn't perform stress tests on your production Web application on a production server. Put a copy of the application on a test server that is similar to the production server. The performance of the Web application will be severely degraded during the stress test since the site will be "hit" by simulated users. Also, make sure you use a test copy of any databases that you're using in the site. Pages that perform updates, inserts, or deletes against the database will change the information in the database during the test.

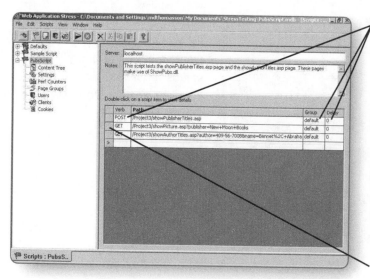

You can add a script item to the list by selecting a Verb (Get or Post) and typing the virtual path to the page. You can also specify a Group that the page should belong to. I'll discuss Page Groups later. The *Delay* column can be used to specify how many milliseconds are allowed to pass before the page is requested. I didn't use a delay on any of my pages.

If you double-click on the square next to a script item, you will be able to specify all kinds of other things about the item.

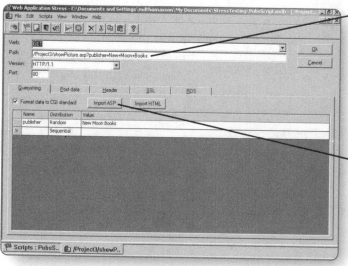

I double-clicked on the second script item, showPicture.asp. Here are all the options I can set about this item. Notice that on the Query String tab I can specify the query string elements the page expects.

If you click on the Import ASP button you will be able to browse for the showPicture.asp page and it will find all the query string elements the page expects for you.

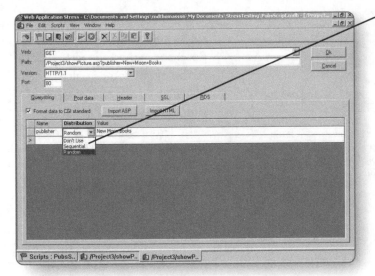

In the Distribution drop down list you can choose how you want to have the query string values fed into the page. Your choices are Don't Use, Sequential, and Random.

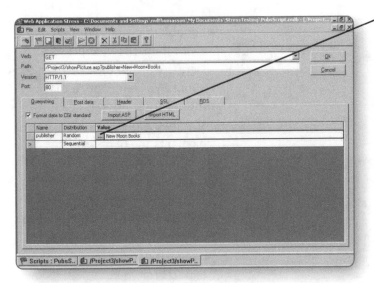

If you click in the Value column, a box with ellipsis (...) will appear. If you want to insert multiple possible query string values, click on the ellipsis.

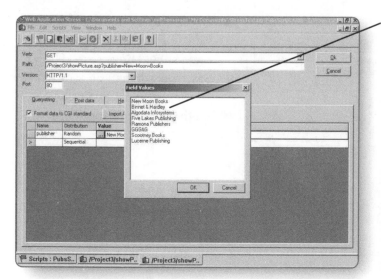

Notice that I simply listed all of the possible values that the query string could contain. The showPicture.asp page expects a publisher name, so I listed all of the possible publisher names from the Pubs database. I get these values by running a query in the query analyzer and pasting the results into this box. When the script runs, the various publisher names will be randomly sent as query string elements to the page.

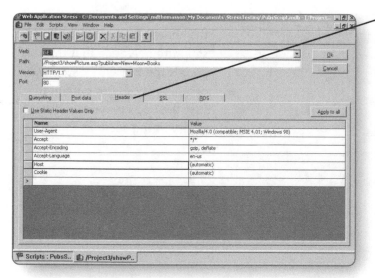

I'll look at the Post tab momentarily. For now I'll look at the Header tab. This is where you can specify any HTTP header information for the page.

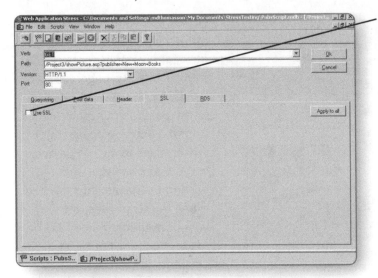

By clicking on the Use SSL check box, you can specify that this page should be accessed using SSL. You will then be able to see the impact that encryption has on the page's performance.

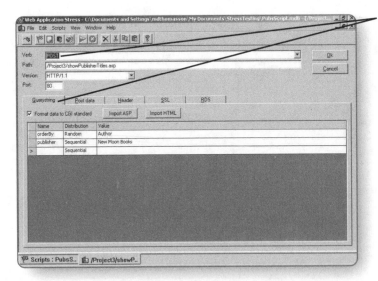

Here are the specifications for the showPublisherTitles.asp script item. Notice that this page expects POST data. You can still specify the parameters that the page expects in the Query String section.

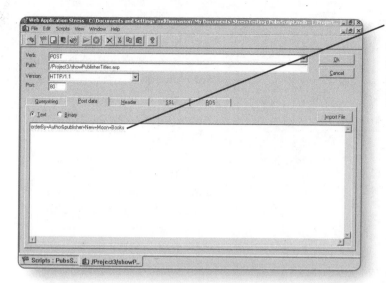

Notice that the parameters you entered on the Query String tab will automatically show up in URL Encoded format on the Post tab.

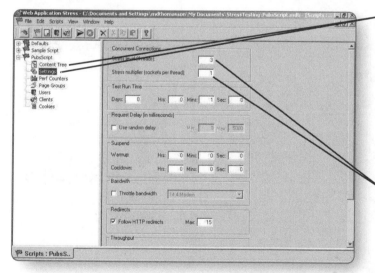

The Content Tree can be used to specify which virtual directory your Web pages are in. We won't be looking at that. Instead, consider the Settings page. This is where you set all the crucial run time information for your stress test.

In the Concurrent Connections section of the page you'll notice that the Stress level and Stress multiplier can be set. This is the section used to increase the number of concurrent hits to your Web site. Microsoft suggests that you don't put more than 100 threads in the Stress level box. If you want to simulate more concurrent connections you can increase the Stress multiplier. The total number of concurrent connections is the stress level multiplied by the stress multiplier. If your Web site requires users with user names and passwords, cookies, or sessions, then you need to make sure that the number of concurrent connections is no larger than the number of users that you specify in the Users section. I'll look at the Users section in a bit.

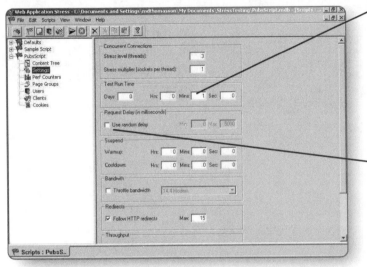

You can specify how long your test should run. I'm only running mine for one minute. You should normally run a test for at least three to five minutes. Complex applications should run 15 to 20 minutes.

Since real users don't click on constantly, you can specify a random delay to simulate the time that users might spend looking at a Web page.

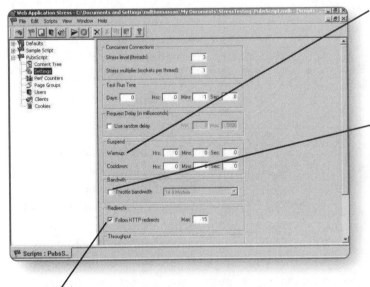

It's not a bad idea to specify a minute or so warm-up time. During the warm-up and cool down the pages are hit but no information is recorded.

You can use bandwidth throttling to simulate the site's performance using different levels of bandwidth.

You can specify whether the test should follow redirects, as well as how many redirects should be allowed.

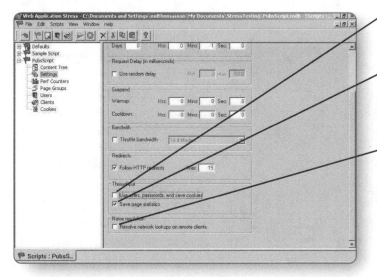

If the site uses users and cookies, check this box.

If you want the WAS tool to generate reports, you must have this box checked.

Click here to have client computers do a DNS lookup to find the Web site.

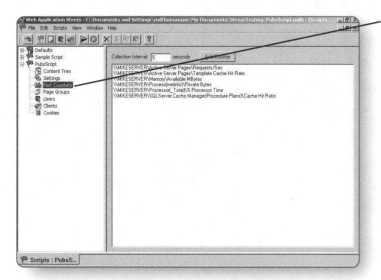

Perf Counters should be added so that you can see what impact the stress had on the various players in your application.

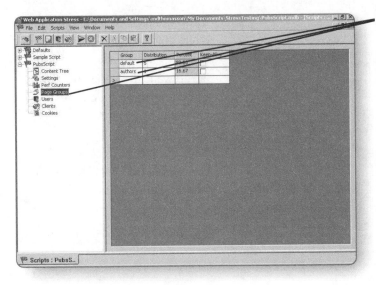

Page Groups can be created to change the frequency with which the different pages in a Web application are hit during a test. In this example I set up two groups. The default group is created for you. I made another group named authors. In this example, script items that have been assigned to the authors group will be hit about 16.67% of the time, the default group will get the rest of the hits. Using page groups you can make the test more realistic because a real Web application will have some pages that get many more hits than others. To assign a script time to a group, change the group setting for the item to whichever group it should be assigned to.

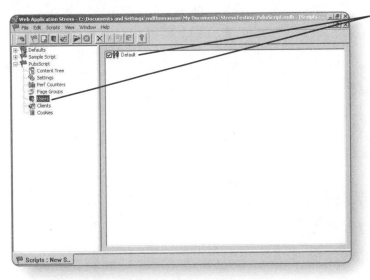

If your Web site is going to use users with user names and passwords, you could specify the user names and passwords allowed on the site by double-clicking on Default in the right-hand frame.

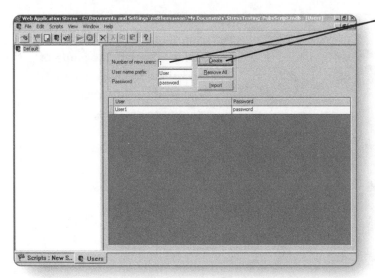

Put in how many users you would like to create, then click on Create. You can then specify a user name and password for each user. Alternatively, you can create users by clicking the Import button and browsing for a .csv file with the usernames and passwords. You can easily generate a comma-separated file with a database.

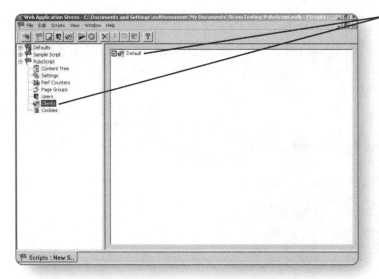

You can add client computers to help hit the Web server by double-clicking on Default and specifying which computers you want to enlist. Each client computer also needs to have WAS installed on it. Add more clients if you want to increase the concurrent connections beyond what one client can simulate. Client computers should not be operating at above 80% processor utilization during the test.

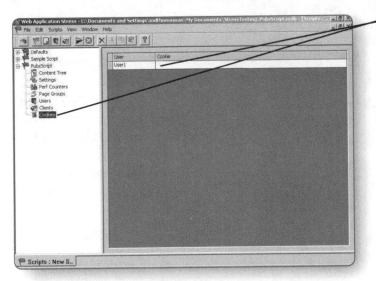

You can create cookies for each user here if your site uses cookies. Specify the name of the cookie followed by an equals sign (=) followed by the value of the cookie.

Running a Stress Test Script

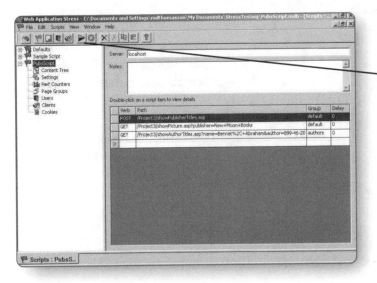

After you've set up a stress test script, you can run the script by clicking on the triangle on the tool bar.

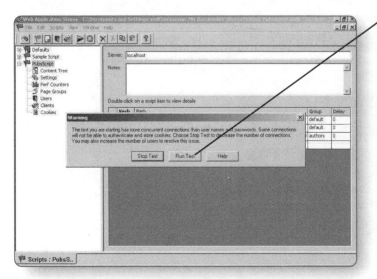

If you didn't create as many users as you have specified concurrent connections, you will get the following message. We aren't using "users" in this site so we can ignore the message by clicking on Run Test.

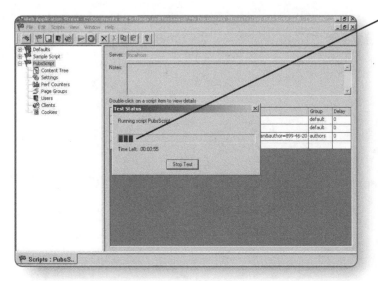

The test will then begin. A progress bar will display the time left on the test.

NOTE

Try browsing the site while the test is running to get an idea of what the site feels like with the specified number of concurrent connections.

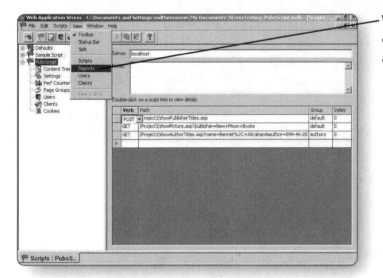

When the test is done you can click on View on the file menu and then Reports.

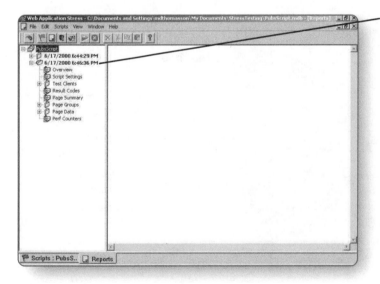

The reports will be named by the time that the report started.

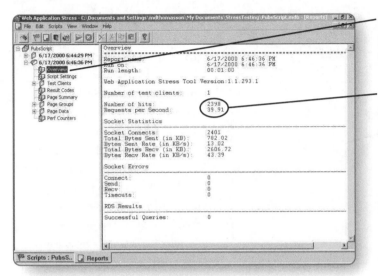

Click on the Overview to find some general information about the test.

Notice that the Total number of hits as well as the Requests per second are shown.

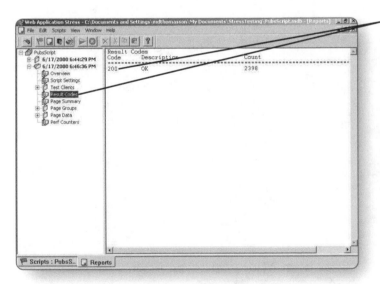

In the Result Codes section of the report you can see the HTTP Status for the hits. In this case, all 2,398 hits had an HTTP 200 status, which means that they were successfully sent. If you see other status (like 404) then there was some error accessing those pages. If that is the case make sure that you set up the script items correctly.

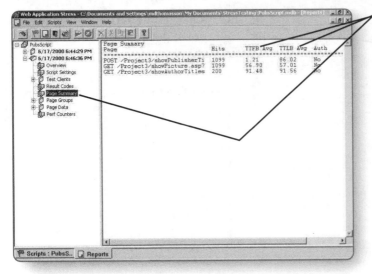

The Page Summary section of the report shows summary information for each of the script items. Besides the number of hits each page got, it shows you the Time to First Byte (TTFB) and Time to Last Byte(TTLB) for each page. The TTFB is the time (in milliseconds) that it took for the first byte of information to be sent back to the client from the server. Likewise, TTLB tells how long it took for the last byte to be sent to the client. These pages didn't take too long. Remember 1000 milliseconds is 1 second.

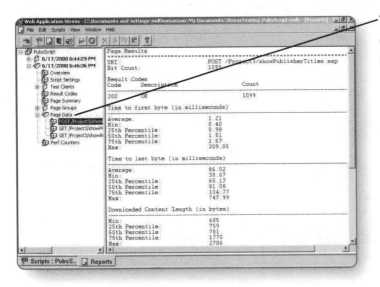

The Page Data section shows detailed information about each page in the test.

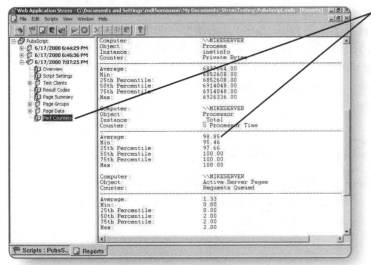

Here is the Perf Counter information from the test. Looks like my CPU is the bottleneck that will prevent my site from getting too many more Requests per Second. Remember that if the %Processor time stays over 80% during the test, you're pushing the processor too hard.

Stress Test Strategies

Generally you use stress tests to do two things: to find out the maximum Requests Per Second that your application can service with the current configuration, and to find out what bottleneck is keeping your application from yielding more requests per second.

Maximum RPS

To find the maximum Requests Per Second your application can handle with its current configuration, gradually add stress (concurrent connections) until the number of Requests per Second levels off or begins to drop. Back off the stress a little. That is the maximum number of Requests Per Second that your site will provide with the current configuration.

Bottlenecks

Bottlenecks are sometimes difficult to find. Here are a few general rules of thumb: If the processors are running over about 80% utilization during the test, they are probably the bottleneck. You can increase the Requests Per Second by adding more processors, or better yet, by adding more servers and using Windows Load Balancing Service to create a *web farm*. If the Active Server Pages Request Queued number fluctuates significantly during the test, you may have some problems with one of your COM components or database calls. Check the Microsoft WAS Web site to get more ideas about identifying bottlenecks.

Third-Party Stress Tools

The Microsoft Web Application Stress Tool works well. However, there are many third-party stress tools available if you want more functionality (or just want to spend more money). Here are some of them:

- AppMetrics.QA by Xtremesoft. See http://www.xtremesoft.com

- Eload by RSW Software. See http://www.rswsoftware.com

- LoadRunner by Mercury Interactive. See http://www.mercuryinteractive.com

- WebHammer by Server Objects. See http://www.serverobjects.com

15

Optimizing Your Web Application's Performance

I'm always on the lookout for ways to increase the performance of my Web applications. This chapter goes over some ways that you can optimize your Web applications. There are often good articles on the Web having to do with this topic as well (check out Appendix B, "Useful ASP Resources"). In this chapter, you'll learn performance tips for:

- ASP
- ADO
- VBScript
- SQL
- COM/COM+
- IIS

Optimizing ASP

Here are some tips to improve the performance of your active server pages.

How Long are Your Active Server Pages?

If your active server pages are several hundred lines long, consider putting some of the code into a COM component. Leave just the presentation type code in the ASP page. On the other side of the coin, however, don't make short active server pages into COM components. There is some overhead involved in executing and managing COM components. If your active server pages are small (100 lines or less) it might be more efficient to avoid incurring the extra COM baggage. Also consider the fact that in order to change a COM component you must recompile the code. This can be tedious if you have to change the component very often.

Watch Those Include Files

Including files using the #Include statement adds code to your active server page. Rename the page (temporarily) so that it has a .stm extension and view it in a browser if you want to see your active server page with all of the included code. Make use of the <Metadata> tag to reference type libraries for components rather that using #Include to reference them. Place the <Metadata> tags in the global.asa file if you will be using the same components in several pages of your application.

Avoid Interspersing ASP and HTML

Although mixing ASP and HTML is unavoidable, try to keep blocks of ASP code and blocks of HTML separate as much as possible. For example:

```
<% If strRequest = "yes" Then %>
<h2><%=username%> your request will be answered via email.<h2>
<% End If %>
```

The preceding code would be much more efficient if written entirely in an ASP block like this:

```
<%
If strRequest = "yes" Then
        Response.Write("<h2>" & username & " your request will be answered via
email.</h2>")
End If
%>
```

I try to put the majority of my ASP code at the top of the page and the HTML code at the bottom.

Use Buffering

Buffering is on by default in IIS 5.0. You can explicitly turn it on by putting `<% Response.Buffer = True %>` at the top of an ASP page. Buffering increases the performance of ASP by sending out information in one big chunk rather than many little chunks. If you have a long page, you can use `Response.Flush` to periodically send out some information to keep users from giving up on the page.

Consider Alternatives to Session Variables

As discussed in Chapter 7, "Application and Session Objects," Session variables limit scalability. For one thing, Session objects are tied to only one server. For another, every user that hits your site will have their own set of Session data in the server's memory. If your site needs to scale (be able to handle more users in the future), consider some of the other approaches to managing state that we discussed in the Chapter 7. If you are not going to use any session variables on a page, put `<% @EnableSessionState = False %>` at the top of the page. If you won't be using Sessions at all in your application, disable session state in IIS.

Don't Leave Empty Events in the Global.asa

You don't have to put the `Application_OnStart`, `Application_OnEnd`, `Session_OnStart`, or `Session_OnEnd` events in your global.asa if you don't want to.

Only put them there if you are going to put code in them. Don't put empty `Session_OnStart` and `Session_OnEnd` events in the global.asa as that causes the ASP interpreter to do unnecessary work.

Client-Side Form Validation

Consider using JavaScript to perform client-side form validation. This will offload work from the server to the client machine. It's not too hard to write cross-browser data validation JavaScript. Most people are using browsers (3.0 level browsers and higher) that can do JavaScript.

Use Server.Transfer When Possible

The new `Server.Transfer` method can be used to transfer control from one active server page to another as long as both pages are on the same server. This method is more efficient and provides greater functionality than the `Response.Redirect` method.

Use ServerVariables Conservatively

The `Request.ServerVariables` method retrieves the entire ServerVariables collection the first time it is used in a page. This is an expensive operation and should only be done when you really need to. Subsequent calls to the `ServerVariables` method in the same page won't need to fetch the collection.

Optimizing ADO

Here are some performance tips related to ActiveX Data Objects (ADO).

Close Your Objects

It's a good practice to close and destroy your ADO objects as soon as you're done using them. Closing connection objects will allow the connection to go back into a connection pool to be used elsewhere. You can disconnect your client-side (adUseClient) recordsets immediately by setting the ActiveConnection property of a recordset equal to nothing. That way you can still use the recordset, but you won't hold a connection open.

Use Firehose Cursors

The default ADO cursor has the following properties: CursorLocation = adUseServer, CursorType = adOpenForwardOnly, and LockType = adLockReadOnly. This type of cursor is known as a *firehose* cursor. It provides the greatest performance but the least functionality. Often this is all you need in your active server page. Don't use updateable, scrollable cursors unless you need to.

Use Native OLE DB Providers

Native OLE DB providers usually provide the best performance and reliability when connecting to a data source.

Use GetString() and GetRows() When Possible

The ADO Recordset object provides the GetString() method to put the information from a recordset into a string and the GetRows() method to put it into an array. By using these methods you can fetch the data from the recordset into a variant string or array and immediately close and destroy the recordset object. Look for opportunities to use these methods.

Change the CacheSize Property

Set the CacheSize property of the Recordset Object to something larger than the default value of one. The CacheSize property determines how many records will be grabbed from the database at once. The closer CacheSize is to the actual number of records that will be returned from the database the better performance will be.

Create Variables That Reference Recordset Fields

If you will be using the values in recordset fields more than once, or if you will be looping through a recordset, you should create local variables that reference the fields. Here's an example (assume that I've already created and opened a recordset named myRecordset):

```
<%
Dim column1,column2,colmnn3
column1 = myRecordset.Fields(0)
column2 = myRecordset.Fields(1)
Response.Write("<table>")
Do While Not myRecordset.EOF
        Response.Write("<tr><td>" & column1 & "</td><td>" & column2 _
        & "</td></tr>")
        myRecordset.MoveNext
Loop
%>
```

Use Stored Procedure Output Parameters

If you only expect to get one or two values back from a query, use a Command object with output parameters rather than having a recordset returned. Doing so will be more efficient than having a recordset returned.

Use adExecuteNoRecords

If you are executing a Command object that won't be returning a recordset, use the adExecuteNoRecords argument when you call the Execute method.

Use the CreateParameter() Method

If you are using a Command object to call a stored procedure that expects or returns parameters, you should explicitly create the parameters using the CreateParameter() method rather than having ADO determine the properties of the parameters for you.

Optimizing VBScript

Here are some ways to increase the performance of VB Script.

Local Variables vs. Global Variables

Although global variables are sometimes necessary, they are not as efficient as local variables. Remember that global variables are those that are declared outside of a procedure and are available to any procedure in a particular class or active server page, while local variables are declared within a procedure. Use local variables inside procedures as much as possible and use globals only when you have to.

ByVal versus ByRef

Pass variables `ByVal` if you don't want the value of the variable to be changed by the procedure your calling. `ByVal` is more efficient than sending variables `ByRef`. If you are creating procedures in COM components that accept parameters from ASP `ByRef` then make sure the parameters are of data type `Variant`.

Avoid Redimensioning Arrays

It turns out that redimensioning arrays with the `ReDim` statement is a costly exercise. In many instances you're better off to create the array with more space than you need than to create a dynamic array and redimension it.

Use Option Explicit

Declared variables are faster than undeclared variables. Use `Option Explicit` to force yourself to declare variables.

Optimizing SQL

Here are some ways to optimize SQL performance.

Break Up Stored Procedures

If you're creating recordset returning stored procedures that use `if` statements to determine which `Select` statement to run, you should create a separate stored procedure for each `Select` statement and put the conditional code in your ASP page or COM component. SQL Server will yield much better performance that way.

Indexes

Create indexes on tables for columns that are frequently used in Order By or Group By statements. Indexes will have a dramatic affect on the performance of your database.

Limit Select Statements

Limit the amount of information sent back to the client from Select statements by specifying which columns should be sent back and by limiting the number of rows returned using the Where clause.

Study Database Design

The design of your database will have a big impact on how well it performs. Is your database normalized? Is it denormalized where it should be?

Optimizing COM/COM+

Here are some tips on making COM/COM+ components perform well.

Only Use Transactions When Necessary

There's additional overhead involved in transactions. Create transactional components for processes that require transactions and create nontransactional components for processes that don't need transactions to occur.

Call SetAbort and SetComplete Often

By calling either SetAbort or SetComplete in each method of your transactional components, you allow COM Services to release resources earlier. You can also go into the Component Services manager and click the check box that says "Automatically deactivate this object when this method returns" in the properties section for each method of a transactional component.

Library versus Server Applications

The default Activation type in COM+ Services is "Server application." That means that your component will run in a separate piece of memory from the client (ASP application) that created it. This will protect the ASP application from crashing if the COM component crashes, however the COM component will not run as fast as it would if it were running in the same process as the ASP application. If you are confident that your COM components won't crash, then you can set the activation type to "Library application," which will cause the component to run in the same memory space as the ASP application that called the component.

Get Property and Set Property Statements

If your component has a lot of properties then you might be better off creating a couple of methods that set or retrieve several properties at a time rather than using individual `Get Property` and `Set Property` statements for each property. Every call to a procedure in a component requires a roundtrip from the application to the component. The fewer roundtrips the better.

Optimizing IIS

Here are some IIS configuration tips.

Disable Server-Side Script Debugging

Make sure that you disable server-side script debugging on your production Web applications. If it is enabled, performance will suffer dramatically.

Use SSL Conservatively

Only encrypt pages that must be encrypted with SSL. SSL requires a lot of extra processing.

A
Setting Up SSL Encryption on IIS

SSL(*Secure Sockets Layer*) is the technology that enables HTTP information to be sent encrypted over the Internet. Basically, SSL encryption involves the use of two keys. A company (or organization, individual, and so on) has a private key on their Web server. The company also has a public key. Information encrypted with the private key can only be decrypted by the public key and visa-versa. When someone hits a page that uses encryption, the Web server will send the public key to the person hitting the site. After that, the Web server sends a unique session key that is encrypted using the private key. The visitor's browser decrypts the session key using the public key. At that point all the information passed back and forth between the client and the server can be encrypted using the unique session key. No one intercepting the HTTP stream will be able to decrypt the information since they will not have the unique key.

SSL provides another feature in addition to the ability to encrypt information sent over the Internet. It also allows a visitor to a Web site to be sure they are really talking to the company they think they're talking to rather than some imposter who's trying to steal their credit card number. The reason they can be sure is that the company's public key has a certificate attached to it that is assigned by an outside agency called a Certificate Authority (CA). The CA is responsible for collecting information from companies that want to use a public key on the Internet. After investigating the company, the CA will sign the company's public key. Whenever someone enters into an encrypted session with the company, they can check the certificate (if they want to) to see which CA signed the certificate and for how long the certificate is valid. Web browsers come with a list of trusted CA's built in. Other CA's can be made trusted by adding their certificate to the browser's list.

Obtaining a Signed Server Certificate

To have your Web site's certificate signed by a Certificate Authority, follow these steps:

1. Go into the Internet Services Manager by clicking on Start, Settings, Control Panel. Double-click on Administrative Tools and then double-click on Internet Services Manager.

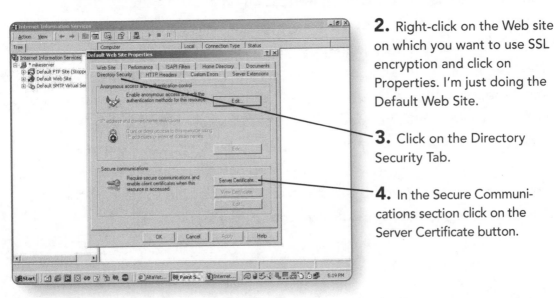

2. Right-click on the Web site on which you want to use SSL encryption and click on Properties. I'm just doing the Default Web Site.

3. Click on the Directory Security Tab.

4. In the Secure Communications section click on the Server Certificate button.

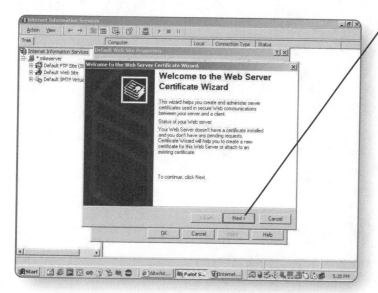

5. The Server Certificate Wizard will start. Click on Next.

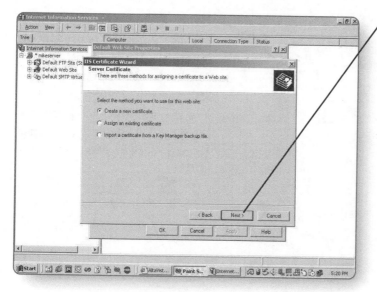

6. On the next screen, click on Next again because you want to create a certificate.

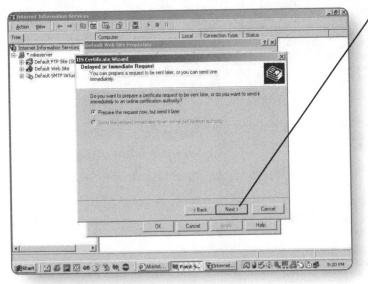

7. Click on Next again.

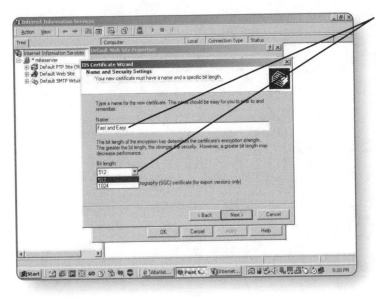

8. Type a name for your certificate. Also select the bit length of your certificate. The longer the bit length, the stronger the encryption. The stronger the encryption, the longer it will take for your pages to load. Click on Next.

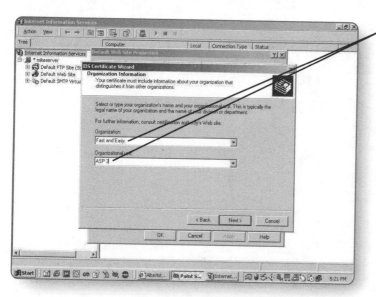

9. Put the legal name of your company or organization here. The organizational unit is optional, but specifies the part of the organization the certificate is for. The CA will ask you to provide documentation supporting that your company is known by the Organizational name you provide. Click on Next.

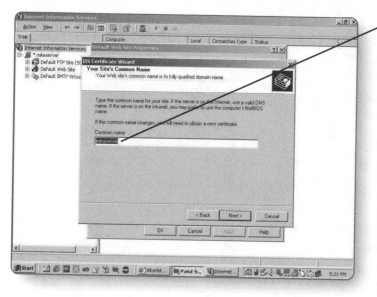

10. THIS ONE IS IMPORTANT: Enter the domain name of the Web site for which you're generating the certificate. Don't type the http:// part. For example, you should enter something like www.mysite.com. If this certificate is for an intranet, you can just type the name of the server if you are going to use that for the site's URL. If you try to use a certificate to encrypt Web sites other than the one specified when the certificate was made, then the browsers will put up all kinds of warning messages to the site's visitors. Because I'm creating a certificate for just my machine, I'm using my machine's name. Click on Next.

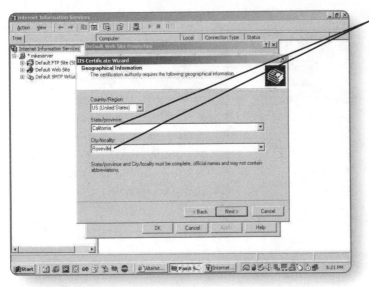

11. Make sure you spell out the state and city names. Click on Next.

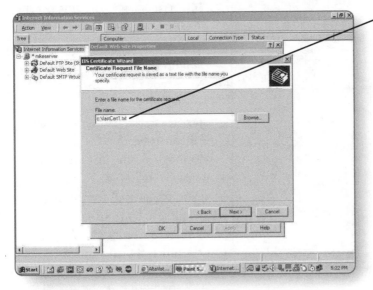

12. Type a name with a .txt extension. Save it wherever you want. This is your Certificate Signing Request (CSR). Click on Next.

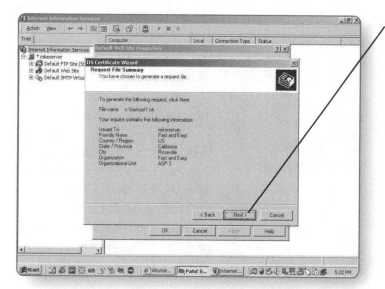

13. Click on Next again.

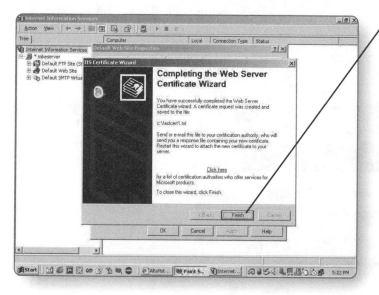

14. Click on Finish.

You have now generated a CSR.

If you open the text file it will look something like this:

Now you need to go to a CA's Web site to request a certificate. Two popular Certificate Authorities are Verisign (www.verisign.com) and Thawte (www.thawte.com), although there are many others. CAs have different methods of assigning certificates. All of them, however, require that you get your CSR to them somehow. Usually you copy your CSR to the clipboard and paste it into a text area on the CA's Web site. For this example I'm obtaining a test certificate from Verisign. If you want to experiment with a certificate (for 14 days) then you can do this to.

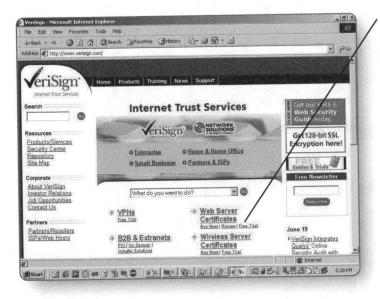

On the Verisign Web site I clicked on Free Trial. I then had to fill out several online forms.

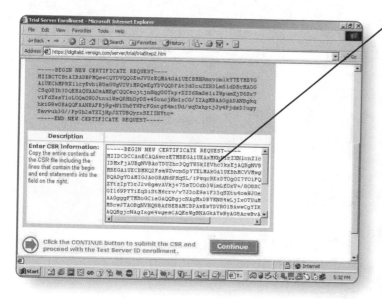

Finally, I came to the page where I had to paste my CSR.

After finishing the online application, I received an e-mail that contained my temporary server certificate. I received the e-mail within an hour. If you're applying for a real certificate it will take several days or even weeks because you will have to send documentation to the CA and they will have to check your documentation. I copied the certificate text from the e-mail and saved it as a text file.

Installing the Certificate

To install the certificate, follow these steps:

1. Go into the Internet Services Manager by clicking on Start, Settings, Control Panel. Double-click on Administrative Tools and then double-click on Internet Services Manager.

2. Right-click on the Web site on which you want to use SSL encryption and click on Properties. I'm just doing the Default Web Site.

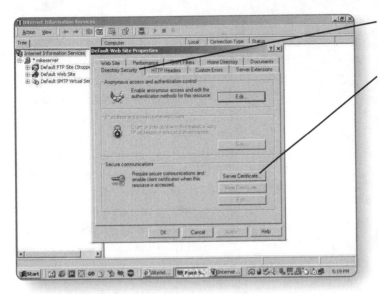

3. Click on the Directory Security Tab.

4. In the Secure Communications section, click on the Server Certificate button.

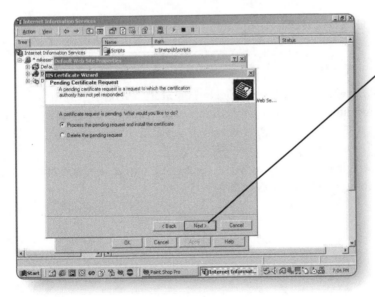

5. The Server Certificate Wizard will start. Click on Next.

6. This time the wizard will let you know that a request is pending. That's because you already generated a CSR. Click on Next.

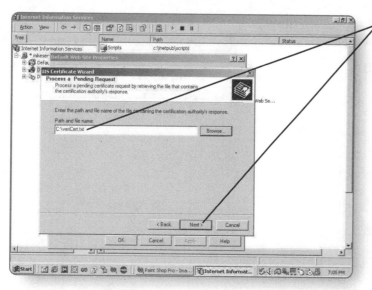

7. Browse to find the text file that contains the certificate. Click on Next. Click on Next on the following screen as well.

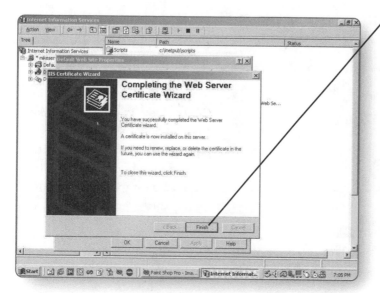

8. The certificate is now installed. Click on Finish.

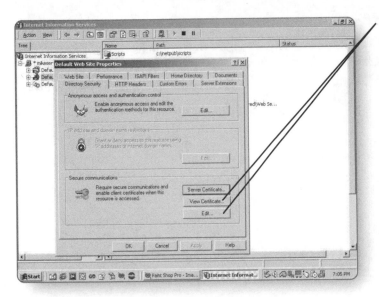

Notice that you can now view the certificate or edit the secure communications settings. At this point, any Web page in your site can use SSL encryption if you so choose.

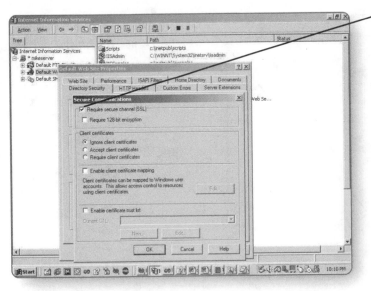

By clicking on the Edit button you can edit the secure communications settings for your Web site. If you click on the box next to Require secure Channel, every page in the Web site can only be viewed using encryption. That's typically not a good idea because encryption requires a lot more processing by the server and slows down your site.

CAUTION

Only require SSL on pages that need to be encrypted. Encrypted pages take much longer to load than nonencrypted pages.

Instead of making the whole Web application require encryption, you can make just the folders in a particular directory require encryption. To do that, right-click on the directory on which you want to require SSL and click on Properties. Click on the Directory Security tab. Click on Edit under Secure Communications and check the Require secure channel (SSL) box. You can also specify SSL settings for an individual Web page by right-clicking on the Web page and following the same instructions.

If you try to access a page that requires SSL without using SSL, you will get the following error.

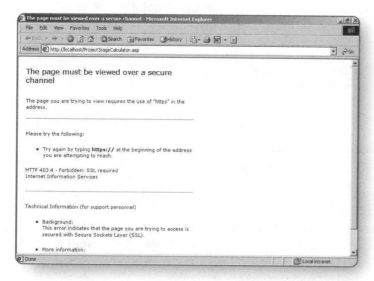

Using SSL to Encrypt Pages

Encrypting pages with SSL is very simple. It requires that you specify the absolute path of a page in your Web site in a hyperlink tag. Instead of typing **http://**, you need to type **https://**. The "s" stands for "secure." The pages in your site will be encrypted until you explicitly turn off SSL by specifying an absolute path in a hyperlink using "http" instead of "https." Here is a page that demonstrates this.

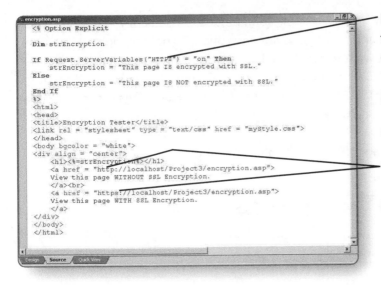

```
<% Option Explicit

Dim strEncryption

If Request.ServerVariables("HTTPS") = "on" Then
    strEncryption = "This page IS encrypted with SSL."
Else
    strEncryption = "This page IS NOT encrypted with SSL."
End If
%>
<html>
<head>
<title>Encryption Tester</title>
<link rel = "stylesheet" type = "text/css" href = "myStyle.css">
</head>
<body bgcolor = "white">
<div align = "center">
    <h1><%=strEncryption%></h1>
    <a href = "http://localhost/Project3/encryption.asp">
    View this page WITHOUT SSL Encryption.
    </a><br>
    <a href = "https://localhost/Project3/encryption.asp">
    View this page WITH SSL Encryption.
    </a>
</div>
</body>
</html>
```

Notice that I check to see if the page is encrypted by checking the value of the "HTTPS" server variable. If the page is encrypted, it returns "on." I then display the appropriate message.

You can see the "http" verses "https" notation in the hyperlinks.

CAUTION

In order for this example to work you must have installed a server certificate on your machine. Additionally, you must change the absolute path specified in the links to match the absolute path of the encryption.asp page on your machine. Since my Visual InterDev project was named Project3 my pages are found at http://localhost/Project3/. If you put your pages in another virtual directory then change the URLs appropriately.

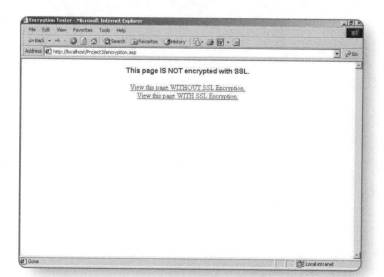

Here is the page in action.

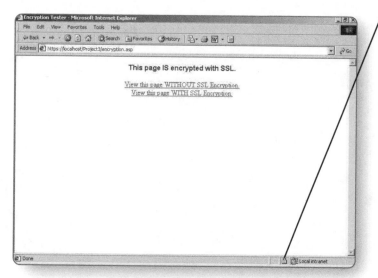

Notice that the "Lock" is on, showing that the page is encrypted.

B

Useful ASP Resources

Here are some useful links related to ASP and web development.

ASP

- 4Guys From Rolla – http://www.4guysFromRolla.com. These guys have lots of good articles related to ASP development. A great place to learn the tricks of the trade.

- ASP 101 - http://www.asp101.com. Check out the Samples section. Articles are ranked according to level of difficulty.

- ASP Today - http://www.asptoday.com. A new article related to ASP is posted every day. Of course you can look at old articles as well. Some great material here.

- ActiveServerPages.com - http://www.activeserverpages.com. Lots of tutorials to learn various aspects of ASP. Charles Carroll also moderates ASP listservers at www.asplists.com.

- Action Jackson - http://www.actionjackson.com. This site has lots of great ASP articles. Most of them are intermediate to advanced level.

- ASP Alliance - http://www.aspalliance.com. A good range of ASP articles.

- Dev Guru - http://www.devguru.com. Lots of great tutorials. The site also has articles on client-side technologies like JavaScript and Cascading Style Sheets.

- Microsoft's ASP White Papers - http://support.microsoft.com/support/activeserver/whitepapers.asp. This site has white papers on ASP, COM, IIS and related technologies.

- Microsoft's ADO Website - http://www.microsoft.com/data/ado. Get the latest on ADO.

VBScript

- Microsoft Scripting Technologies - http://msdn.microsoft.com/scripting. This site has the latest versions of VBScript and JScript. It also has documentation and tutorials.

SQL

- Swynk.com - http://www.swynk.com/sysapps/sql.asp. This site has some great material on SQL Server and other Back Office products. Has SQL Server FAQ's and a SQL Script library.

- The SQL Server Pro - http://www.inquiry.com/techtips/thesqlpro. Ask SQL Server questions or browse answers by category.

- SQL Server Magazine - http://www.sqlmag.com. Read articles online.

Visual Basic/ COM/COM+

- 15 Seconds - http://www.15seconds.com. This site covers just about everything related to Microsoft web development. Has lot's of good articles on building COM Components. They show how to use many commercially available components and have an extensive list of component vendors.

- Microsoft's Code Center - http://msdn.microsoft.com/code. Find lots of code samples having to do with ASP, VB, SQL, ADO and so on.

- About.Com - http://visualbasic.about.com/compute/visualbasic. Lots of info about Visual Basic and VBScript.

Java/JavaScript

- Scoop on Java - http://home.att.net/~baldwin.r.g/scoop/index.htm. Dick Baldwin is a professor in Texas. He has some great tutorials on Java, JavaScript, XML and other technologies.

- JavaScripts.com - http://www.javascripts.com. Lots of tutorials and sample scripts.

COM Component Vendors

- Cyscape - http://www.cyscape.com. They make BrowserHawk, the ultimate browser capabilities component. This will tell you everything you ever wanted to know about a browser.

- ASP Email - http://www.aspemail.com. Email components with a range of features.

- Persits Software - http://www.persits.com. Best known for its ASP Upload component that facilitates the uploading of files from client to server. Many other components are available from Persits as well.

- Automated Solutions Group - http://www.active4.com. These guys have lots of components for sale. One of the coolest is a component that will output ASP pages as .pdf files on the fly. They also make a credit card authorization component.

Web Application Stress Tool (WAS)

- Web Application Stress Tool Home - http://webtool.rte.microsoft.com. Download the WAS tool here. They also have documentation, white papers, and a WAS Knowledge Base to browse.

HTML/DHTML

- W3C Web Style Sheets - http://www.w3.org/Style/CSS/. A great place to learn about Cascading Style Sheets (CSS).

- HTML Goodies - http://htmlgoodies.earthweb.com. Great tutorials. This is the place to learn about HTML. Also has lots of information on JavaScript and CSS.

- Dynamic HTML Resource - http://www.htmlguru.com. A pretty impressive DHTML site.

- The Dynamic Duo - http://www.dansteinman.com/dynduo. A site dedicated to Cross-Browser dynamic html.

- Web Review CSS - http://webreview.com/wr/pub/guides/style/style.html. A chart showing what CSS techniques will work on what browser.

C

Using the CD-ROM

The CD-ROM that accompanies this book contains the Microsoft Web Application Stress Tool (WAS), a 90 day trial Version of Microsoft Visual InterDev 6.0, and all of the sample files generated by the author. The specially designed Prima Tech interface will assist you in navigating the CD-ROM and/or installing the contents on your computer.

Running the CD

To make the CD more user-friendly and take up less of your disk space, no installation is required to view the CD-ROM. This means that the only files transferred to your hard disk are the ones you choose to copy or install.

Windows 95/98/2000/NT

1. Insert the CD-ROM in the CD-ROM drive and close the tray.

2. Via the Windows Explorer, double click on the CD-ROM.

3. Double Click on start_here.html.

The Prima License

The first window you will see is the Prima License Agreement. Take a moment to read the agreement, and if you agree, click on I Agree to accept the license and proceed to the user interface. If you do not agree with the license, click on I Disagree.

The Prima User Interface

The opening screen of the Prima user interface contains a two-panel window. The left panel contains the structure of the programs on the disc. The right panel displays a description page for the selected entry in the left panel.

Resizing and Exiting the User Interface

To resize the window, position the mouse over any edge or corner, hold down the left mouse button, and drag the edge or corner to a new position.

To close and exit the user interface, simply close your browser window.

Index

License Agreement/Notice of Limited Warranty